STRATEGIC MANAGEMENT
IN
SCHOOLS AND COLLEGES

Edited by
David Middlewood and Jacky Lumby

P·C·P
Paul Chapman
Publishing Ltd

Paul Chapman Publishing Ltd
144 Liverpool Road
London
N1 1LA

British Library Cataloguing in Publication Data

Strategic management in schools and colleges.
(Educational management: research and practice)
1. Strategic planning
2. School management and organization – Great Britain
3. Universities and colleges – Great Britain – Administration
I. Middlewood, David II. Lumby, Jacky
371.2'00941'09049

ISBN 1 85396 374 7

Typeset by Palimpsest Book Production Limited, Polmont, Stirlingshire, Scotland
Printed and bound in Great Britain.

ABCDEFGH 321098

CONTENTS

SERIES EDITOR'S FOREWORD

As we approach the new millennium, the pace of change affecting educational institutions shows no sign of slackening. National governments, anxious about the performance of schools and conscious of the link between educational achievement and economic growth, continue to impose new demands and to expect 'results' within tough and often unrealistic timescales. These requirements range widely and may include the curriculum, teaching and learning, staff management, budgeting and external relations, all within a framework of 'school improvement'.

In England and Wales, and in many other English-speaking countries, the responsibility for implementing national reforms rests largely with the leaders of individual institutions. The shift to self-managing schools, and incorporated colleges, means that the role of intermediary bodies, such as the local education authorities, has been much reduced. Principals, senior staff and lay governors are expected to lead their institutions towards the fulfilment of school objectives within the framework of national policies.

Because the levers of control are largely held at institutional level, it is both possible and desirable for leaders to adopt a strategic approach to management. This stance involves taking a holistic view of the organisation and planning for the long term within a framework of clearly articulated values and objectives. Strategic management requires the ability to integrate different aspects of the school to ensure the best possible educational outcomes.

The development of effective managers in education requires the support of literature which presents the major issues in clear, intelligible language while drawing on the best of theory and research. The purpose of this series is to examine the management of schools and colleges, drawing on empirical evidence. The approach is analytical rather than descriptive and generates conclusions about the most appropriate ways of managing schools and colleges on the basis of research evidence.

The aim of this series, and of this volume, is to develop a body of literature with the following characteristics:

- Directly relevant to school and college management.
- Prepared by authors with national and international reputations.
- An analytical approach based on empirical evidence but couched in intelligible language.
- Integrating the best of theory, research and practice.

Strategic Management in Schools and Colleges is the second volume in the series and it is underpinned by the view that a strategic approach is essential if leaders are to handle, and integrate, the plethora of internal and external initiatives. Self-management presents serious challenges for managers but also provides the potential for self-determination in a way that was simply not possible before this fundamental reform. Strategy was formerly the business of local or regional government but is now very much the responsibility of internal leaders. The purpose of this book is to support managers in developing the strategic approach which is vitally important to successful self-management.

Tony Bush
University of Leicester
September 1997

PREFACE

At the end of the 1990s, as we approach the millennium, a book on strategic management may seem to be particularly relevant because of the topic's requirement to take account of the future. As the future in education faces ever-increasing change and an ever-faster pace of change, the need is greater than ever for managers and leaders who will be skilled in the ability to influence their institutions' futures.

Equally relevant, as far as the future is concerned, the shift in many countries over recent years to the self-management of schools and colleges has brought a double-edged pressure. On the one hand there is greater freedom for schools and colleges to shape their own futures; on the other, there is a far greater necessity in a self-managing world with an emphasis on performance for individual schools and colleges to succeed – or close down.

In England and Wales, the legislation of the Education Reform Act (ERA) in the late 1980s and the incorporation of further education colleges in the early 1990s mean that schools and colleges now have sufficient experience for research into that experience to be relevant. Since strategic management concerns itself with longer time frames than operational management, institutions and their managers are now in a position to learn from those first years of, for example, initial strategic planning.

During the 1990s, requirements and pressures have been placed upon schools and colleges to produce development plans and/or strategic plans by bodies such as the Office for Standards in Education (Ofsted) and the Further Education Funding Council (FEFC). The introduction of a new qualification for headteachers in schools (NPQH) has also recognised the critical importance of strategic management through making it the compulsory and most important element of what is needed for effective school leadership.

To all these factors supporting the need for a book such as this can be added the fact that very little literature exists at present upon strategic management which is specific to schools and colleges. There is ample literature from the business world, some of which of course is relevant to education and referred to by contributors in this volume. However, there is much in that literature which is clearly not relevant and there is, therefore, a need to examine the situation of schools and colleges specifically.

Strategic management involves taking a view of the whole organisation, its key purpose, its direction and its place in its environment. In so doing, strategic managers must consider carefully their accountability to a wide variety of stakeholders who are involved in the education that their institution provides. These stakeholders may range from taxpayers at the national level to local employers and parents, as well as, most notably, students and children themselves. This area of accountability is one where business differs from education in the nature of who the stakeholders are and the nature of their relationship with the managers themselves. The theme of accountability therefore is a recurring one in this volume and most contributors see it as a key aspect of the strategic issue with which they are concerned.

Strategic management as described above has relevance to all educational institutions, regardless of size and composition. A small rural primary school, for example, with three teachers has the same imperative to review its key purpose, its place in its local community, to look at the opportunities and challenge of the future and be concerned about its growth or survival as does a large FE college or secondary school in an urban area, competing for students with neighbouring rival institutions. The NPQH requirements recognise this, of course. This book therefore will have relevance for managers in all educational institutions whatever their size.

Many aspects of strategic management are generic and the title of this volume, *Strategic Management in Schools and Colleges,* reflects the editors' belief that the issues involved are meaningful to managers in all educational institutions. However, there are a few areas where the processes are markedly different between statutory schooling and further education. In a few cases, therefore, chapters have been commissioned that are phase specific; these relate to those on the formal planning processes and the specific governance of schools.

The purpose of this book is to harness relevant research and theory in order to enhance management practice in education. It aims to avoid that kind of literature which prescribes 'best practice' for managers but provides little empirical support for such prescriptions. The editors' intention is to provide information and ideas from the most recent research and to stimulate and suggest practical ways of developing an aspect of the role of those managing in schools and colleges. The book is meant to enrich and provide possibilities, not to deter by setting up a normative picture of the ideal, which no ordinary human could achieve! All chapters have been specifically commissioned for this volume.

The book is organised in four sections each of which addresses broad aspects of strategic management. Section A examines strategic management in terms of definitions and purposes, as well as some of the major factors affecting its effectiveness. An overview of strategic management and thinking is followed by studies of vision and mission, and organisational culture. Section B focuses on the critical aspects of implementing strategy, including some of those most relevant to the educational context today such as marketing and resources. The importance of planning is examined separately for schools and for further education colleges.

Section C concentrates on the management roles undertaken by people in implementing strategy. The vital importance of collaborative management is examined first and then the contributions of leaders, middle managers and school governors. Section D studies the least examined part of strategic management, that of evaluating and reviewing its effectiveness. Approaches to review are examined first, followed by a study of the place of external inspection in the process and a final reflective analysis of strategic change.

Some criticisms of recent years have focused on the gap between the managerialism of leaders and the key purpose of a school or college, i.e. teaching and learning. The editors readily acknowledge the central importance of teaching and learning which should be the focus for educational leaders. They also believe that the ability to know the future direction of that teaching and learning, to identify and hold to that path over the next few years are of major importance.

The editors are grateful to all the contributors whose work is featured in this book for their co-operation. We also wish to thank Tony Bush as series editor for his personal support and professional expertise offered so generously to us, Marianne Lagrange of Paul Chapman Publishing for her support and advice, and Christopher Bowring-Carr for preparing the index. Finally, we express our warmest thanks to Joyce Palmer and Debbie Simister for their invaluable work in producing the manuscript and to Jacqui and David (from David and Jacky respectively!) and other family members for their encouragement, patience and support.

David Middlewood and Jacky Lumby
October 1997

NOTES ON CONTRIBUTORS

Tony Bush is Professor of Educational Management and Director of the Educational Management Development Unit at the University of Leicester. He was formerly a teacher in secondary schools and colleges and a professional officer with a local education authority. He was Senior Lecturer in Educational Policy and Management at the Open University before joining Leicester in January 1992. He has published extensively on several aspects of educational management. His main recent books are *Managing Autonomous Schools: The Grant Maintained Experience* (1993, with M. Coleman and D. Glover, Paul Chapman), *The Principles of Educational Management* (1994, with J. West-Burnham, Longman), *Theories of Educational Management* (1995, Paul Chapman) and *Managing People in Education* (1997, with David Middlewood, Paul Chapman).

Carol Cardno is Professor of Educational Management and Head of the School of Education at UNITEC Institute of Technology, New Zealand. She has a wide experience of teaching and managing having taught in primary and secondary schools, and held several senior management positions and the position of principal in a secondary school before establishing an Education Management Centre at UNITEC in 1991. Carol is the author of *Collaborative Management in New Zealand Schools* (1990, Longman Paul), *Effective Performance Appraisal* (1997, with Eileen Piggot-Irvine, Longman) and several papers on topics related to her research interests which are staff appraisal, organisational learning, collaborative management and management development.

Marianne Coleman has extensive experience in education, mainly teaching in secondary schools, and also working in the advisory service of a large LEA. She is co-author of *Managing Autonomous Schools: The Grant Maintained Experience*. She has also published a range of materials as part of the EMDU's distance-learning MBA, including 'Marketing in education' and 'Women in educational management'. She has published articles on gender issues in management and contributed chapters to the widely read *Principles of Educational Management* (1995, T. Bush and J. West-Burnham) and *Managing People in Education* (1997, T. Bush and D. Middlewood). She has also written on the subject of mentoring. She is currently engaged in comparative research projects in China and South Africa.

Michael Creese taught physics before becoming the headteacher of a

13–18 school in his native county of Suffolk. He then moved into governor training and was awarded his doctorate for a thesis on governor–teacher relationships. His book *Effective Governors – Effective Schools; Developing the Partnership* was published in 1995. He now works as a freelance consultant/researcher and is currently conducting research into the role of governors in school improvement.

Peter Earley was a schoolteacher originally. He then worked for many years at the National Foundation for Educational Research undertaking a number of projects in the areas of educational management, governance and professional development. He is currently a senior lecturer in the Management Development Centre at the Institute of Education, University of London, where he is also an associate director of the International School of Effectiveness and Improvement Centre. He is currently researching school governing bodies and their role in school improvement. His most recent publications include *Improvement through Inspection: Complementary Approaches to School Development* and *OFSTED Inspections: The Early Years* (both edited with Fidler and Ouston and published by David Fulton in 1996).

Keith Foreman was the principal of two community colleges in Cambridgeshire and Leicestershire before joining the Educational Management Development Unit of Leicester University in 1994 as Senior Tutor. He is a consultant to schools and LEAs, and was a member of the DES School Management Task Force from 1989 to 1992. His research interests lie in the broad field of school leadership.

Nick Foskett has taught in both secondary and post–16 sectors and has held middle and senior management posts in a range of educational institutions, including roles as marketing manager. He is currently Senior Lecturer in Education at the University of Southampton, and Director of the Centre for Research in Education Marketing. His work includes management training and staff development with school and college managers, heads and principals, and he has provided marketing consultancy to schools, colleges, universities and government organisations. His specific interests lie in marketing and strategic planning in education, and he has researched and published extensively in these fields.

Valerie Hall is Reader in Education in the Graduate School of Education, University of Bristol. She currently manages the taught doctor of education (EdD) programme at the University of Bristol, the first of its kind in Europe. She has taught in schools, colleges and universities for over 30 years. During the past 20 years she has been involved in a number of research projects, including the POST Project looking at the selection of secondary heads, the CROSH Project (changing role of the secondary head) and the SMT Project (senior management teams in secondary schools). Her latest book, *Dancing on the Ceiling: A Study of Women Managers in Education,* describes her study of education management from a gender perspective.

Brian Hardie has taught children and adults in a variety of schools and universities for 35 years. Ten years were spent in three secondary schools including being a head of department. Fifteen years were spent teaching in primary schools first as a teaching deputy and subsequently as head of a middle school. In three universities he has taught master's students education management for over ten years in the UK, USA and Israel. He has published the books *Marketing in the Primary School* (1991, Northcote House) and *Evaluating in the Primary School* (1995, Northcote House) as well as contributing to edited volumes.

Edith Jayne is currently running the portfolio of education leadership and management courses at the University College of St Mark and St John in Plymouth after similar appointments at two other universities. She began her career teaching early years and then heading an innovative community nursery school (in the USA). Following childrearing breaks, she then spent a decade doing educational research for the Inner London Education Authority. Her research interests are in school effectiveness and women leaders.

Jacky Lumby is a lecturer in educational management at the Educational Management Development Unit at Leicester University. She has previously taught in a range of educational settings, including schools, community and further education. Prior to joining Leicester University, she worked in a training and enterprise council with responsibility for the development of managers in both business and education. Current projects include research in the management of vocational education in China and human resource management in South African schools. She has published articles on the management of the curriculum and the development of managers in further education and also on the development of headteachers. She has published within EMDU's distance-learning MBA and was a contributor to the previous volume in this series, *Managing People in Education* (1997, T. Bush and D. Middlewood).

David Middlewood is a senior tutor in educational management and Director of School and College-based Programmes at the Educational Management Development Unit of the University of Leicester. He taught in schools and community colleges for 25 years, including nine years as a headteacher, before joining Leicester University in 1990. His special interests are appraisal (in which he has extensive research experience), staff selection and development and management structures. His publications include work on appraisal, human resources and development planning, and most recently *Managing People in Education* (1997, with Tony Bush), the first volume in this series. Current research involves human resource management in South African schools.

Tim Simkins is Head of the Centre for Education Management and Administration in the School of Education at Sheffield Hallam University. He has more than 20 years' experience teaching, consulting, researching and writing on education planning and management both in the UK and a number of overseas countries, and is currently Chair of the British Educational Management and Administration Society. His particular interests are in strategic and resource management in education and the management of educational change in developing countries.

Section A: developing a strategic approach

1

STRATEGIC MANAGEMENT IN EDUCATION: AN OVERVIEW

David Middlewood

INTRODUCTION

In this chapter, I wish, first, to examine the context of strategic management in education and suggest that understanding the paradoxes and tensions in that context is essential for effective strategic managers in schools and colleges. The chapter then discusses some key elements in strategic thinking itself. Such an approach, i.e. thinking strategically, is relatively new in education and involves much more than the planning process, important though that is. Strategic planning is then considered as a critical element of management, with a particular emphasis on its links with, and relevance to, the actual day-to-day work of the school or college.

THE CONTEXT OF STRATEGIC MANAGEMENT IN EDUCATION

Self-governance

The international trend in the management of education systems towards greater autonomy and self-governance for institutions has changed the demands upon those who manage those institutions. The role of the state in education is significantly adjusted and its leaders may be 'in the middle of a process of reconsidering its functions and its scope' (Bollen, 1996, p. 6). Choices have to be made at a national level about what is feasible, as well as desirable, and decisions, increasingly likely to include financial ones, have to be taken at the institutional level. The role therefore of intermediary bodies, such as regional councils or LEAs, becomes

1

decreased or marginalised and individual schools and colleges find themselves in the 'wild' climate, described by Carlson (1964). In such a climate, organisations 'struggle for survival. Their existence is not guaranteed, and they do cease to exist. Support for them is closely tied to performance and a steady flow of clients is not assured' (*ibid.*, p. 267).

As schools and colleges take over many of the tasks that were once carried out by others outside them, the size of the individual institution becomes important. On the one hand, the issue of the very small rural primary school, in several countries, encapsulates the dilemma of the socialising aspect of education versus the practical viability of the means of provision. Such schools may be viable only through the regional authority offering financial support as part of their overall management of educational provision in an area. On the other hand, in further and higher education in particular, and in secondary education to some extent, some institutions are becoming larger, sometimes through mergers/amalgamations. The main reason for this is likely to be the financial advantages of shared facilities and thereby provision of learning conditions at lower cost.

The requirement to manage an overview of an individual institution's provision, both now and in the future, has passed from regional bodies to individual schools and colleges. Whereas in the previous 'domesticated' climate the broad thrust and direction of educational provision and the place of an individual institution in that system were determined outside the school or college, leaders and managers in those institutions must now be responsible for this. Following the incorporation of further education colleges in England and Wales, the responsible body (FEFC) required colleges to develop their individual strategic plans, showing how they were fulfilling their responsibility for the management of their own direction. In state schools, the first attempt at a national standard for school leaders (National Professional Qualification for Headteachers – NPQH) placed 'strategic management' at the top of its priority list of requirements.

Market orientation

This overall context of greater autonomy for educational institutions has been accompanied by a significantly increased market orientation for schools and colleges, especially in England and Wales where the Education Reform Act 1988 (ERA) and subsequent legislation emphasised explicitly consumerist approaches:

> The underlying dynamic is that schooling is shifting from a public service driven by professionals towards a market-driven service, fuelled by purchasers and customers. In Britain, this market economy for schooling is in its infancy. In the USA and Canada, the development is in its birth stages. But the development is clear and discernible in the developed world.
>
> (Murgatroyd and Morgan, 1993, p. 1)

This market orientation in education carries one inherent contradiction in particular, that of greatly increased devolution of decision-making and resources management versus greater central government prescription (e.g. a statutory National Curriculum for schools). Some control from the centre is inevitable in state education in any case because the main source of funding is central government.

These contradictions are important in affecting the strategic management of educational institutions. Schools and colleges are not in an open market, free to change course according to sudden environmental changes; nor can they simply close down and begin again. Their purposes are prescribed for them in terms such as school improvement (Ofsted, 1995) or improved quality of student learning (FEFC, 1996). This prescription caused by funding control means that schools' and colleges' strategies and strategic plans operate within defined limits, compared with some business organisations, and may have tightly constrained and uniform requirements imposed upon them. For example, the FEFC states that it does not approve the strategic plans of individual FE colleges in England and Wales but colleges 'share their plans with the Council' (*ibid.*, p. 3). However, the whole of the document's thrust is that plans will be the basis for funding applications, for assessing (externally) the quality of education provided and the council 'needs assurance that strategic plans are robust and soundly based' (*ibid.*). The robustness is later defined as based on evidence, integration of plans and financial forecasts in significant detail. The notion of unpredictability is acknowledged through a recognition of 'risk analysis'. Institutions are asked to quantify risk factor variations in terms of projected student numbers (*ibid.*), i.e. because of public fund implications.

General climate of rapid change and uncertainty

As discussed above, public service policies will always impinge upon the strategic management of the delivery of those services but, additionally, in the late 1990s *all* organisations (private sector, manufacturing and service industries also) are operating in a climate of unprecedented pace of change and of uncertainty. This context is described by writers such as Drucker (1990), Handy (1994) and many others, and the context for educational managers in particular by Bush (1997). For example, Bush (*ibid.*, p. 4) points out how a vocational approach to the educational curriculum may be 'difficult to define in the context of such rapidly changing work patterns'. Changing patterns of employment in schools and colleges, such as the increase in fixed-term contracts, part-time staff and ancillary staff 'alternatives', have reflected the changes that are occurring in the world of work generally.

In this context of a plethora of changes, the performance of schools and colleges and therefore of those responsible for performance is carried out under intense public scrutiny. The focus on the 'visible outputs' of schools and colleges means that managers have to develop, plan and implement strategies with the attention of both central and local stakeholders firmly upon them.

TENSIONS IN THE CONTEXT AFFECTING STRATEGIC MANAGEMENT

In addition to management problems arising from limited resources and the consequent temptation for management strategy to be resource driven, at least four tensions may be discerned in the educational context within which schools and colleges operate.

Competition versus collaboration

The market orientation presupposes that competition between organisations will drive up standards, in direct contrast to a previous culture of collaboration. However, the research of Busher and Saran (1993, p. 190) led them to conclude that there was evidence that 'teachers are co-operating more closely and more widely than ever before with colleagues in other schools nearby'. They also concluded that, within institutions, the more effective leaders were those who used collaborative approaches, rather than those who relied upon new legislative powers. The notion of partnerships has become widespread in educational management, but in a 'managed' rather than a 'free' market, it is a concept that in some circumstances will be starkly in contrast with survival! For example, if a number of secondary schools exist in one town and there are surplus school places overall, some may have to succeed at the expense of others.

Change versus stability

Because of the need to ensure continuity for students' development and learning, especially in the formative years of statutory schooling, schools strive to provide a stable environment. Because of the requirement to implement many educational changes and in a time when societal changes occur rapidly, this is all the more important. Schools do not have the luxury of closing down, rethinking their strategy and then restarting, because of the entitlement of their main clients to continuous education. However, in strategic management terms, it means that schools have to some extent tended to plan for the future by looking at the past. In responding to pressures from society and government the emphasis can be on incremental change or hurried policy mandates (Stoll and Fink, 1996).

The challenge for strategic managers may be, as Stoll and Fink (*ibid.*) argue, to link a model for managing change to a radically new approach to learning – one which is based on the world of the future, not the world which has disappeared.

Transformation versus transaction

The business of schools and colleges is education which, by its nature, has elements of idealism in it, a concern to 'improve' people, and this in itself is necessarily a long-term aim – especially in the years of statutory schooling. At the same time, the political and social imperatives are for short-term goals and achievements, and the daily processes of learning and teaching must focus upon the transactional elements. Assessment of performance therefore ideally needs to balance these two elements (Middlewood, 1997), but pressures to respond to urgent demands may predominate, leading to what, for example, Hopkins *et al.* (1994) have described as the situation of the 'meandering school', one which has tackled many changes but has lost sight of its overall direction.

This is closely linked with what I see as a fourth tension.

Professionalism versus institutional worker

The concern about the deprofessionalising of teachers in schools and colleges has been the subject of debate in the 1990s, and focuses upon a clash of values. Elliott and Crossley's (1997) research in further education found a considerable gap between senior managers' focus upon quantitative performance indicators required of them from external agencies and lecturers' concern for student welfare. Formal quality assurance systems are seen by those who teach the students as marginalising the emphasis on the quality of what actually occurs during student learning. Elliott and Crossley (*ibid.*, p. 88) believe that 'confusing learner-centred approaches with a client-led approach' is caused by a failure of communication between two groups, with the willingness of lecturers to comply with external directives being mistaken for an acceptance that such systems improve quality of learning. Limb (1992, p. 167) has pointed out that 'values of the academic culture may be inconsistent with strategic planning's emphasis on sensing, serving and satisfying the market'.

Similarly in schools, the work of Fullan (1991), Hargreaves (1992) and Hopkins *et al.* (1994) has stressed the centrality of teachers' ownership for real change to occur, but even those who believe teachers are improving the quality of schooling for students may see this as being *in spite of* the climate. Busher and Saran (1993, p. 191) claim that

> preserving what seemed to be effective practice prior to 1988 but adapting it to the new legislative environment, accepting those aspects of the new system which cannot be avoided but managing them with well-tried processes, teachers have found ways to begin to change the environment minutely and locally and so to allow themselves to colonise it further. Through this, they have raised the quality of schooling for pupils, providing it as equitably as the harsh winds of a value-laden free market mechanism and an ideologically driven central control will allow.

THE CRITICAL IMPORTANCE OF DEVELOPING STRATEGIC THINKING

I have suggested thus far that the first element in strategic thinking in educational management is the realisation of the special contextual factors involved in the 'business of education'. It is tempting to envisage this in negative terms, i.e. of schools and colleges being placed in a market-orientated context which is alien to them. However, the positive view is that the demand for education is assured and the possibilities for influencing the form of its delivery are exciting! At the beginning of a new century, the realisation of the opportunity and the need to be more than reactive is the next element I shall consider in effective strategic management.

Being proactive

In the early years of greater autonomy for schools and colleges, it was inevitable that some individual organisations had to be reactive to survive. Abbott (1993) describes a situation of a school with a negative reputation and declining pupil numbers which suddenly had to face the opening of a new city technology college (CTC) in the area (funded directly by a mix of government and industrial sponsorship). The opening of the CTC 'encouraged us to get our house in order. One immediate and obvious response was to improve the quality and quantity of advertising material' (*ibid.*, p. 149). The implication is that not only did the school realise that it needed to improve its provision but that advertising that provision had now also to be part of its strategy. As the headteacher noted, 'we had never been in the business of selling the school. Once the CTC started, we had to promote the school' (*ibid.*, p. 151). The school knew that if it was successful in attracting additional numbers, other schools were bound to suffer, the final outcome in the area likely to be closures and/or amalgamations. Clearly, a longer-term strategy for survival, and preferably growth, needed to be developed.

This may be seen as the second important aspect of strategic thinking – realising that it is essentially *proactive*. Rather than merely being reactive to events and circumstance, the effective strategic manager aims to 'control' the future of the organisation within a framework. 'Strategic control sets the framework while operational control involves the day-to-day management' (Scott, 1985, p. 134). Evans (1996, p. 209), describing the need for strategic planning for a reasonably stable comprehensive school, points out that development planning and curriculum reviews had 'sought to respond to changes emanating from the 1988 Education Act'. She discerned a need for a comprehensive rationale for decisions about the school's future and states (*ibid.*) clearly

> the motive for evolving a strategic approach to planning at Richard Aldworth School was based upon a desire to be proactive rather than reactive. This was coupled with a realisation of the importance of attempting to establish some explicit overall direction for the school which would guide it through the plethora of change and uncertainty.

However, being proactive is a state that, by definition, involves constant renewal and the effective strategic manager is one who constantly encourages debate, aiming for continual organisational renewal. Pascale (1990) argued that having a strategy was no guarantee of success but that lasting success was impossible without one. In the educational context, his arguments would mean that the strengths of successful schools or colleges can become the roots of their weakness if they persist with perceptions formed in the period of success, particularly if these perceptions remain unquestioned. Such schools or colleges may resist change and fail to see environmental changes occurring around them. If recruitment is buoyant and income seems assured, the temptation is to assume that actively seeking to influence the future is not necessary, particularly since the public and political focus is more likely to be on 'failing' schools and colleges in an overt thrust to raise standards.

This idea is reinforced by the research of Hopkins *et al.* (1994) who categorised schools according to the response to and capacity for change, one category being that of the 'promenading school', exhibiting features of those described above, i.e. tending to be complacent with current success. Furthermore, in examining strategies to support schools through the merging of research into school effectiveness and school improvement, Hopkins and Lagerweij (1996) pointed to the need for strategies not only to assist failing schools to become at least reasonably effective but also ones for assisting effective schools to remain so.

Constancy of purpose and mission

The key to maintaining effective strategy whilst being able to renew constantly is seen as *constancy of purpose* by Peters and Waterman (1982) and Peters (1988). This aspect for some strategic managers, such as Limb (1992), is expressed through a mission statement. In her work at an FE college, Limb (*ibid.*, p. 168) saw the mission as something which 'defines purpose and embodies our educational philosophy and value. It is a reference point by which we make decisions, determine implementation strategies and policy, judge behaviour and evaluate our performance. It informs and guides our strategic direction'. The relevance of mission statements is discussed in more detail by Keith Foreman in Chapter 2.

Characteristics of strategic thinking.

Mintzberg (1995, p. 82) describes strategic thinking as essentially 'seeing'. The strategic manager must see 'ahead and behind, above and below, beside and beyond' but 'for a thinker to deserve the label *strategic*, he or she must also *see* it *through*'. Mintzberg reasoned that, since the full consequences of creative visions could never be understood ahead of time, 'seeing through' was a more accurate concept than 'thinking through' (*ibid.*, p. 83). This 'seeing through' aspect of strategic management is the reason for a significant section of this book being devoted to implementation of strategy.

'Seeing', of course, also carries the other implication of the ability of the strategic thinker to make intelligent guesses about the future. This ability therefore involves an element of risk-taking. For Mintzberg therefore there is a clear need for strategic managers to balance boldness of vision in anticipating scenarios and the realistic understanding of what will be involved in implementing action in those scenarios.

Mintzberg's arguments, along with those of Hanford (1995), Fidler (1996) and Weindling (1997), make it possible to show the clear differences between strategic thinking and the operational management which ensures the day-to-day running of the school or college (see Table 1.1).

Table 1.1   Differences between strategic and operational thinking

Strategic thinking is	Operational management thinking is
Longer term	Short term, immediate
In whole organisation terms	Concerned with the section needing attention
Reflective	To lead to action quickly
Looking to use fully whole organisational capabilities	Looking to use accessible resources
Conceptual	Concrete
Creative, breaking new ground	Ongoing, routine
More concerned with effectiveness	More concerned with efficiency
Identifying opportunities	Resolving existing problems
Constantly examining the external environment	Focusing on the internal context
Demonstrating a 'hands-off' approach	Demonstrating a 'hands-on' approach
With a 'helicopter' perspective	With an 'on-the-ground' perspective

It is worth stating here, however, that the differences denoted in Table 1.1 do not indicate a simplistic distinction of roles, i.e. one person or persons conceiving the strategy, other people implementing it. Mintzberg's notion of 'thinking as seeing' implies a notion of sharing with others so that possible consequences can be foreseen. Strategic thinking, although it is a requirement of leaders, is not the sole prerogative of individual heads or principals; others have their part to play too. Peter Earley's chapter in this book, for example, examines middle managers' roles in this. Likewise, strategic management is one part only of what being a leader involves. Some of these issues are explored in more detail in the third section of this book. If the strategic manager's thinking remains detached from implementation, there is a risk that it will remain purely theoretical, and based solely upon rational assumptions about change. McLaughlin's (1990, p. 12) study in the USA found that the higher the level of the policy-maker, the less the linkage between policy and change of practice: '[the] study demonstrated that the nature, amount, and pace of change at the local level was a product of local factors that were largely beyond the control of higher-level policymakers'. Thus, the decentralisation of policy control to semi-autonomous schools and colleges helps to reinforce the critical importance of *context* for strategic managers and suggests that what is needed is what Hopkins and Lagerweij (1996, p. 66) called a strategy that is 'implementation friendly'. They use school improvement as an example of a strategy which has failed on occasions because some implementers did not recognise that it was the *process* of managing improvement that was as important as specific changes for improvement.

Only in recognising this central link between strategy and its implementation process can the strategic manager become effective. This notion underpins approaches to strategic planning, on which a later section of this chapter focuses.

The importance of values

The consistent link between strategy and its implementation lies in the values of the school or college – 'what is important to us' (West-Burnham, 1994, p. 86). Marsh (1993) links values with vision and mission as part of an organisation's strategic 'Purpose Statement', although placing these after an analysis of customer needs. In Marsh's model, the critical success factors will address how far vision, mission and values are being met, as well as customer needs and wants. However, in the educational contexts described earlier, the issue of 'whose values?' may well arise at critical implementation stages. In England and Wales, legislation for schools in 1996 enabled comprehensive secondary schools to introduce an element of selection into their intake. This possibility of selecting some pupils on ability criteria and thus improving results is clearly at odds with the original aims and ideals of schools committed to all-ability intakes. Tensions in values are inevitable in such schools as they strive to achieve their aims of becoming thriving, successful locally attractive schools. These aspects of values are addressed by Keith Foreman in terms of leadership and Tony Bush in relation to organisational culture in Chapters 2 and 3, respectively.

Accountability to stakeholders

Strategic managers of schools and colleges have to recognise the accountability of their visions, plans and their implementation, especially perhaps in the public sector because public funding is being used, and because of the moral imperatives inherent in managing education. One dimension of accountability is that executed through what Russell (1995) calls the rational position, i.e. the world of external inspection, publication of results, requirements to report to various bodies. The legitimacy of this accountability may be clear but it can be based on assumptions that are not necessarily founded on the actual requirements of those to whom the manager is accountable. Martin's (1995, p. 9) research found, for example, that many parents do not wish to be involved in decision-making in schools yet, as she points out,

> public policy and legislative trends in several countries and educa-
> tional jurisdictions in the industrialised world have been to give
> parents increasingly more power over educational decisions . . . in
> the latter 1980s, Britain, Australia, New Zealand, British Columbia,
> Alberta, Quebec and Chicago all enacted provisions which gave
> parents as a group a relatively more powerful role in educational
> affairs than they had previously.

However, the other dimension of accountability to which the strategic manager must give attention is the one without which no mission or plan can succeed. It is what Russell (1995, p. 11) calls 'empowered, personal accountability'. Unless those who work in the schools or colleges are motivated through this to bring about real improvement, the rational accountability will be merely facilitating routine reporting and responding to minimum demands. In devising an action plan, for example, Russell suggests that features of the ideal future for the organisation may be taken as indicators and evaluation headings. In this way, the ideals may be linked with the objectives and gain continued support from the individuals who co-ordinate action.

Effective strategic management therefore moves beyond an instrumental notion of accountability for the efficiency and effectiveness of the school or college to foster, in addition, a liberating conceptualisation.

STRATEGIC PLANNING: COMPONENTS AND ISSUES

This chapter, and indeed this book, is based upon the premise that strategic management is much more than strategic planning and, although 'there is no clear consensus in the literature as to what strategic management actually comprises' (West-Burnham *et al.*, 1995, p. 62), the two terms are often used interchangeably. However, strategic planning is critically important as a means of integrating strategy and its implementation and in schools and colleges can be described as 'mapping a route between the perceived present situation and the desired future situation' (West-Burnham, 1994, p. 82). One secondary head, interviewed about strategy by Parker (1997), was fond of quoting *The Koran*: 'If you do not know where you are going, anywhere will do.' This head saw the broad strategic plan as providing that knowledge of where the school was going.

Need for planning to adapt to changing circumstances

According to Hall *et al.* (1995, p. 176), organisations are now 'comfortable with the notion of emergent planning i.e. strategies that follow broadly agreed tracks but which flex and respond to competitor and customer trends as they emerge'. The case study of a large FE college by Cowham (1994) paid special attention to how strategic planning might help in the period of turbulence, in the first year after colleges' incorporation. Observing the ambiguities and conflicts inherent in the strategic implementation phase, the consultant's view was that strategic planning offered many benefits for the individual college, particularly as its process enabled a college to have coherence in response to an 'unstable and threatening external environment' where the responses should be 'practical and pragmatic' (*ibid.*, p. 290).

Environmental scanning

Caldwell and Spinks (1992) make it clear that leadership in autonomous schools involves keeping abreast of trends and issues, threats and opportunities and discerning the mega-trends. This scanning of the environment within which the school or college does and will operate is likely to include not only those aspects close to hand, such as local competition, but also those discerned as having influence both from a national (e.g. government legislation) or even international level (e.g. technological development).

Limb (1992, p. 177) lists 17 'external factors affecting strategic planning at Milton Keynes College'. These included one at international level ('The single European market in 1992'), eight at national level (e.g. government papers on employment, on skills and actual legislation), five at local level (e.g. the county council's reorganisation plans) and three direct (e.g. 'the legacy of neglect in the physical environment, equipment and resources of Milton Keynes College during the seventies and eighties').

Similarly, Henley College, Coventry (1997, p. 3) uses a regional labour market and skills trends analysis to estimate a shift in demand: 'With the demographic shift in the age composition of the local population it may be expected that demand for school leaver courses will drop. However, there may be a corresponding demand in courses for young adults and those in the pre-retirement/early retirement groups.' The college's plan also examines the future agenda of further education at a national level in order to draw conclusions for its own framework for action.

Generic strategies

Murgatroyd and Morgan (1993, p. 25) argue that schools which choose a strategy and work 'within this strategy frame to build loyalty, commitment, understanding and ownership of the strategy are more likely to produce successful students'. This is because individual schools need to develop their own special place in the market situation, which comes from a strong personal or cultural identity. Four factors are seen as determining decisions about choice of strategy – access, resources, curriculum and management. The four generic strategies of schooling proposed by Murgatroyd and Morgan are shown in Figure 1.1.

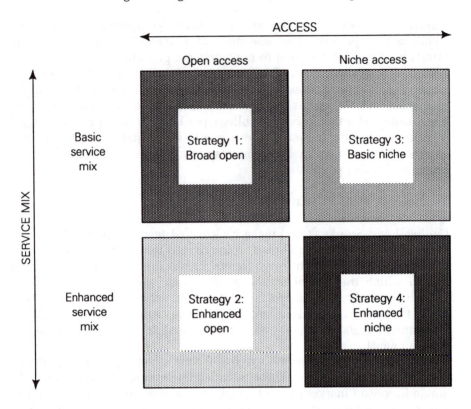

Figure 1.1 The four generic strategies of schooling. *Source*: Murgatroyd and Morgan, 1992. Reprinted by permission of Open University Press.

However, such a model may not be able to remain constant since circumstances beyond the organisation's control may force a change. For example, the Technology Schools Initiative (TSI) in England and Wales meant that some schools felt they were forced to develop an 'enhanced niche' strategy because government funding was available for technology curriculum focus and the funding was vital for marketing the school in a competitive situation. 'We have open competition between schools here, which means that any vision which does not include effective marketing is not in touch with reality. We need, for example, to be oversubscribed' (secondary head quoted in Parker, 1997, p. 27). The reasons therefore for the chosen niche could be, at least initially, opportunist.

Clearly, Murgatroyd and Morgan's model is for schools and largely based upon curricular choices. Other institutions, such as some further education colleges, may need to develop strategies about, for example, place, i.e. considering where a college site would be most advantageous for the market available.

Strategic analysis and choices

Strategic analysis of the organisation's current and future position provides the basis for making decisions about possible ways ahead. Fidler (1996, p. 89) argues that this analysis must include 'an examination of the organisation's culture. Its taken-for-granted ways of doing things need to be made explicit so as to recognise the values-in-use in the organisation'. Johnson and Scholes' (1993) model (see Figure 1.2) is a valuable one, not least because it stresses the interdependence of analysis, choice and implementation. Indeed, Johnson and Scholes (*ibid.*) point out that strategic choice, analysis and implementation may well not be separate stages but occurring simultaneously. Implementation of strategic planning may be integral to the actual strategic choices. It is clearly important to establish clear links between the longer-term strategic plans and short and medium-term processes for planning, for four main reasons. To

- monitor and evaluate effectiveness and efficiency of the operations;
- enable directions or emphasis to be switched when circumstances require;
- meet current accountability demands of stakeholders while progress is being made; and
- ensure a closer link with day-to-day operational activities of the organisation than something 'distant' would be able to.

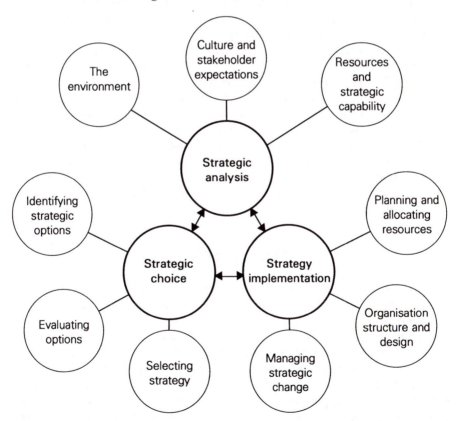

Figure 1.2 The Johnson and Scholes summary model of strategic management. *Source*: Johnson and Scholes, 1993. Reprinted by permission of Prentice Hall Europe.

The FEFC's strategic planning model for colleges in England and Wales (FEFC, 1992) proposes a five-year strategic plan which is 'informed' by *annual* review and evaluation of performance against implementation targets and 'delivered' by implementing the plan through *annual* operating statements. Bearing in mind the issues discussed earlier concerning a conflict of values, Cowham (1994, p. 279) describes the FEFC model as 'simplistic and bureaucratic in its approach'.

In any case, even if planning is rational, change is emphatically not guaranteed to be so! Cowham's (*ibid.*) study showed that a range of perspectives could be seen operating in the environments affecting the college. As West-Burnham *et al.* (1995, p. 62) point out: 'One of the greatest dangers of strategic planning is that it is perceived as having no direct relationship with the realities of work in the classroom. Indeed, a cynical view of planning in general is that "we formulate the strategic plan and then get on with the actual job".' The extent to which this view can be avoided will depend upon a number of factors, including the effective management by those in key roles (discussed in detail in the chapters in Section C of this book) and the actual process of planning (examined by Edith Jayne and Jacky Lumby in Chapters 6 and 7, respectively).

However, Fidler (1996) suggests that there are two distinct approaches to the process of strategic planning. One he calls the 'grand design' 'whereby the future direction is planned out in general terms before the details are subsequently worked out. The other, in contrast, seeks to "sum the parts" by producing detailed plans from sub-sections . . . before trying to synthesise the resulting overall direction . . . indicated in these plans' (*ibid.*, p. 86). Although these two do not necessarily correspond to a 'top-down' versus 'bottom-up' style, it is easy to see that either could have significant influence on the attitudes held to strategic planning within an organisation. The problem for managers is to reconcile the ownership of stakeholders with the risk of fragmentation of the plan if, for example, the second approach is attempted because of internal dissatisfaction with the current situation.

CONCLUSIONS

Developing a strategic mode of thinking is essential for leadership and management of schools and colleges in the twenty-first century. Strategic management is much more than strategic planning and it would be dangerous for autonomous schools and colleges if they were to assume that devising a strategic plan indicated that most of the work was complete. As argued in this chapter, implementation cannot be separated from planning and the effective strategic manager remains alert to the constant linkage between what is happening in the organisation *now* and the trends, issues and consequent need for change. All models of strategic planning inevitably assume some degree of rationality. Perhaps the value of such planning 'is as much about the development of the capacity to plan as it is about outcomes' (West-Burnham, 1994, p. 97). However, it is useful to try to indicate the relationships between vision, strategy, medium-term plans and day-to-day activities as in Figure 1.3.

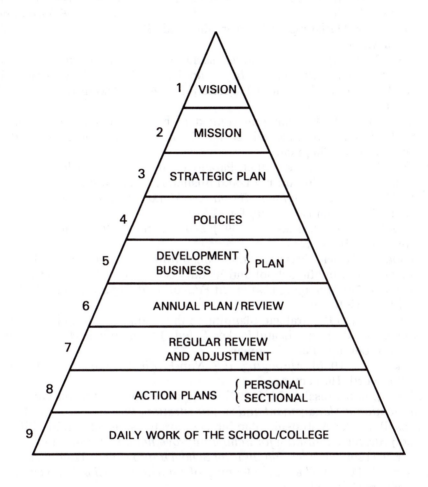

Figure 1.3 Relationship of strategic aspects to the daily work of an organisation

Jacky Lumby's final chapter of this book examines the management of such change processes. The strategic manager needs to be aware that of the nine levels shown in Figure 1.3, none is fixed for ever. Nevertheless, the levels show not only the relationship between vision and daily operations but also illustrate a ratio of likelihood for change. Levels 1–3 are least likely to change, certainly not with any regularity. Levels 4 and 5 need regularly updating. Levels 6–8 involve continual adjustment whilst level 9 (described by Parsons *et al.*, 1994, p. 9, as 'the regular hurly-burly') involves the ultimate excitement and frustration of the business of education itself, i.e. the interaction of learners and teachers, and other stakeholders. It is ensuring the relevance and quality of this everyday experience to the longer-term future of the school or college which is the enduring challenge for the strategic manager.

REFERENCES

Abbott, I. (1993) The opening of a city technology college. In Smith, M. and Busher, H. (eds.) *Managing Schools in an Uncertain Environment: Resources, Marketing and Power*, Sheffield, Sheffield Hallam University for BEMAS.

Bollen, R. (1996) School effectiveness and school improvement: the intellectual and policy context. In Reynolds, D., Bollen, R., Creemers, B., Hopkins, D., Stoll, L. and Lagerweij, N. (eds.) *Making Good Schools*, London, Routledge.

Bush, T. (1997) The changing context of management in education. In Bush, T. and Middlewood, D. (eds.) *Managing People in Education*, London, Paul Chapman.

Busher, H. and Saran, R. (1993) Paradoxes of power under local management of schools. In Smith, M. and Busher, H. (eds.) *Managing Schools in an Uncertain Environment: Resources, Marketing and Power*, Sheffield, Sheffield Hallam University for BEMAS.

Caldwell, B. and Spinks, J. (1992) *Leading the Self-Managing School*, London, Falmer Press.

Carlson, R. (1964) Environmental constraints and organisational consequences: the public school and its clients. In Baldridge, J. and Deal, T. (eds.) (1975) *Managing Change in Educational Organisations*, Berkeley, Calif., McCutchan.

Cowham, T. (1994) Strategic planning in the changing external context. In Crawford, M., Kydd, L. and Parker, S. (eds.) *Educational Management in Action*, London, Paul Chapman.

Drucker, P. (1990) *Managing the Non-Profit Organisation*, London, Butterworth-Heinemann.

Elliott, G. and Crossley, M. (1997) Contested values in further education, *Educational Management and Administration*, Vol. 25, no. 1, pp. 79–92.

Evans, B. (1996) A strategic plan for a comprehensive School. In Fidler, B. (ed.) *Strategic Planning for School Improvement*, London, Pitman.

Fidler, B. (1996) *Strategic Planning for School Improvement*, London, Pitman.

Fullan, M. (1991) *The New Meaning of Educational Change*, New York, Teachers College Press.

Further Education Funding Council (1992) *Circular 92/01*, Coventry, FEFC.

Further Education Funding Council (1996) *Circular 96/34*, Coventry, FEFC.

Hall, P., Norris, P. and Stuart, R. (1995) *Making Management Development Strategically Effective*, Peterborough, Silver Link Publishing.

Handy, C. (1994) *The Empty Raincoat*, London, Hutchinson.

Hanford, P. (1995) Developing director and executive competencies in strategic thinking. In Garratt, B. (ed.) *Developing Strategic Thought*, London, HarperCollins.

Hargreaves, A. (1992) Cultures of teaching: a focus for change. In Hargreaves, A. and Fullan, M. (eds.) *Understanding Teacher Development*, London, Cassell.

Henley College, Coventry (1997) *Strategic Plan, 1997–2000. External Analysis*, Coventry, Henley College.

Hopkins, D., Ainscow, M. and West, M. (1994) *School Improvement in an Era of Change*, London, Cassell.

Hopkins, D. and Lagerweij, N. (1996) The school improvement knowledge base. In Reynolds, D. *et al.* (eds.) *Making Good Schools*, London, Routledge.

Johnson, G. and Scholes, K. (1993) *Exploring Corporate Strategy* (3rd edn), Hemel Hempstead, Prentice-Hall.

Limb, A. (1992) Strategic planning: managing colleges into the next century. In Bennett, N., Crawford, M. and Riches, C. (eds) (1992) *Managing Change in Education*, London, Open University Press.

Marsh, J. (1993) *The Strategic Toolkit*, IFS International, London.

Martin, Y. (1995) What do parents want? *Management in Education*, Vol. 9, no. 1, pp. 9–11.

McLaughlin, A. (1990) The Rand change agent study revisited, *Educational Researcher*, Vol. 19, no. 9, pp. 11–16.

Middlewood, D. (1997) Managing appraisal. In Bush, T. and Middlewood, D. (eds.) *Managing People in Education*, London, Paul Chapman.

Mintzberg, H. (1995) Strategic thinking as seeing. In Garratt, B. (ed.) (1996) *Developing Strategic Thought*, London, HarperCollins.

Murgatroyd, S. and Morgan, C. (1992) *Total Quality Management and the School*, Buckingham, Open University Press.

Office for Standards in Education (1995) *Governing Bodies and Effective Schools*, London, DFE.

Parker, R. (1997) *Role of school leaders in monitoring and evaluating*, MBA dissertation, University of Leicester.

Parsons, C., Howlett, K. and Corbett, F. (1994) *Institutional Development Planning*, Lancaster, Framework Press Publications.

Pascale, R. (1990) *Managing on the Edge*, London, Viking Press.

Peters, T. (1988) *Thriving on Chaos*, London, Macmillan.

Peters, T. and Waterman, R. (1982) *In Search of Excellence*, London, Harper & Row.

Russell, S. (1995) Accountability: paralysis or liberation? in *Management in Education*, Vol. 9, no. 1, pp. 17–18.

Scott, J. (1985) Ownership, management and strategic control. In Elliott, K. and Lawrence, P. (eds.) *Introducing Management*, Harmondsworth, Penguin Books.

Stoll, L. and Fink, D. (1996) *Changing our Schools*, Milton Keynes, Open University Press.

Taylor, T. and Harrison, J. (1990) *The Manager's Case-Book of Business Strategy*, Oxford, Butterworth-Heinemann.

Weeks, R. (1994) The deputy head and strategic planning. In Crawford, M., Kydd, L. and Parker, S. (eds.) *Educational Management in Action*, London, Paul Chapman.

Weindling, D. (1997) Strategic planning in schools: some practical techniques. In Preedy, M., Glatter, R. and Levacic, R. (eds.) *Educational Management: Strategy, Quality and Resources*, Buckingham, Open University Press.

West-Burnham, J. (1994) Strategy, policy and planning. In Bush, T. and West-Burnham, J. (eds.) *The Principles of Educational Management*, Harlow, Longman.

West-Burnham, J., Bush, T., O'Neill, J. and Glover, D. (1995) *Leadership and Strategic Management*, Harlow, Longman.

2

VISION AND MISSION

Keith Foreman

INTRODUCTION

Contemporary orthodoxy demands that leaders shall possess personal visions of a brighter future for themselves and their organisations, and will be able to communicate and demonstrate them with vigour, persuasiveness and conviction. Governments, congregations, shareholders, members, customers, clients, patients, parents, local communities, the media and so on expect it of them. Without vision, there can be no clear direction, no corporate way forward – and no commitment. Vision is the distinguishing feature of the leadership role.

Leadership has been defined as 'the art of mobilizing others to want to struggle for shared aspirations' (Kouzes and Posner, 1996, p. 30). Visions are about dreams, hopes, possibilities – in sum, a better future. Leaders are expected to show the way. In two surveys across four continents, of the characteristics which respondents most admired in their political, business, educational, religious and community leaders, Kouzes and Posner found that 'being forward looking' – providing a sense of direction and concern for the future – and 'inspiring' – not merely dreaming about but enthusiastically communicating a vision increasingly shared – were consistently near the top (Table 2.1).

Yet, in apparent paradox, they also found that developing a shared vision is the least frequently practised of leadership skills. Leaders told them that 'inspiring a shared vision is the leadership practice with which they feel most uncomfortable' (*ibid.*, p. 124). The researchers believe that this is so because most people have attributed something mystical to the process. 'They see it as supernatural, as a grace or charm that comes from the gods' (*ibid.*).

Table 2.1   Characteristics of admired leaders

Characteristics	1995 respondents: percentage of people selecting	1987 respondents: percentage of people selecting
HONEST	88	83
FORWARD-LOOKING	75	62
INSPIRING	68	58
COMPETENT	63	67
Fair-minded	49	40
Supportive	41	32
Broad-minded	40	37
Intelligent	40	43
Ambitious	13	21
Loyal	11	11
Self-controlled	5	13
Independent	5	10

Source: Based on Kouzes and Posner, 1996.

In a similar vein, Collins and Porras (1991), following their survey of 75 business organisations, describe vision as an 'elusive, yet vitally important, component of corporate success'. But they also conclude that

> most mission statements are terribly ineffective as a compelling, guiding force. In fact, most corporate statements we've encountered – be they called mission, vision, purpose, philosophy, credo or the company way – are of little value. They don't have the intended effect. They don't grab people in the gut and motivate them to work toward a common end. They are usually nothing more than a boring stream of words.   (*Ibid.*, p. 30).

Michael Fullan (1992, p. 83) suggests that vision-building 'permeates the organisation with values, purpose and integrity for both the what and how of improvement' (see Figure 2.1) but adds that 'it is never an easy concept to work with largely because its formation, implementation, shaping and re-shaping in specific organisations is a constant process . . . Vision building is a highly sophisticated dynamic process which few organisations can sustain'.

This chapter attempts to explain the 'vision thing', as President Bush rather sceptically described it, for educational managers, and suggests that, while academics and other researchers have insisted that vision, mission, credo, goals, philosophy, core values and beliefs are fundamental to success, the whole area remains somewhat cloudy and confused. It is something that leaders know they must do – i.e. provide direction and an improved future for the organisation – because the literature on manage-

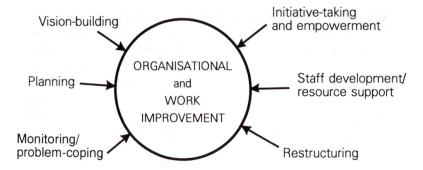

Figure 2.1	The vision-building factors
Source: Adapted from Fullan, 1992

ment tells them so, and because it is expected of them. Indeed in public sector schools and colleges it is increasingly *required* of them by governments demanding improvement. For instance, in the compulsory training module for the National Professional Qualification for Headship, the Teacher Training Agency (TTA, p. 6) expects aspirant headteachers in England and Wales to be able to

- lead by example, provide inspiration and motivation, and embody for the pupils, staff, governors and parents the *vision*, purpose and leadership of the school.
- create an ethos and provide educational *vision* and direction.

But, precisely how to do it in the competitive and unstable world of today and in a multitude of unique contexts remains both unclear and under-researched.

ORIGINS

Much of the literature on vision comes from the business sector and is based on American research and aspiration. It was Warren Bennis and Burt Nanus (1985, p. 101), two US professors, who brought the term into the forefront of leadership literature:

All of the leaders to whom we spoke seemed to have been masters at selecting, synthesising, and articulating an appropriate vision of the future . . . If there is a spark of genius in the leadership function at all, it must lie in this transcending ability, a kind of magic, to assemble – out of all the variety of images, signals, forecasts and alternatives – a clearly articulated vision of the future that is at once single, easily understood, clearly desirable, and energising.

Starratt (1993, p. 7), reviewing the advent of the term vision, suggested that previous writers would have rejected it as being 'too fuzzy, too unquantifiable, too impossible to operationalize in one or two variables. It smacks of religious fervour. It is something one would associate with that other psychiatrically suspect category, "charisma"'. He categorised previous generations of leadership writing as 'instrumental' models which focused on behavioural and strategic aspects of leadership. 'There was little concern for the unique substance of leadership, as though styles and skills . . . would carry the day in all organisations and under most circumstances' (*ibid.*, p. 4).

In an earlier survey, Starratt (1988, p. 3) studied the origins of visions of great leaders. He found a common thread running through every great and powerful vision. Each:

> has its roots in those deep, core meanings about human life, its dignity, grandeur, beauty, value etc. It tends to be expressed in myth, poetry, metaphor. It is concerned with values such as freedom, honour, selflessness, altruism, loyalty, devotion to fatherland (or community), integrity, dignity of the person, equality, peace and harmony among peoples, the rule of law, the elevation of reason and civility, wisdom, self government, courage, character, a perfect performance, creative expression, harmony with nature etc.

But it is the language of such visions – grandiose and remote – which presents difficulties for today's leaders and their prospective followers.

Stacey (1992, p. 130) acknowledges the benefits of vision for organisations but also warns of some dangers: 'Though leaders are told to develop vision the advice on how to do it is not concrete enough and may lead to bewilderment and frustration. No one really knows how we are supposed to form a vision':

- A single vision may in the end be destructive because it does not take into account changes which affect the basis on which the vision was originally constructed.
- Vision-building places heavy burdens on leaders and may lead to follower dependency or groupthink and the perpetuation of the belief that the success of organisation relies on one or two gifted individuals.
- The process distracts the organisation away from learning and interacting in groups (adapted from Stacey, *ibid.*, pp. 137–40).

VISION IN EDUCATIONAL LEADERSHIP

Writings on the importance of vision in educational leadership emerged in the 1980s. In *The Self-Managing School*, Caldwell and Spinks (1988) described the results of research into highly effective schools in Tasmania and South Australia. Coming as it did in the very early days of the movement towards local management it proved highly influential. In their 'Collaborative school management cycle' they suggested that the vision of the school leader would, in time, be embodied in a statement of philosophy, a set of assumptions, values, beliefs which support learning and teaching. Goals, policies, plans, priorities, budgets and everyday activities should be consistent with the school's philosophy. They asserted that it was desirable that all in the school community be committed to goals as well as the vision and philosophy of the school, and provide extensive guidance on how this might be achieved (*ibid.*, pp. 36–56).

In *Creating an Excellent School,* Hedley Beare and his colleagues at the University of Melbourne (Beare *et al.*, 1989) summarised studies of educational leadership over the previous decade (Roueche and Baker, 1986; Block, 1987; Scheive and Schoenheit, 1987; etc.). They offered ten generalisations, the first three of which are relevant here:

- Outstanding leaders have a vision for their organisations.
- Vision must be communicated in a way which secures commitment among members of the organisation.
- Communication of vision requires communication of meaning.

(Beare *et al.*, 1989, p. 16)

They suggest that, in a school, the vision of a school leader

- includes a mental picture of a possible and desirable future of the school
- will embody the leader's own view of what constitutes excellence in schooling
- includes a mental image of a possible and durable future state for the broader educational scene and society in general
- reflects different assumptions, values and beliefs
- must be 'institutionalised' so that it shapes the everyday activities of the school.

(*Ibid.*, pp. 118–24)

Roland Barth (1990, p. 47) summed it up when he said that 'a school without visions is a vacuum inviting intrusion'.

DEFINITIONS

But before proceeding further it is essential to be clear about the meanings of such words as vision, vision-building mission and objectives. For some writers they are virtually interchangeable; for others they are quite distinct. In this chapter, the following definitions apply:

- *Vision* An image of what might be; an ideal which is unique to the person or the organisation and recognises dissatisfaction with the present. It is a catalyst for action, and reflects core values: 'A vision is a preferred future, a desirable state. It is an expression of optimism despite the bureaucratic surroundings or evidence to the contrary' (Block, 1987, p. 103).
- *Vision-building* The process of creating agreement about the future of an organisation, by shaping and reshaping over time ideas which point to improvement, and the means of getting there. Shared visions are the result of a collective exercise of vision-building, which inspires and ensures corporate commitment: 'Creating a vision forces us to take a stand for a preferred future' (*ibid.*, p. 104).

- *Mission* A public statement which defines the *purpose* of an organisation: why it exists and what that means for customers – both internal and external: 'The organisation's statement of purpose, intentions and priorities: its direction . . . the basis for planning and decision making' (Stott and Walker, 1992, p. 50).
- *Objectives (including targets, aims, goals, strategies)* Statements of outcomes, more or less measurable, which visions or missions *may* produce. They are most frequently contained in a development, action or business plan.

Sergiovanni (1991, p. 57) sums up the difference in these words:

> Vision . . . should not be constructed as a strategic plan that functions as a 'road map' charting the turns needed to reach a specific reality . . . [but] be viewed more as a compass that points the direction to be taken, that inspires enthusiasm and that allows people to buy into and take part in the shaping of the way.

PERSONAL VISION-BUILDING

Creating a personal vision statement is recommended by a number of writers. Covey (1990, p. 44) tells us to 'begin with the end in mind'. This is framed as a personal vision statement – an inside-out view – and is, he suggests, highly motivating because it provides a sense of direction.

Kouzes and Posner (1996, p. 104) suggest that intuition plays an important role: 'Intuition is the well spring of vision, the bringing together of knowledge and experience to produce new insights.' It is not, they suggest, a logical activity, which explains why some researchers and writers ignore it, and why some senior managers dismiss it as being too 'soft' to acknowledge openly. Nor is it a mystical process: 'It is the bringing together of knowledge and experience to produce new insights' (*ibid.*, p. 105).

Making a personal vision statement may take considerable courage. Block (1987, p. 106) asserts that 'to avoid creating a vision for oneself is to protect oneself from disappointment and failure. It is hard to comprehend how pervasive this wish for protection is . . . To choose autonomy and create your own vision is to choose a risky path'. Nevertheless, he claims that making a personal statement *for the organisation to which you belong* is an essential leadership step because it signifies dissatisfaction with the current situation, opens up potential conflict, demands actions and becomes a benchmark.

The first message is that personal vision-building is an essential starting point. The second is that, without the ability to communicate that vision so that others see and want to achieve it, then the ideal remains merely a dream.

VISION-BUILDING FOR ORGANISATIONS

The characteristics of successful visionary leaders

Hoyle (1995) suggested three essential characteristics of educational leaders who succeed as visionaries:

- The capacity to be compassionate and to care for others. Even those visionaries who are impatient to make visions happen must demonstrate this. The model is the *servant leader.*
- The capacity to communicate, often not so much by what is said but by actions. Words, nevertheless, are important. They need to energise others into action. Listening, equally essential, is the other side of the coin.
- The capacity to persist in the face of resistance, failure and disappointment (adapted from, Hoyle, *ibid.*, p. 56).

Enlisting the support of others

Techniques for gaining the commitment of people in the organisation to a common vision have been well rehearsed in the literature. Murgatroyd and Morgan (1993), strong advocates of TQM, give guidance to school leaders such as:

- talk-up the power and importance of vision; and
- focus the minds of staff on key words representing the leaders' vision of what the school could become (adapted from Murgatroyd and Morgan, *ibid.*, pp. 93–5).

But the most crucial fact arising from research is that vision cannot be imposed or mandated from above. Vision-building is about enrolling the interests and aspirations of others. But here lies the problem: the translation of personal dreams which animate and enthuse into something which enlists the support of others through appealing to their wants and values. For many, it is not a natural role.

Holmes (1993, p. 17) concluded that

very few school leaders admit to being visionaries and many feel uncomfortable with the whole notion of vision. To many, the word smacks of ideology or even of fanaticism . . . it is related to a well-embedded distrust of charisma and fervour in public life in ideological terms, which is frequently resisted, perhaps feared.

Kouzes and Posner (1996) suggest that this discomfort may be caused by lack of training or opportunity, and insist that the skills of inspiring or communicating a vision can be learned:

1) Begin by being receptive and sensitive to others, listening to their hopes and fears and making use of 'a human longing for meaning and fulfilment' (*ibid.*, p. 132).

2) Give life to a vision by using powerful and emotive language – metaphors, figures of speech, examples, stories, anecdotes, quotations, slogans, adopting a positive and energetic approach, with warmth and affection.
3) Demonstrate a personal conviction and belief in the vision (*ibid.*, pp. 99–147).

It seems entirely reasonable to suggest that aspiring leaders should deliberately focus their training and development on vision-building skills. However the problem remains that there can be no guarantee that on appointment as principal/headteacher, for example, they will be successful in persuading stakeholders in that specific context to struggle for the future which the vision seeks to identify.

The role of the principal/headteacher

The evidence arising from studies of vision-building in schools and colleges indicates that headteachers and principals see themselves as the source of a vision for their institutions, working through various processes of consultation, to enlist the support of their staff. They are, after all, *expected* to be leaders. But their success is questionable.

Evidence about the function of vision in England and Wales was gathered by the School Management Task Force Professional Working Party (Bolam *et al.*, 1993). Twelve headteachers were interviewed and asked to describe their vision for their schools. All were able to describe some form of vision – 'more or less articulately'. However, the components of the vision which most of the headteachers described were 'neither surprising, nor striking, nor controversial. They were closely in line with what one might expect of the British system of education' (*ibid.*, p. 35). In other words vision was not specific to the school. Furthermore, in most of the schools, comparatively few teachers were able to speak with any confidence about the elements of the vision:

> This would suggest that, as a general rule, the headteachers of their schools had not consciously and deliberately set out to communicate their vision to colleagues and to ensure that its influence permeated every aspect of organisational life. Only in four of the schools were staff very clear as to what the headteacher stood for and wished to see happen. (*Ibid.*, p. 36)

In contrast, in their study of successful high schools in the USA, Wilson and Corcoran (1984, p. 83) concluded that

> leaders in these schools not only effectively use the more commonly mentioned bureaucratic devices of rules, procedures and authority relations to establish or reinforce a set of desired behaviours on the part of staff or students, but they also are attuned to the importance of cultural links – those activities that provide a consistency of the belief system and consensus about the direction in which the school

is headed. It is the ability to focus all the brief interactions . . . around a vision of the school that contributes to the dynamism of these organisations. No one style offers a solution. Nor is it a single individual who provides an answer. By . . . matching leadership style with the character of the school community, and recognising the leadership potential of staff, the formal leaders in these schools have made major contributions to their success.

One conclusion from these studies might be of significant cultural differences between approaches to vision-building in the USA and England and Wales and raises questions about training, expectations and practice.

Leadership in further education

Further education in England and Wales has faced extraordinary challenges in the past decade. Funding, very much controlled by the Further Education Funding Council (FEFC), is largely dependent on performance against required criteria. Governing bodies of FE colleges are *required* to determine 'their educational character and mission' (FEFC, 1994, p. 14). A principal is expected to ensure that a clear *mission* for the college is established so that no one is in doubt about the future. Gorringe (1986, p. 238), Principal of Norton Radstock College, expressed it in these terms:

In essence, the vision is of a college in which managers are strategic thinkers and planners, not controllers; where each employee recognises his/her contribution to such things as status and remuneration; where thinking about quality, and elimination of wasteful practices, is second nature; where initiative is regularly used to meet our customers' needs; where the accepted right thing is whatever enables us to serve individuals and employers; and removing barriers to learning is the greatest good.

In practice, however, the reality is that vision in the FE context is greatly restricted by the requirements and financial controls wielded by the FEFC. Mission, in the FE sense, expresses something of the uniqueness of a college, but is essentially a business statement to ensure its future existence. But evidence as to the effectiveness of mission statements in business and education is not persuasive.

MISSION

In business

The effectiveness of mission statements in industry was researched by Collins and Porras (1991). In their study of 25 leading US companies, they described four approaches to creating a *mission*:

1) *Targeting*   Setting a clear, defined target and aiming for it; quantitative or non-quantitative: 'To be a $1 billion company in four years' (a doubling in size) (Wal-Mart).

2) *Common enemy*   Creating a goal focused on defeating a successful competitor, usually a bigger company leading the field: 'Yamaha Wo Tsubusu (We will crush, squash and slaughter Yamaha)' (Honda). They suggest that companies recognise the value of motivations based on David and Goliath and the urge to win. The downside is how long can you sustain a war effort and what happens when you are Goliath?

3) *Role model*   Setting a bright prospect for small to medium-size companies in their industry: 'To be the IBM of the real estate industry' (Trammel Crow). The risk is setting role models which do not generate powerful and motivating images for organisational members (the subsequent decline of IBM is a case in point).

4) *Internal transformation*   Setting a target of internal change which will allow the organisation to remain or become healthy – more likely to be effective when an organisation must change in order to survive: 'To contrive a convergence of the strength of our research venture with the teaching of our undergraduates' (Stanford University).

In all these, the authors insist that a vivid, vibrant, engaging and specific description of what it will be like when the mission is achieved is essential. It transforms words into pictures – so that 'people carry around a clear, compelling image in their heads' (*ibid.*, p. 47). For non-quantative missions 'picture painting' is essential. Yet, as we have seen, these researchers found mission statements to be ineffective as a guiding force.

In education

There is little evidence as to the use of mission statements in education and their effectiveness. Mission and vision are key components of total quality management. In the USA, a TQE (total quality education) strategy has been advocated by a number of American writers including, for instance, Downey *et al.* (1994). They insist (*ibid.*, p. 30) that an educational organisation requires a mission which

> must describe purpose, why are we in the school business and what that means for students and other customers – internal (e.g. parents) and external (e.g. businesses and industry). Our mission describes our aim (to what end) and our actions (what do we do). Most important, it provides the criteria for making choices.

They propose mission statements for school systems, schools, departments, taskforces, committees and *every individual* associated with their work.

Sagor and Barnett (1994, p. 5) provide an example of a mission statement from 1) a school district in Iowa and 2) a school in San Diego:

> Our mission is to provide effective instruction in basic skills, to develop the potential of all students, to nurture a sense of individual

worth, and to build a foundation for lifelong learning in a changing world. The district, in partnership with the community, is committed to serve all students with academic, cultural, vocational, and activity programs that meet the highest standards of educational excellence.

Our mission is to prepare all students to become lifelong learners who are self-supporting, responsible, participating members of American and world societies.

However, these statements are extremely general and not specific to these particular organisations – which links to the problem identified by Bolam *et al.* (1993) (see above).

In their survey of the perceptions of Singaporean heads of department about mission statements in their schools (10 primary, 9 secondary), Stott and Walker (1992) found similar problems:

- Central government policy was strongly influential in the formulation of the statement.
- The statement was most frequently drawn up by either a core of management staff or the whole staff – there was no parental involvement, for instance.
- Worthy intentions were often expressed in ambiguous terms.
- There was much uncertainty about the use of mission statements in planning processes.
- There was an apparent failure to revise or update statements even during a period of major changes in Singaporean schools (adapted from Stott and Walker, *ibid.*, pp. 55–6).

In an analysis of how headteachers/principals have tried to secure support of staff towards a common goal, Murgatroyd and Morgan (1993, p. 69) were also highly critical of the use of mission statements: 'Such statements tend to be long and complex, and often the result of compromises among a staff with competing and different interests. Many are not inspiring . . . are rarely "owned" by anyone and . . . often not remembered.'

Peeke (1994, pp. 9–11) summarised the benefits that have been claimed for mission statements in further education. They should

- encourage the development of a clear sense of purpose
- facilitate decision-making
- facilitate communication both internally and externally
- aid evaluation activity
- clarify marketing strategy.

The process of mission building may be seen as 'a powerful method of promoting organisational change' (*ibid.*, p. 11) but success depends on how well it is contrived, communicated and operationalized – and on the quality of the statement itself. Peeke (*ibid.*, p. 9) concludes with the view that mission was

an important part of strategic analysis . . . influential in guiding organisational action through the process of strategy implementation.

It is likely, however, that strategic management is not yet widely practised within British Further Education, at least, and that the mission statements of most colleges have failed to impact strongly on organisational processes.

CONCLUSION

Vision and mission in public sector schools and colleges are essential but problematic aspects of leadership. The determination of central governments to improve educational systems has put great pressure on educational leaders. They are required to be transformational and visionary, and also to have the capacity to bring about change, much of it generated by governments themselves. It cannot, therefore, be surprising that many vision statements are not very specific to individual institutions. Nevertheless, leaders must find ways of inspiring staff towards improvement. Without some sense of direction which captures both minds and hearts, teachers will indeed be working in a vacuum. Schlechty (1990, p. 137) put it in a nutshell when he said: 'Teachers will not be inspired by goals like reducing drop out rates or improving test scores. They will, however, respond to the challenge to invent schools in which teachers and students have increased opportunities for success.'

Even in a context of tight central controls, there is still the opportunity for corporate vision-building. Bell and Harrison (1995, p. 4) express the position in this way:

> Major threats and the intervention of 'outsiders' have forced change on every educational institution in the UK in recent years. Department for Education and Funding Council circulars have regularly carried veiled (or, in some cases, plainly stated) threats on the lines of 'conform and improve, or perish' . . . Heads of institutions have had to develop new skills and structures which not only take account of institutional culture, but which also enable action to be taken quickly in order to implement new regulations. The fact that changes have been imposed . . . in no way reduces the need for vision because, without it, planning becomes haphazard or disappears under the weight of day-to-day burdens.

Nevertheless it is still necessary to face up to the real problems and dangers of vision-building which have been outlined above – finding a balance between rationality and intuition, avoiding dependency by followers, the need to be adaptable as circumstances change, the avoidance of vagueness and overgeneralisation inherent in both vision and mission statements and making them specific and unique to any institution. It may not come as a surprise to find this chapter ending with a number of questions still to be answered:

- How does the newly appointed educational leader, needing to articulate a vision, best go about it?

- How is vision best communicated to the complacent and those resistant to change?
- How can the interest and active co-operation of governors and parents be gained in building a school's vision?
- How can students be involved in the formulation of a school/college vision?
- How can the support of FE lecturers be harnessed for a college mission which is fundamentally serving the needs of central government?
- What, precisely, is the relationship between a leader's vision and an organisation's culture?
- What can be done to train educational leaders for vision-building?
- How can the values, needs and motives of staff and students be incorporated within a school/college vision/mission?
- How can the different visions of departments or curriculum areas be best fitted into a corporate vision?

Vision, after all, 'appeals to the emotional and spiritual resources of an organisation' (Bennis and Nanus, 1985, p. 102) and it is these that successful leaders seek to tap.

REFERENCES

Barth, R. (1990) *Improving Schools from Within*, San Francisco, Calif., Jossey-Bass.

Beare, H., Caldwell, B. and Millikan, R. (1989) *Creating an Excellent School*, London, Routledge.

Bell, J. and Harrison, B.T. (1995) *Finding a Practical Theory for Managing Education: Why Vision?*, David Fulton, London.

Bennis, W. and Nanus, B. (1985) *Leaders,* New York, Harper & Row.

Block, P. (1987) *The Empowered Manager*, San Francisco, Calif., Jossey-Bass.

Bolam, R., McMahon, A., Pocklington, K. and Weindling, D. (1993) *Effective Management in School*, London, HMSO.

Caldwell, B.J. and Spinks, J.M. (1988) *The Self-Managing School*, London, Falmer Press.

Collins, C. and Porras, J. (1991) Organisational vision and visionary organisations, *California Management Review*, Fall, pp. 30–52.

Covey, S. (1990) *Principle Centred Leadership*, New York, Simon & Schuster.

Downey, C.J., Frase, E.F. and Peters, J.J. (1994) *The Quality Education Challenge*, Thousand Oaks, Calif., Corwin Press.

Fullan, M. (1992) *The New Meaning of Educational Change*, London, Cassell.

Further Education Funding Council (1994) *Guide for College Governors*, Coventry, FEFC.

Gorringe, R. (1986) A vision and culture for the future. In Gorringe, R. and Toogood, P. (eds.) *Changing the Culture of a College, Coombe Lodge Report*, Vol. 24, no. 3, Bristol, The Staff College.

Holmes, G. (1993) *Essential School Leadership: Developing Vision and Purpose in Management*, London, Kogan Page.

Hoyle, J.R. (1995) *Leadership and Futuring: Making Visions Happen*, London, Corwin Press.

Hutchinson, B. (1993) The effective reflective school: visions and pipedreams in development planning, *Educational Management and Administration*, Vol. 21, no. 1, pp. 94–9.

Kouzes, J.M. and Posner, B.Z. (1996) *The Leadership Challenge*, San Francisco, Calif., Jossey-Bass.

Murgatroyd, S. and Morgan, C. (1993) *Total Quality Management and the School*, Milton Keynes, Open University Press.

National Standards for Headteachers (1997) London, Teacher Training Agency.

Peeke, G. (1994) *Mission and Change. Institutional Mission and its Application in the Management of Further and Higher Education*, Buckingham, SRHE/OUP.

Roueche, J. and Baker, G. (1986) *Profiling Excellence in America's Schools*, Arlington, Va.: American Association of School Administrators.

Sagor, R. and Barnett, B.G. (1994) *The TQE Principal: A Transformed Leader*, Thousand Oaks, Calif., Corwin Press.

Scheive, L. and Schoenheit (1987) *Yearbook of Association for Supervision and Curriculum Development*, Alexandria, Va.: American Association of School Administrators.

Schlechty, P.C. (1990) *Schools for the Twenty-First Century*, San Francisco, Calif., Jossey-Bass.

Sergiovanni, T. (1991) *The Principalship: a reflective practice perspective*, Boston, Allyn & Bacon.

Stacey, R.D. (1992) *Managing the Unknowable*, San Francisco, Calif., Jossey-Bass.

Starratt, R.J. (1988) Dimensions of the principal's leadership: vision and dramatic consciousness, Paper presented to the Southern Tasmania Council for Educational Administration.

Starratt, R.J. (1993) *The Drama of Leadership*, Bristol, Penn., Falmer Press.

Stott, K. and Walker, A. (1992) The nature and use of mission statements in Singaporean schools, *Educational Management and Administration*, Vol. 20, no. 1, pp. 104–110.

Wilson, B.L. and Corcoran, B.C. (1984) *Successful Secondary Schools*, London, Falmer Press.

3

ORGANISATIONAL CULTURE AND STRATEGIC MANAGEMENT

Tony Bush

WHAT IS ORGANISATIONAL CULTURE?

The concept of 'culture' stresses the informal features of organisations rather than their official aspects. It focuses on the values, beliefs and norms of people in the organisation and how these individual perceptions coalesce into shared organisational meanings. Culture is manifested by symbols and rituals rather than through the formal structure of the organisation. Deal's (1985, p. 605) definition of culture is similar to those offered by many other writers:

> Culture is an expression that tries to capture the informal, implicit – often unconscious – side of . . . any human organisation. Although there are many definitions of the term, culture in everyday usage is typically described as 'the way we do things around here'. It consists of patterns of thought, behaviour and artefacts that symbolise and give meaning to the workplace.

Harris (1992, p. 4) claims that culture is central to educational organisations:

> Theorists argue that educational administration has a technical management aspect but is mainly about the culture within an organisation. This culture includes the rituals which occur (or should occur) within an organisation . . . Educational managers . . . are taken to be those capable of shaping ritual in educational institutions.

The interest in culture as an increasingly significant aspect of school and college management may be explained, in part, as dissatisfaction with the limitations of the traditional bureaucratic model. The latter's emphasis on the technical aspects of institutions appears to be inadequate for schools and colleges aspiring to excellence. The stress on the intangible world of values and attitudes helps to produce a more balanced portrait of educational institutions:

> Every organisation has a formally instituted pattern of authority and an official body of rules and procedures which are intended to aid the achievement of those goals. However, alongside this formal aspect of the organisation are networks of informal relationships and unofficial norms which arise from the interaction of individuals and groups working within the formal structure.
>
> (Harling, 1989, p. 20)

The developing importance of culture arises partly from a wish to understand, and operate more effectively within, this informal domain of the values and beliefs of teachers and other members of the organisation. Morgan (1986) and O'Neill (1994) both stress the increasing significance of cultural factors in management. Beare *et al.* (1989, p. 173) claim that culture serves to define the unique qualities of individual organisations: 'An increasing number of . . . writers . . . have adopted the term "culture" to define that social and phenomenological uniqueness of a particular organisational community . . . We have finally acknowledged publicly that uniqueness is a virtue, that values are important and that they should be fostered.'

Schools and colleges in many countries have become 'self-managing' during the 1990s and this reinforces and enhances the notion that they are unique entities. It is likely that self-management will be accompanied by greater individuality and, in Britain, this has been one of the explicit aims of the government's educational policy (Bush, 1995).

The shift towards self-management also facilitates the adoption of a strategic approach. Because the main aspects of management are located at school and college level, governing boards, principals and senior staff are able to integrate the management of finance, staff, curriculum and external relations to achieve the institution's strategic aims. It also enables managers to align strategy with the culture of the organisation.

The concepts of strategy and culture are closely linked. Schneider and Barsoux (1997, p. 106) claim that their definition of culture, 'solutions to problems of external adaptation and internal integration', could be taken as a fitting description of strategy. They argue that the strategic direction of the organisation is conditioned by its culture. 'Different approaches to strategy . . . reflect different underlying cultural assumptions' (*ibid.*). Weick (1985, p. 382) goes further to suggest that culture and strategy are twin concepts: 'It is as if there were a common set of issues in organisations that some of us choose to call culture and others choose to call strategy.'

MAIN FEATURES OF CULTURE
Values and beliefs

Culture emanates from the values and beliefs of members of organisations. These values underpin the behaviour and attitudes of individuals within schools and colleges but they may not always be explicit. Nias *et al.* (1989, p. 11) argue that, in primary schools, 'beliefs are indeed so deeply buried that individuals do not even know what they are'. These individual beliefs are thought to coalesce into shared values to create organisational culture. This assumption is reflected in much of the literature on culture: 'Shared meaning, shared understanding and shared sensemaking are all different ways of describing culture . . . These patterns of understanding also provide a basis for making one's own behaviour sensible and meaningful' (Morgan, 1986, p. 128). As Morgan suggests, shared values provide the foundation for the ethos or culture of a school or college. When the culture is widely known and understood, the organisation's members constantly reinforce it through their discourse and actions. Events and behaviours are interpreted using cultural norms. Conformity with these norms may be 'rewarded' by approval or 'membership'.

The concept of shared meanings does not necessarily mean that individual values are always in harmony with one another. 'There are often many different and competing value systems that create a mosaic of organisational realities rather than a uniform corporate culture' (*ibid.*, p. 127). The existence of multiple cultures is more likely in large, multipurpose organisations such as universities and colleges (Sergiovanni, 1984).

Where different cultures co-exist, teachers and other staff may give their primary loyalty to subunits such as departments rather than the organisation itself. Fullan and Hargreaves (1992, pp. 71–2) argue that some schools develop a 'balkanised' culture made up of separate and sometimes competing groups:

> Teachers in balkanised cultures attach their loyalties and identities to particular groups of their colleagues. They are usually colleagues with whom they work most closely, spend most time, socialise most often in the staffroom. The existence of such groups in a school often reflects and reinforces very different group outlooks on learning, teaching styles, discipline and curriculum.

This issue may be particularly significant in vocational education with its commitment to different, and often separate, disciplines. Bridge (1994, p. 194) refers to 'staff teams possessing different cultural values' at his London further education college.

In formulating strategy, school and college leaders should be sensitive to the values and beliefs of organisational members. Vision, aims and policies that match the culture of the institution are much more likely to become operational than strategies which are inconsistent with those values. In this way, culture serves to 'steer' the organisation by restricting strategic options to those which match its unique ethos. 'Rationality in decision-making is limited, or . . . culture-bound' (Schneider and Barsoux, 1997, p. 108). Where there are multiple cultures, the strategic management process is likely to be even more constrained and problematic.

Shared norms and meanings

The concept of culture emphasises the development of shared norms and meanings. Interaction between members of the organisation, or its subgroups, eventually leads to behavioural norms that gradually become cultural features of the school or college. Morgan (1986, p. 129) claims that 'the nature of a culture is found in its social norms and customs'.

Nias *et al.* (1989, pp. 39–40) show how group norms were established in their case-study primary schools:

> As staff talked, worked and relaxed together, they began to negotiate shared meanings which enabled them to predict each others' behaviour. Consequently each staff developed its own taken-for-granted norms. Because shared meanings and ways of behaving became so taken for granted, existing staff were largely unaware of them. But they were visible to newcomers . . . Researchers moving between schools were constantly reminded of the uniqueness of each school's norms.

These group norms sometimes allow the development of a monoculture in a school with meanings shared throughout the staff. As we noted earlier, however, there may be several subcultures based on the professional and personal interests of different groups. These may have internal coherence but experience difficulty in relationships with other groups whose behavioural norms are different. Wallace and Hall (1994, pp. 28, 127) identify senior management teams (SMTs) as one example of a group culture with clear internal norms but often weak connections to other groups and individuals:

> SMTs in our research developed a 'culture of teamwork' . . . A norm common to the SMTs was that decisions must be reached by achieving a working consensus, entailing the acknowledgement of any dissenting views . . . there was a clear distinction between interaction inside the team and contact with those outside . . . [who] were excluded from the inner world of the team.

Rituals and ceremonies

Culture is typically expressed through rituals and ceremonies which are used to support and celebrate beliefs and norms. Schools, in particular, are rich in such symbols as assemblies, prize givings and, in many voluntary schools, corporate worship. Hoyle (1986, pp. 150, 152) argues that ritual is at the heart of school culture: 'Symbols are a key component of the culture of all schools . . . [they] have expressive tasks and symbols which are the only means whereby abstract values can be conveyed . . . Symbols are central to the process of constructing meaning.'

Beare *et al.* (1989, p. 176) claim that culture is symbolised in three modes:

- **conceptually or verbally**, for example through use of language and the expression of organisational aims;
- **behaviourally**, through rituals, ceremonies, rules, support mechanisms, and patterns of social interaction;
- **visually or materially**, through facilities, equipment, memorabilia, mottoes, crests and uniforms.

Turner (1990, p. 6) suggests that 'ritual is a key mechanism for binding members into the organisation and getting acceptance of activities and experiences which one might expect them rationally to question'. He distinguishes between 'consensual' and 'differential' rituals. The former help to develop shared values while the latter reinforce loyalty to subgroups. Rituals (*ibid.*) demonstrate to members what is important about the society to which they belong:

> The rituals of an organisation create the dramatic style of its culture and are an overt performance to the inside and outside world. The most important function of ritual is to indicate what is highly valued and what is of less value, what are the dominant concerns and what are peripheral, what are central goals and what are marginal.

The relationship between goals and culture is an important aspect of strategic management and we will return to this issue later.

Heroes and heroines

Culture is reflected in the achievements of heroes and heroines who embody the values and beliefs of the organisation. These honoured members typify the behaviours associated with the culture of the institution. Only successes consistent with the culture are likely to be celebrated. 'Choice and recognition of heroes . . . occurs within the cultural boundaries identified through the value filter' (Campbell-Evans, 1993, p. 106).

Beare *et al.* (1989, p. 191) stress the importance of heroes (and anti-heroes) for educational organisations: 'The heroes (and anti-heroes) around whom a saga is built personify the values, philosophy and ideology which the community wishes to sustain . . . The hero figure invites emulation and helps to sustain group unity. Every school has its heroes and potential heroes.'

CULTURE AND MANAGEMENT STRUCTURES

Structure may be regarded as the physical manifestation of the culture of the organisation. The values and beliefs of the institution are expressed in the formal pattern of roles and role relationships established by the school or college. Morgan (1986, p. 131) argues that a focus on organisations as cultural phenomena should lead to a different conceptualisation of structure based on shared meanings: 'Culture . . . must be understood as an active, living phenomenon through which people create and recreate the worlds in which they live . . . organisations are in essence socially constructed realities that rest as much in the heads of their members as they do in concrete sets of rules.'

Structure is usually expressed in two distinct features of the organisation. First, individual roles are established and there is a prescribed or recommended pattern of relationships between role holders. Turner (1990, p. 4) argues that structures are not 'real' but are 'myths' or 'interpretations of reality': 'The [organisation] chart is assumed to reflect what exists in the organisation, people act as though it were true, it structures how people should behave in given situations, but it is in the end not the reality but a frame of thinking – another term for a myth.'

Secondly, there is a structure of committees, working parties and other bodies which have regular or *ad hoc* meetings. These official encounters present opportunities for the enunciation and reinforcement of organisational culture. Hoyle (1986, pp. 163–4) stresses the importance of 'interpretation' at meetings:

> Ostensibly formal meetings are called to transact school business either in a full staff meeting or in various subcommittees and working parties. But meetings are rich in symbolic significance both *as* meetings and in the forms they take . . . The teachers have the task of interpreting the purposes of the meeting and they may endow a meeting with functions which are significant to them.

The larger and more complex the organisation the greater the prospect of divergent meanings, leading to the development of subcultures and the possibility of conflict between them:

> The relationship between organisational structure and culture is of crucial importance. A large and complex organisational structure increases the possibility of several cultures developing simultaneously within the one organisation. A minimal organisational structure, such as that found in most primary schools, enhances the possibility of a solid culture guiding all areas of organisational activity.
>
> (O'Neill, 1994, p. 108)

The development of divergent cultures in complex organisations is not inevitable but the establishment of a unitary culture with wide and active endorsement within the institution requires skilful leadership to ensure transmission and reinforcement of the desired values and beliefs.

Hargreaves (1995, pp. 30–1) emphasises the close and interactive relationship between cultures and their underlying structures, or 'architecture':

> A structural change often has cultural consequences; a shift in culture may alter social structures. Cultures and their architecture are subject to constant pressure towards change by internal and external factors . . . The impact of much externally imposed change is structural rather than cultural, since it is easier to legislate about people's work situation and practices rather than their values and beliefs.

Strategic change is often manifested through new or amended structures. Leaders may adopt these reshaped frameworks in order to secure implementation of their policies or, more ambitiously, to underpin their own cultural assumptions. This may not succeed unless the new structure also takes account of current cultural realities and the values of the staff: 'The organisation's structure and design can be used to reinforce leader assumptions but is rarely an accurate initial basis for embedding them because structure can usually be interpreted by the employees in a number of different ways' (Schein, 1997, p. 247).

MANAGING ORGANISATIONAL CULTURE

Culture is an elusive aspect of organisations. It is a shadowy concept compared with the apparent certainty of structures. Yet it is widely regarded as an important dimension that requires 'managing' if it is to contribute to the organisation's success. In this section, we examine how culture can be managed.

AUDITING CULTURE

An important preliminary stage in managing culture is to establish the main cultural features of an organisation. This may be a valuable task for an incoming leader, helping to ascertain the nature of the prevailing culture and the extent to which subcultures exist. Lewis (1996, pp. 14–15) claims that auditing culture is an essential task if it is to be managed effectively. She identifies several diagnostic techniques:

- Study of behaviour as an embodiment of values and assumptions.
- Examination of the communication rules of an organisation.
- Assessment of the myths, rituals, symbols and language of the organisation.
- Developing a cultural profile, including employee views of management style.
- An organisational culture index based on a staff survey.

While advocating these approaches, Lewis (*ibid.*) points to certain limitations:

> Behaviour is not always a good indicator of values and underlying assumptions . . . profiles . . . will not uncover the organisation's culture . . . People's basic assumptions are often unconscious and their espoused theories are often not the same as their theories in use . . . culture profiles . . . could form part, but not the whole, of a technique for diagnosing culture.

Lewis (*ibid.*, p. 16) concludes that diagnosis has not been a significant feature of cultural analysis because 'managers are no longer concerned about the kind of culture they have, but only about the kind of culture they want to have'.

Gale and Cartwright (1995, p. 3) comment that any assessment of culture needs to take account of the impact of 'masculine' cultures on women and on the ways in which women may influence or change culture.

Generating culture

Leaders have a central role in generating culture, either to reinforce existing norms or to modify or radically change cultural assumptions. However,
as Preston (1993, p. 18) asserts, 'gaining control of organisational culture is
a difficult business'. Brown (1992, p. 6) claims that effective leadership
depends on understanding culture and on being prepared to be proactive
to develop it:

> Excellent leaders are not merely aware of their organisation's basic
> assumptions, they also know how to take action to mould and refine
> them. This process of cultural management appears to have been
> achieved through the skilful use of artefacts, stories, myths and
> symbolic actions to reinforce desired patterns of thought and behav-
> iour.

One way of generating culture is to focus on the aims of the school or
college. The statement of purposes, and their espousal in action, serve to
reinforce the values and beliefs of the organisation (Bush, 1995). Where
goals and values are consistent the institution is likely to cohere: 'A clear
description of the aims of a school, college or any section within it helps
to provide a common vision and set of values. Well-stated aims will seize
everybody's interest. Such aims will help in creating a strong culture'
(Clark, 1992, p. 74).

As Clark (*ibid.*) suggests, the process of goal-setting should be linked to
organizational values. The core values help to determine the vision for the
school or college. The vision is expressed in a mission statement which in
turn leads to specific goals. This is an essentially rational process but it
operates within an overt framework of values.

Official goals are often vague and tend to be inadequate as a basis for
guiding decisions and action. Much then depends on the interpretation of
aims by participants. This is likely to be driven by the values of the inter-
preter. Where there is a monoculture within the organisation, a consistent
policy is likely to emerge. If there are competing cultures, the official aims
may be subverted by members of subunits who interpret them in line with
their own sectional values and goals (Bush, 1995).

Leaders may also be able to generate culture through structural change.
Preston (1993, p. 21) argues that 'management development structures
could provide cultural symbols for managers within an organisation' but
questions whether it works as well for other employees. Hopkins (1996, p.
37) notes the problematic nature of the relationship but points to how
structure may influence culture:

> Significant structural changes, especially ones that bring teachers
> into working more closely together, will affect how teachers talk to
> one another and define their professional relationships. It is through
> the new relationships and the content and style of talk arising from
> structural changes that the culture begins to shift.

Linking culture to strategy

Strategy is the term used to describe the overall, or synoptic, management of organisations. It generally operates over an extended timescale and guides decision-making during that period. Strategy provides the link between the vision of the organisation and its operational management and helps to ensure integration between different parts of the school or college.

The strategy has to take account of the prevailing culture of the organisation but it may also be necessary for leaders to seek to shift the culture if strategic objectives are to be achieved. Bridge (1994, p. 191) examines the relationship between culture and strategic planning at his London college:

> I have endeavoured to use the corporate planning process as a key tool in moulding and modifying the organisational culture of STC corporation. Many staff seem impervious to the existence of a particular culture in their section, school or faculty. Consequently, the process of consulting upon and building up a strategic plan has required us to hold a mirror to the organisation and develop greater self-awareness amongst our staff.

Hopkins (1996) has developed a linear model for linking strategy and culture. The school's priorities lead to a strategy chosen to achieve them. This produces a period of turbulence leading to a change in internal conditions and, ultimately, a change in culture (see Figure 3.1).

PRIORITY → STRATEGY → TURBULENCE → INTERNAL CONDITIONS → CULTURE

Figure 3.1   Linking strategy and culture: a linear model
Source: Adapted from Hopkins, 1996, p. 34

An alternative conceptualisation is to regard both strategy and culture as vehicles for the dissemination of organisational values. The beliefs and values of leaders coalesce to form a vision of the future of the organisation. This vision is expressed in a mission statement or set of aims which subsequently becomes operational through more specific goals. The overall plan to achieve these goals may be regarded as strategy. Subsequent decisions are expected to be consistent with this strategy.

This rational strategic model operates alongside the informal dimension of culture. This latter concept is also underpinned by core values but operates through rituals and symbols rather than via a formal goal-setting process. The establishment of a distinctive culture as a unique feature of the organisation provides the 'glue' which holds individuals and groups together. Aims which are consistent with this ethos are likely to be pursued while those which contradict prevailing norms may be ignored or given a low priority.

Turner (1990, p. 9) claims that culture 'is the set of core values and proclaimed standards, the stated goals, the published mission, the organisational ideology', leading to a clear image of the school or college. Mission statements play an important part in establishing culture but the stated goals must be operational if they are to be meaningful:

> Goals, mission statements, or ideologies . . . create a focus for the cohesive bonds of organisational culture, expressed through the symbol of myth, ritual and language. If the mission statement is dissonant with the practice . . ., this is a clear source of organisational weakness. The establishment of core values is a task of extraordinary significance for management . . . If the task is badly done, and statements do not coincide with practice, then that is bad management.
>
> (*Ibid.*, p. 10)

If culture is to be unique, and strategies to be distinctive, schools and colleges need to go beyond restating general educational aims. The goals should be linked directly to the specific needs, and core values, of the school. Hargreaves (1995) identifies three categories of school culture:

1) *Welfarist* Weak by academic criteria but staff focus on expressive outcomes, including low rates of delinquency.
2) *Formal* High academic press but assigns little value to the expressive domain.
3) *Hothouse* This might be associated with differential effectiveness. Certain students may wilt under the pressure but others might flourish within such an ethos.

While such 'ideal types' are not unique, they indicate broad values which provide a starting point for the development of distinctive cultures.

Changing organisational culture

Hargreaves (1995, p. 41) argues that changing school culture could have the effect of promoting school improvement. Collegial or collaborative cultures are widely advocated to secure the implementation of change but Hargreaves stresses the need to link collaboration to clear school aims.

Cultures which contradict the aims of the organisation's leaders may serve to prevent change. Reynolds (1996, pp. 153–4) refers to one school where the culture was 'posing severe difficulty for any purported change attempts'. He points (*ibid.*) to 'multiple barriers to change', including:

- staff wanted 'top-down' change and not 'ownership'.
- 'we've always done it this way'.
- individual reluctance to challenge the prevailing culture.
- staff blaming children's home background for examination failure.
- numerous personality clashes, personal agendas and fractured interpersonal relationships.

This saga illustrates the difficulty of imposing cultural change. Turner (1990) says that the notion of managers changing culture is problematic. He acknowledges the pressure on leaders to 'mould' culture but rejects the belief that 'something as powerful as culture can be much affected by the puny efforts of top managers' (*ibid.*, p. 11).

The further education system in England and Wales provides a graphic example of imposed change. Incorporation of colleges in 1993, and subsequent dramatic shifts in funding patterns, presented a severe test of managerial competence. Many college leaders recognised that the existing culture would be a barrier to change. One principal points to the need to proceed cautiously:

> [It is] dangerous . . . for managers to move too fast on cultural change. Many of us have observed . . . the damaging effect upon college cultures of management initiatives that are fast, too autocratic, or involve changes that are too radical. The resulting damage to colleges is great as they fail to respond and overheat, with resulting entrenchment of existing cultures and staff returning to the values they 'always held'.
>
> (Bridge, 1994, p. 197)

Bridge (*ibid.*, p. 194) responded to this dilemma by allowing, or encouraging, people to leave in order to foster cultural change: 'It is almost impossible to have too much selective early retirement and targeted voluntary redundancy within an FE college. As a way of moulding the culture, the process of easing out inappropriate staff members seems, if anything, more potent than the recruitment of new blood.'

Despite the acknowledged difficulties of promoting new cultures, some writers have produced recipes for change. Turner (1990, p. 17) identifies several characteristics, including the following:

- promulgate the mission statement of the organisation.
- identify two or three 'trade mark' characteristics.
- provide effective leadership of the development through reflection, creative thinking and constant monitoring.
- pick out the people in key roles, perhaps the telephonist and receptionist, and train them to front cultural change.
- begin by working in areas where there is least resistance.

Limb (1994, pp. 230–1) suggests several steps, including 'inspiring a shared vision', enabling others to act and modelling the way to change. Gorringe (1994, p. 186) presents six 'management tools' for culture change:

- clarity of purpose: a clear vision.
- presentation: of vision and strategy.
- a published action plan.
- confidence building: supporting and guiding people to act effectively.
- leadership: setting the vision and strategy, and leading in the process of implementation.
- a focus on underlying principles: referring back to the values which guide management action.

All these commentators stress the role of the leader in developing and sustaining culture. Heads and principals have their own values and beliefs arising from many years of successful professional practice. They are also expected to embody the culture of the school or college.

Hoyle (1986, pp. 155–6) stresses the symbolic dimension of leadership and the central role of heads in defining school culture. Nias *et al.* (1989, p. 103) claim that heads are 'founders' of their school's culture. They refer to two of their case-study primary schools where new heads 'dismantled' the existing culture in order to create a new one based on their own values.

Leaders have the main responsibility for generating and sustaining culture and communicating core values and beliefs both within the organisation and to external stakeholders. Sergiovanni (1984) claims that the cultural aspect is the most important dimension of leadership. Within his 'leadership forces hierarchy', the cultural element is more significant than the technical, human and educational aspects of leadership (*ibid.*, p. 9):

> The net effect of the cultural force of leadership is to bond together students, teachers, and others as believers in the work of the school . . . As persons become members of this strong and binding culture, they are provided with opportunities for enjoying a special sense of personal importance and significance.

CONCLUSION: CULTURE AND STRATEGY

The concept of culture is a valuable tool which aids organisational analysis. The recognition that school and college development needs to be preceded by attitudinal change is salutary and consistent with the oft-stated maxim that teachers must feel 'ownership' of change if it is to be implemented effectively. Externally imposed innovation often fails because it is out of tune with the values of the teachers who have to implement it: 'Since organisation ultimately resides in the heads of the people involved, effective organisational change implies cultural change' (Morgan, 1986, p. 138).

The emergence and subsequent maturation of self-management in education provides an appropriate context for strategic management. With more levers of power located within school and colleges, leaders are able to connect finance, staff, curriculum and marketing to develop a clear strategy for organisational development. Self-management may also lead to greater differences between schools as leaders stress the distinctiveness of their institutions. An important manifestation of this individuality is the unique culture of the school or college.

There are three ways in which culture and strategy may relate. First, both are underpinned by values, leading to a clear vision of the future of the school or college. The main difference concerns the ways in which these beliefs are operationalised. The values provide the vision which informs strategy and leads to consistent decision-making; an ostensibly rational process. The beliefs also lead to norms which gradually coalesce to form the culture of the organisation. This latter process is much more uncertain and elusive than strategic planning.

Secondly, culture is an important dimension of the context within which strategy operates. The strategic plan should match the culture of the organisation if it is to receive the active support of staff. Schein (1997) argues that culture can act as a 'brake' on strategic change. Leaders may wish to adopt strategies which they perceive to be beneficial but cannot do so because they are inconsistent with the culture of the organisation (*ibid.*, p. 381):

> [Leaders] cannot implement those strategies because such implementation requires assumptions, values, and ways of working that are too far out of line with the organisation's existing assumptions. In some cases, the organisation cannot even conceive of certain strategic options because they are too out of line with shared assumptions about the mission of the organisation and its way of working.

Where leaders ignore or underestimate the cultural norms of the organisation, and promote strategies incompatible with the dominant ethos, there is likely to be conflict, or micropolitics, and the probability of weak implementation or failure. In practice, however, leaders are likely to operate a form of 'strategic myopia' (Lorsch, 1985) and limit their options to those likely to be consistent with the organisation's culture:

> Cultural assumptions are the product of past successes. As a result they are increasingly taken for granted and operate as silent filters on what is perceived and thought about . . . Culture constrains strategy by limiting what . . . senior managers are able to think about and what they perceive in the first place.
>
> (Schein, 1997, p. 382)

Thirdly, culture need not be unitary as long as the subcultures do not come into direct conflict. While leaders may wish to promote an overall ethos, recognition of the value of alternative cultures may enrich the organisation. Subunits may have developed distinctive cultures linked to their subject or discipline. In colleges, for example, the engineering and law departments may have different value systems arising from their professional backgrounds. A strategy of mutual tolerance and compatibility is likely to be more effective than attempts to 'weed out' the alien culture.

Culture is an important dimension of organisations but it has to be understood within the broader framework of strategic management. Just as leaders have to acknowledge the subtlety of organisational culture, a rational strategic process, such as development planning, is also vital if the school or college is to prosper.

REFERENCES

Beare, H., Caldwell, B. and Millikan, R. (1989) *Creating an Excellent School: Some New Management Techniques*, London, Routledge.

Bridge, W. (1994) Change where contrasting cultures meet. In Gorringe, R. (ed.) *Changing the Culture of a College*, Blagdon, Coombe Lodge Reports.

Brown, A. (1992) Organisational culture: the key to effective leadership and organisational development, *Leadership and Organization Development Journal*, Vol. 13, no. 2, pp. 3–6.

Bush, T. (1995) *Theories of Educational Management* (2nd edn), London, Paul Chapman.

Campbell-Evans, G. (1993) A values perspective on school-based management. In Dimmock, C. (ed.) *School-Based Management and School Effectiveness*, London, Routledge.

Clark, J. (1992) *Management in Education*, Lancaster, Framework Press.

Deal, T. (1985) The symbolism of effective schools, *Elementary School Journal*, Vol. 85, no. 5, pp. 605–20.

Fullan, M. and Hargreaves, A. (1992) *What's Worth Fighting for in Your School?* Buckingham, Open University Press.

Gale, A. and Cartwright, S. (1995) Women in project management, *Leadership and Organization Development Journal*, Vol. 16, no. 2, pp. 3–8.

Gorringe, R. (1994) Foreword. In Gorringe, R. (ed.) *Changing the Culture of a College*, Blagdon, Coombe Lodge Reports.

Hargreaves, D. (1995) School culture, school effectiveness and school improvement, *School Effectiveness and School Improvement*, Vol. 6, no. 1, pp. 23–46.

Harling, P. (1989) The organisational framework for educational leadership. In Bush, T. (ed.) *Managing Education: Theory and Practice*, Milton Keynes, Open University Press.

Harris, C. (1992) Ritual and educational management: a methodology, *International Journal of Educational Management*, Vol. 6, no. 1, pp. 4–9.

Hopkins, D. (1996) Towards a theory of school improvement. In Gray, J., Reynolds, D., Fitz-gibbon, C. and Jesson, D. (eds.) *Merging Traditions: The Future of Research on School Effectiveness and School Improvement*, London, Cassell.

Hoyle, E. (1986) *The Politics of School Management*, Sevenoaks, Hodder & Stoughton.

Lewis, D. (1996) The organizational culture saga – from OD to TQM: a critical review of the literature, *Leadership and Organization Development Journal*, Vol. 17, no. 1, pp. 12–19.

Limb, A. (1994) Inspiring a shared vision. In Gorringe, R. (ed.) *Changing the Culture of a College*, Blagdon, Coombe Lodge Reports.

Lorsch, J. (1985) Strategic myopia: culture as an invisible barrier to change. In Kilmann, R., Saxton, M. and Serpa, R. (eds.) *Gaining Control of the Corporate Culture*, San Francisco, Calif., Jossey-Bass.

Morgan, G. (1986) *Images of Organization*, Newbury Park, Calif., Sage.

Nias, J., Southworth, G. and Yeomans, R. (1989) *Staff Relationships in the Primary School*, London, Cassell.

O'Neill, J. (1994) Organisational structure and culture. In Bush, T. and West-Burnham, J. (eds.) *The Principles of Educational Management*, Harlow, Longman.

Preston, D. (1993) Management development structures as symbols of organisational culture, *Personnel Review*, Vol. 22, no. 1, pp. 18–30.

Reynolds, D. (1996) Turning around ineffective schools: some evidence and some speculations. In Gray, J., Reynolds, D., Fitz-gibbon, C. and Jesson, D. (eds.) *Merging Traditions: The Future of Research on School Effectiveness and School Improvement*, London, Cassell.

Schein, E. (1997) *Organizational Culture and Leadership* (2nd edn), San Francisco, Calif., Jossey-Bass.

Schneider, S. and Barsoux, J. (1997) *Managing Across Cultures*, Hemel Hempstead, Prentice-Hall Europe.

Sergiovanni, T. (1984) Cultural and competing perspectives in administrative theory and practice. In Sergiovanni, T. and Corbally, J. (eds.) *Leadership and Organizational Culture*, Chicago, Ill., University of Illinois Press.

Turner, C. (1990) *Organisational Culture*, Blagdon, Mendip Papers.

Wallace, M. and Hall, V. (1994) *Inside the SMT: Teamwork in Secondary School Management*, London, Paul Chapman.

Weick, K. (1985) The significance of cultural culture. In Frost, P., Moore, L., Louis, M., Lundberg, C. and Martin, J. (eds.) *Organizational Culture*, Beverley Hills, Calif., Sage.

Section B: effective implementation of strategy

4

LINKING MARKETING TO STRATEGY

Nick Foskett

MARKETS, MARKETING AND INSTITUTIONAL AUTONOMY

The growth of institutional autonomy with its associated responsibility for planning has been an international phenomenon within education over the last decade. The delegation of management responsibility has been but one element in the creation of quasi-markets (Bartlett and Le Grand, 1993) by governments in pursuit of a range of political goals. This has seen a shift in the nature of accountability in schools and colleges. The traditional emphasis on professional accountability (accountability to the profession of teaching and its self-established values and aims) has been replaced by both increasing political accountability and market accountability. Schools and colleges have been caught in the middle of an ideological struggle within right-wing administrations between, on the one hand, libertarian ideologies emphasising the concepts of choice and individualism, the reduction of government 'control' and the removal of the perceived protectionism of professionalism in state services and, on the other hand, conservative ideologies emphasising strong central control. 'Marketisation' has pursued the 'three Es' of efficiency, economy and effectiveness, seeking the downward cost pressures of competition, but has also developed in an environment in which strong government funding and curriculum policies have severely distorted the nature of the market.

Active marketisation is well exemplified by developments in England and Wales following, in the case of schools, the Education Reform Act 1988 and, for further education institutions, the Further and Higher Education Act 1992. In schools open enrolment has given parents a theoretical right to make a free choice of school for their child, while formula funding under the local management of schools (LMS) initiative directly links school income to pupil numbers. In addition the encourage-ment of diversity of school type with the development of *inter alia* grant-maintained (GM) schools (soon to be 'foundation schools') has extended choice for parents. While the reality of parental choice is questionable (e.g. Gewirtz *et al.*, 1995), competition between schools has clearly developed. In the postcompulsory field competition between providers has always been inherent. However, government expansion of the FE sector in the period 1993–97, steered through the funding models of the Further Education Funding Council (FEFC), has seen pressure for colleges to increase student numbers by nearly 30 per cent while having a substantial 'efficiency gain' imposed. A strongly competitive environment has been created, therefore.

Competition, the market and self-management have come to institutions hand in hand. The 'new managerialism' (Clarke and Newman, 1992) of the 1990s is predicated on accountability and effectiveness in the market-place, and planning and strategy are now essential components of manage-ment (both pragmatically and statutorily!). Linking strategy and planning to the market, however, is problematical. Across education, experience of planning is limited, knowledge of marketing as a concept and as a manage-ment skill is poorly developed, and the realities of education markets mean governments not only impose tight constraints on the market-place but also 'move the goalposts' quite frequently. Furthermore, since the 'market' is a mechanism designed to minimise 'producer control', there is an inherent tension between formal and rational planning approaches and market processes.

The relationship between marketing and strategy is complex. The Institute of Marketing defines marketing as 'the management process which identifies, anticipates and supplies customer requirements efficiently and profitably'. Identifying and anticipating customer require-ments is clearly an input into the planning and strategising process, while the 'supply' element involves managing delivery of the institution's service or product. Strategy must be informed by market considerations, therefore, yet many other factors are also of importance in developing institutional strategy, for schools and colleges have wide social and humanitarian objectives. The market may be important, but it is not the sole consideration in planning. In the context of FE, for example, the FEFC (1997) has identified a number of factors which impact on strategy, including the overall direction of the institution, needs and market analy-sis, the mix of staff skills, finance and estate management issues and broader factors of responsiveness, partnership and the local labour market.

Planning and marketing are intimately linked, therefore, but are not synonymous, so that senior managers must make judgements about the importance of market considerations in their planning. This chapter examines the challenges of linking marketing to strategy both in schools and in further education. After examining the nature of marketing, it considers a range of planning approaches which build responsiveness to the market into institutional planning from first principles. The principles it considers relate to schools and colleges of all sizes, for planning and strategising in relation to the market are essential equally to small primary schools and large FE colleges, differences between them lying only in the scale and complexity of the strategising process.

THE NATURE OF MARKETING

But what *is* 'marketing'? Marketing is a problematic concept not just for those working in education. Most institutions clearly identify marketing as an important management function, yet diversity in interpreting the term leads to diversity and contradictions in the way schools and colleges participate in their own market(s). Just as 'consumers' (parents + pupils/students) possess inherent advantages or disadvantages in the market because of differences in their 'cultural capital' (Bourdieu and Wacquant, 1992), so institutions vary in their 'institutional cultural capital'. Some schools and colleges possess not only high 'market value' because of their educational outputs and perceived market status but also have the skills, knowledge, attitude of mind and institutional culture to participate effectively in the market – others do not. Of key importance in this is the view of marketing held by key managers.

Three perspectives on marketing may be identified. *Product-orientated* organisations are concerned primarily with the product or service that they have skills and expertise in producing, and the customer's perspective is subordinate to this aim. This is the traditional perspective in professional services such as education, where the view of the professional as the 'expert' who dictates what the customer receives is commonplace. Indeed, in education the customer may not be seen as the pupil or parent anyway, but as an academic discipline ('I'm a science teacher') or as society as a whole. In product-orientated organisations marketing, if present at all, is seen as 'selling' and as a relatively unimportant activity.

The second perspective on marketing is that of *sales orientation*. Such organisations have a strong product focus, but recognise that selling is central to their survival. Such a sales-orientated culture is often the marketing stereotype, and the imagery of 'a bewildering bazaar' in education (Brighouse, 1992) and 'Kentucky-fried schooling' (Hargreaves and Reynolds, 1989) reflects such a perspective. The first response of an educational institution moved from the market-protected positions of monopoly power (e.g. impermeable school catchments or LEA allocation of particular courses to particular FE colleges), or of a great excess of demand over supply (e.g. applications to higher education in the 1970s) is to seek to sell what it already offers very vigorously.

The third perspective is that of a *marketing orientation*, in which the satisfaction of customer 'wants' is central. In education, each institution has a very diverse range of customers, including pupils/students, parents, government, professional bodies and 'society', and market orientation indicates a focus on all these groups. Such an orientation has considerable implications for an organisation and its management, for it represents a holistic philosophy. Marketing is not an activity of the 'sales' team, but is central to the organisation's whole approach.

Such a broader perspective on marketing encompasses issues of *quality and community responsiveness*, for both are essential in meeting customer wants. Neither of these is as alien a concept as 'selling' to most educationists. Indeed, they may reflect the very essence of education to many. It is possible, therefore, to produce a model of what 'marketing' is which includes traditional educational values as well as the discipline of the market-place. This can be represented as a *marketing triad* model (Foskett, 1996) (see Figure 4.1), which presents the concept of marketing as a 'field', with an individual's or organisation's precise conceptual location representing a balance of perspectives between quality, recruitment and community responsiveness aims. Such a position will depend on 'micro-market' conditions, and will be subject to change. An institution under threat from declining pupil numbers, for example, might focus its marketing perspective on the bottom left of the model, while those in a more secure market position might be located more centrally or towards one of the other apices.

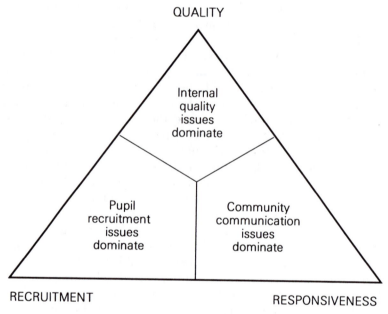

Figure 4.1   The marketing triad model
Source: Foskett, 1996

This view of marketing in education can be extended to incorporate an important concept that has emerged from small business marketing (Payne *et al.*, 1995). *Relationship marketing* recognises that small organisations (and *all* schools are small organisations) actually sell not just a simple product or service to their 'customers' but a relationship which is built on partnership, mutual trust and confidence. It emphasises that marketing is about a relationship built over time between individual people inside and outside the organisation, and not a distant, impersonal link between the 'customer' and the 'corporation' (Stokes, 1996). Such an approach to external links characterises much of what primary and secondary schools have tried to do for many years for sound 'educational' reasons, without the word 'marketing' being mentioned. As O'Sullivan and O'Sullivan (1995) suggest, such a view of marketing means that 'even while claiming an innocence of marketing, or more vehemently, an antipathy towards it, [schools] are actually rather good at it'. Relationship marketing seems an especially helpful perspective and approach for schools and colleges, therefore.

MARKETING AND THE PLANNING PROCESS – STRATEGIC MARKETING

How can marketing be built into planning in a school or college? An important concept is that of *strategic marketing*, which refers to the development of an institutional strategy integrating a marketing orientation. Two strategic planning models can be used to illustrate this idea, and can be applied to schools or colleges of any size – the thinking and envisioning processes are the same for all, differences lying only in the detail and complexity of the process.

First, Gray (1991) sees marketing not as a process servicing a strategic plan but as an underpinning philosophy that drives the plan and hence the medium and short-term operational 'tactics' of promotion. The organisational structure, both for marketing and for other management functions, derives from this plan, rather than acting as a limiting factor upon it. Furthermore, other strands within the strategic plan (e.g. 'curriculum') are themselves derived from marketing analysis techniques. Set against these principles, Gray (*ibid.*) sees strategic planning as comprising three stages:

1) The development of *an institutional plan*, driven by a marketing perspective and linked tightly to the school or college's mission, which itself is market focused.
2) The development of *thematic plans* for each broad component of the institutional plan, e.g. curriculum.
3) The production of a *marketing plan* which integrates the future marketing research needs of the institution with the short-term and medium-term marketing processes linked to promotion and external communications.

Each of these stages is itself operationalised through a rational planning model of review, analysis, planning, implementation/monitoring and evaluation, a familiar process to all involved in institutional planning.

Secondly, Hanson and Henry (1992, p. 258) distinguish clearly between 'strategic marketing' and 'project marketing'. Project marketing ('the most practised form of marketing' – *ibid.*) deals with short-term activities that do not necessarily relate to any long-term strategy. In contrast, strategic marketing 'emerges out of a sequence of well-planned research and operational steps' (*ibid.*) linked to long-term vision (Figure 4.2).

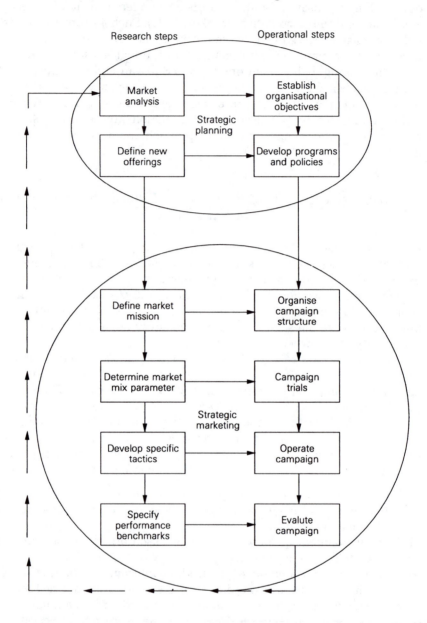

Figure 4.2   The strategic marketing planning process
Source: Hanson and Henry, 1992

This two-phase model sees the institutional plan developing from market analysis as a first stage, with the development of goals, strategies and tactics, followed by implementation and evaluation against specific performance benchmarks as a second stage. This reflects a 'marketing orientation', and this perspective has been emphasised in relation to both the FE sector and schools in recent guidance on marketing practice (e.g. Evans, 1995; Pieda, 1996; FEFC, 1997; FEFC/NAO, 1997).

EDUCATION MARKETING IN PRACTICE – THE STATE OF THE ART ?

But how far have schools and colleges developed in relation to these models of strategic marketing? The following sections consider the research evidence about current practice, and identify a complex and variable pattern.

Marketing in schools

The extent of research on marketing in schools reflects a preoccupation with demand-side issues, and in particular with parental choice (e.g. Carroll and Walford, 1997). However, the research of Foskett (1995), Gewirtz *et al.* (1995), James and Phillips (1995) and Glatter *et al.* (1996) identifies the relatively undeveloped strategisation of secondary schools in relation to the market. They have identified the following:

- A highly variable interpretation of 'marketing', with a strong 'product-centred' philosophy as teachers and managers 'struggle to reconceptualise an alien concept' (Foskett, 1996, p. 39).
- An *ad hoc* approach to marketing, with an emphasis on project marketing rather than strategic marketing.
- A perception of marketing as a crisis management approach to short-term recruitment changes, using 'superficial and short-term solutions to problems even when in the long term such strategies may be socially and educationally unhelpful' (Gewirtz *et al.*, 1995, p. 157).
- The absence of any coherent form of marketing research.
- A slow cultural shift towards accepting (pragmatically, but not necessarily philosophically) the role of the market.
- Most schools have by default adopted an undifferentiated marketing strategy, seeking to be all things to all people, in which they emphasise community, care, personal attention and the pursuit of value added for individual pupils, rather than identifying distinctive factors which set them apart from their 'competitors'. Glatter *et al.* (1996, p. 22) explain this by indicating that popular schools 'have no incentive to differentiate further' while less popular schools seek 'not to sharpen but to blunt any difference and thereby share the mutual benefits arising from being similar'.

Primary schools are often very small organisations and face many of the operational and management issues that small businesses face – small turnover, limited staff numbers, few opportunities for staff management specialisation, and a small and precisely defined market. While studies of marketing in primary schools are limited in number (e.g. Stokes, 1996;

Minter, 1997), practice appears to reflect that of secondary schools, only to a more marked extent. A strong commitment to educational values drives them together with the establishment of strong relationships with the community. The role of word-of-mouth promotion is so important that a selling orientation is of little assistance, so many primary schools have by default, and without reference to the 'canons' of marketing, adopted a strategy that is 'relationship marketing'.

Marketing in further education

Marketing has become a major preoccupation of FE institutions in the period since incorporation (post-1992). Strategic planning is a key requirement within the funding formula of the FEFC (FEFC, 1995), and this is expected to reflect a college's response to the market. In large colleges a substantial marketing function has been developed with specialist marketing teams, while in smaller colleges the inclusion of marketing within wider remits of middle and senior managers is more common. Research into marketing in FE has examined both organisational and functional aspects of practice (Smith *et al.*, 1995; Foskett and Hesketh, 1996; Pieda, 1996), and a number of patterns can be identified:

- Considerable diversity of organisational structures.
- A focus on short-termism and project marketing, with a lack of integration between strategic planning and market intelligence.
- The development of a wide range of expertise in promotional activities.
- A distinction between markets with many competitors (contiguous markets) and markets with no competitors (parallel markets) in terms of the sophistication of the marketing function.

LINKING MARKETING AND STRATEGY

Against this landscape of education marketing it is appropriate to ask how schools and colleges might build more effective links between marketing and strategy. It is important to recognise that this link is bidirectional, with market perspectives informing strategy, which in turn informs marketing practice. Each of these directions will be examined here.

Linking strategy to the market

If strategy is to be driven by a market-orientated perspective then it must be informed by knowledge and understanding of the market(s) within which the school or college operates or might wish to operate. *Needs analysis* and *market analysis* represent two strands of *marketing research*. Needs analysis is the identification of individual customer requirements, both real and potential, or broader market needs in relation to, for example, labour market intelligence. Market analysis seeks to identify the characteristics of specific markets in terms of

- market size, parameters, character, change and future development;
- competition, present and future, and the behaviour of competitors; and
- buyer behaviour and the decision-making of potential 'customers'.

Such 'market intelligence' may be obtained formally through a market research programme or informally through gathering information from inside or outside the organisation. The scale of marketing research can be tailored to the resources of the institution, and need not be large. While large amounts of data *can* be useful, using *some* information, albeit limited, is better than using none in the planning process. Once obtained, FEFC (1997) suggest that such information can be used in two main ways:

- As *confirmatory* evidence, either confirming or contradicting current understandings and intentions.
- As *anticipatory* evidence, to provide information which enables new or changed provision to be made.

Evidence from Smith *et al.* (1995) and Foskett and Hesketh (1996) suggests that the use of formal marketing research is not well developed as yet in the FE sector. While its importance and value are recognised, colleges suggest that they do not have the resources to undertake or 'buy in' information. Developments have been strongest in the use of inquiry and enrolment data, and the role of TECs and other bodies in providing labour market information (LMI) is becoming well established (Pieda, 1995). Using the data to influence strategy, though, is difficult because of a lack of formal systems to feed data into the planning process, a lack of expertise in interpreting and analysing such information and the slow responsiveness of colleges who are locked into timescales of years rather than the shorter timescales of market change. Such market intelligence tends, therefore, to be used mainly to identify short-term tactical changes in relation to a pre-existing marketing strategy.

In schools a more marked absence of needs and market analysis has been demonstrated (Bagley *et al.*, 1996). This in part reflects the more limited resource base of schools, the limited number of markets within which they operate and the compulsory nature of schooling. However, it is also a function of the more intimate engagement of schools with the communities they serve, enabling the assimilation of informal intelligence more readily. Schools have smaller catchment areas, a more easily identifiable clientele and built-in communication systems with parents. Developments have largely been limited to parental response questionnaires (e.g. Martin, 1995), but this should not be seen as a deficit model – many small schools including many primaries have a very good sense of their market through 'keeping an ear to the ground'.

At the opposite extreme, the technology for sophisticated marketing research is available and may be of value to larger institutions. The potential of information technology for supporting marketing research is now being recognised, both in terms of market mapping using geographical information systems (GIS) (Harvey, 1995), and as a tool for database marketing (Aitken, 1996). Such approaches are unlikely to be cost-effective for most secondary schools and all primary schools, however, and will remain the domain of the FE college and the independent school.

Linking marketing to strategy

Within a formal planning process the translation of broad institutional strategy into operational strategies and tactics is a key requirement in seeking to achieve long-term aims. This represents the second stage in Hanson and Henry's model (Figure 4.2), and Kotler and Fox (1995) identify three elements of market strategy formulation (target market strategy; competitive positioning strategy; marketing mix strategy). These are considered here, together with general strategy issues of personnel, organisation and finance.

Target market strategy

This involves identifying specific segments of the total market that the institution intends to focus on. In postcompulsory education such strategisation is relatively unconstrained, and colleges may choose to specialise in specific programmes (e.g. engineering), specific markets (e.g. 16–19-year-olds) or specialist niches (e.g. boat building), or they may choose a comprehensive strategy where they offer a wide range of provision.

Schools are more constrained by the legal requirements of delivering the National Curriculum, but the ability to extend this curriculum, to develop specialist expertise, and to 'select' up to 20 per cent of their intake by chosen criteria has facilitated some differentiation. Murgatroyd and Morgan (1993) have identified four generic marketing strategies that schools might adopt. A *broad, open strategy* is one in which a school does not seek to differentiate itself from its 'competitors', emphasising only that it does these things better. The target market, therefore, is *all* pupils in a locality. The three other strategies represent different degrees of differentiation, and hence have a more precise target market. An *enhanced open strategy* involves some peripheral additional provisions (e.g. a third foreign language, team sports); a *basic niche strategy* involves an emphasis on a particular area of expertise within the broad curriculum (e.g. a strong science or IT emphasis); an *enhanced niche strategy* involves the focus of the school shifting to a particular area (e.g. a technology college; a drama/arts school).

Competitive positioning strategy

This involves the identification of distinguishable features of the institution that make it distinctive from its competitors operating in the same market segments. Glatter *et al.* (1996) identify seven forms of school diversity. This is extended and refined here to identify eight options for competitive positioning strategy for schools:

- Structural diversity – (LEA, grant-maintained or private).
- Curricular diversity – developing specialisms or emphasising particular elements of the curriculum (e.g. performing arts, technology, sport).
- Style diversity – emphasising particular approaches to teaching, learning or discipline.
- Religious/philosophical specialisation (e.g. faith-based schools).
- Gender.
- Ability range diversity – either through selection by ability, or by setting or streaming.
- Age range diversity (e.g. 11–16, 11–18).
- Achievement diversity – an emphasis on the achievement of high results in absolute sense, as measured, perhaps, by performance in public examination league tables, or in a relative sense in relation to concepts of value added.

In practice, most schools choose a mix of these factors to emphasise, and it is this combination which makes an individual school distinctive or unique. In further education, although the potential range of strategies used for competitive positioning is similar, particular emphasis tends to be placed on diversity of curriculum, style and achievement, as illustrated by contrasts between, for example, a grammar school sixth form, a sixth-form college and a general further education college all providing A-level programmes. In addition, in FE, competitive positioning in relation to price is possible, both in terms of direct costs (e.g. course fees), indirect associated costs (e.g. costs of transport to the institution) and non-monetary costs (e.g. required entry grades).

Marketing mix strategy

The concept of the marketing mix is well established in commercial marketing settings. The marketing mix represents the combination of elements that the institution presents to its potential consumers to promote itself, and in commercial settings is characterised by the '4 Ps':

- *Product* The nature of the product or service that is being offered (in the case of education this is both the course/programme and the wider experience of education/training and school/college life that is provided).
- *Place* The location of purchase or delivery (on-site or off-site).
- *Price* The price demanded for the service or product.
- *Promotion* The combination of promotional strategies (e.g. advertising) used to present the product or service.

In relation to service sector marketing, this is sometimes extended to '5Ps' by the addition of the following:

- *People* The individuals delivering the service to customers (teachers/lecturers and support staff).

Kotler and Fox (1995) extend this idea to '7Ps' in the context of education marketing by adding the following:

- *Process* The manner and style in which teaching, administrative and support processes are provided.

- *Physical facilities*   The nature of the facilities both for teaching and other components of student/pupil life (e.g. sports facilities, common-room areas).

In the context of schools James and Phillips (1995) have demonstrated that the development of marketing mix strategy is rarely *explicitly* developed, and this has been confirmed for primary schools (Minter, 1997). However, an analysis of promotional materials from schools shows its *implicit* presence in strategy. Schools are using clear and distinctive 'marketing mixes' by default and without referring to the term by name. In the context of further education, Foskett and Hesketh (1997) have demonstrated contrasting patterns of marketing mix development between institutions in parallel and contiguous markets, with overt and explicit focus on the marketing mix in colleges in contiguous markets, but a pattern similar to that found in schools prevailing in colleges in parallel markets.

The development of a promotional strategy is an important element of the marketing mix, although it is important that it is founded in an understanding of how and why pupils/parents choose as they do. Recent research (e.g. Foskett and Hesketh, 1996) has identified the key promotional pathways in relation to school and FE recruitment (open days, teacher guidance and visits from staff from the receiving institution are the main information routes), and two principles of importance in planning promotional strategy:

1) Pupils and their parents obtain information from both direct promotional channels under the control of institutions (e.g. open days), and from indirect pathways such as word-of-mouth and community perceptions. The latter require long-term external relations management and the pursuit of quality within the institution, yet may be more influential than the direct controllable channels.
2) Promotional literature, such as prospectuses, while essential to enable institutions to compete, is of little importance in influencing choice. Choice, where it occurs, is usually based on some form of personal contact (for example an open day or a visit to a college).

Personnel, organisation and finance for marketing

Producing a strategy requires management decisions on the deployment of people and resources. Cowell (1984) has identified four features of a service sector organisation that has developed a marketing orientation – the presence of an 'attitude of mind' that places the client at the centre of the organisation's philosophy; the use of an array of techniques to analyse the market; the use of a range of promotional methods tailored to the market; and the existence of an organisational and operational structure that 'manages' the marketing process. Two key components of this latter dimension are 1) the structure of the marketing organisation and 2) the budget allocation method used to support marketing.

Gray (1991) has suggested that the marketing organisation found in most schools focuses on roles and activities that existed prior to marketisation with the lead role falling to the headteacher. More recently, Foskett (1995) has identified four models of marketing organisation within schools:

1) The *chief executive model*, in which the headteacher takes decisions, provides the drive and the ideas and defines the *modus operandi* of marketing.
2) The *SMT model*, in which the senior management team is the focus of decision-making, but with no individual taking responsibility for the whole marketing function.
3) The *marketing manager model*, in which responsibility is delegated to a senior member of staff, usually a deputy headteacher, but sometimes to a middle manager in the school.
4) The *advisory committee model*, in which the development of policy and practice is delegated to a working group that is broader than the SMT in constitution.

These organisational types are not discrete, and combined models often exist. However, the dominance of the first three structures in secondary schools, and of the chief executive model in primary schools, is clear, indicating that consultation and collaboration outside senior management in relation to marketing is not well developed. Marketing appears to be seen in schools as something that senior managers do.

In FE the rapid response of colleges has led to a wide range of organisational structures, resulting from what Smith *et al.* (1995) identify as two key tensions:

1) 'Advanced' marketing-focused superstructures at the corporate centre versus 'primitive' PR-orientated substructures at faculty, school and departmental level.
2) An administrative approach to promotion, 'most prominently displayed by the established . . . sixth form college' (*ibid.*, p. 110) versus a more competitive market-orientated approach.

It is clear that contrasts in individual institutions' markets drive different organisational solutions. In highly competitive contiguous markets, Pieda (1996) and Foskett and Hesketh (1996; 1997) both emphasise the relative success of structures where lead responsibility lies with a member of the SMT (usually a vice-principal), either with or without a senior marketing manager. For such organisations 'the implicit model is that of the commercial world' (Smith *et al.*, 1995, p. 110). In less competitive parallel markets, a model of devolved marketing can be successful. Such a model is 'more limited . . . in reach and language. Its aim is to sustain historic advantage . . . Its focus is on maintaining, and enhancing, reputation and esteem' (*ibid.*).

The role of finance in linking marketing and strategy has traditionally been underplayed in the literature. Davies and Scribbins (1985) identified a number of approaches to funding marketing in FE, while Gray (1991) has emphasised the importance of marketing plans being fully costed. In the context of both schools and colleges, Foskett (1995) has identified five approaches to marketing budgeting:

1) *Remainder budgeting* Budget a fixed amount in the annual institutional budget, then allocate this to marketing tasks on an *ad hoc* basis. The total budget is dictated by the demands of other budgetary areas, and is historically based.

2) *Opportunity budgeting* Allocate the funding on an *ad hoc* basis throughout the year without identifying a global sum in the budget, drawing funds from other budget headings.

3) *Planned budgeting* Budget a fixed sum linked to the prioritised needs of the institutional plan, or marketing plan.

4) *Competition budgeting* Allocate a budget determined by a recognition of what competitor institutions appear to be spending.

5) *Per capita budgeting* Allocate a budget proportional to pupil/student numbers.

In the context of schools, the dominant approach is that of remainder budgeting, reflecting the comparatively low priority still accorded to marketing, although the growth of planned budgeting can be strongly identified (Foskett, 1995). In FE institutions, planned budgeting is more commonly identified, with competition budgeting occurring in some colleges in the most active and aggressive markets. As with organisational structure, the choice of methodology is dependent on a range of factors unique to each school or college's internal and external environment. Just as the budgetary methodology varies, so the budget allocation itself varies. In 'for-profit' organisations the marketing budget typically lies in the range of 5–25 per cent of turnover, but values of 1–5 per cent are more typical of FE colleges and sums of less than 1 per cent are the norm for most schools. However, this reflects direct marketing budgets, and it may be contended that in an organisation that is truly market orientated almost all the budget is marketing related.

CONCLUSION

Linking strategy with marketing has become an important part of institutional planning for educational organisations, with a two-way link, in that marketing informs strategy and the resulting strategy in turn drives marketing and promotional practice. This process is explicit in some schools and colleges, but is implicit and undertaken without specific reference to the term marketing in others. The school and college system is characterised by great diversity in marketing practice and organisation. The conclusions about marketing in FE by Smith *et al.* (1995, p. 110) apply equally to schools:

> marketing is on the march, [but] . . . institutions are at different stages of development in marketing terms, marketing philosophies are often poorly articulated, marketing functions have yet to be adequately defined and the organisation of marketing remains inchoate (and occasionally illogical).

However, Smith *et al.* (1995) and Foskett and Hesketh (1997) warn against assumptions that there is a simple model of marketing organisation, and emphasise the tight linkage between an institution's precise micromarket conditions and its response. In particular, Smith *et al.* (1995) stress three key ideas:

1) *Horses for courses* The structure and approach to marketing must build from the existing culture initially and has to 'go with the grain rather than against it'.
2) *Fitness for purpose* Institutions must develop an approach that is appropriate to their circumstances, and must not be driven by the bandwagon of marketing. What is appropriate for a small primary school is not appropriate for a large secondary or an FE college, and *vice versa*. Equally, this is not an excuse for lack of response.
3) *Marketing is not a political tool* Marketing is not a tool for driving through changes emanating from other organisational aims.

Recent attempts to identify 'good practice' in marketing in FE (Smith *et al.*, 1995; Pieda, 1996; FEFC/NAO, 1997) have struggled to draw out broad principles without recourse to a narrow commercial model of marketing. While this is appropriate to some both in the school and FE sector, for many schools and for some colleges an approach based more firmly in the concepts of 'relationship marketing' may be more helpful. Since most educational institutions are small primary schools, the integration of a 'marketing orientation' will come with the recognition that sophisticated marketing research, large promotional programmes and gimmicky marketing are unhelpful and unnecessary, and that well managed external relations building confidence in the community about the quality of the school and about the sophistication of relationships with pupils and parents are the essence of effective marketing.

REFERENCES

Aitken, G. (1996) College customer profiling comes of age, *Education Marketing*, Issue 8, pp. 24–6.

Bagley, C., Woods, P. and Glatter, R. (1996) Scanning the market: school strategies for discovering parental perspectives, *Educational Management and Administration*, Vol. 24, no. 2, pp. 125–38.

Bartlett, W. and Le Grand, J. (1993) *Quasi-Markets and Social Policy*, Basingstoke, Macmillan.

Bourdieu, P. and Wacquant, L. (1992) *An Invitation to Reflexive Sociology*, Oxford, Polity Press.

Brighouse, T. (1992) External relations and the future. In Foskett, N. (ed.) *Managing External Relations in Schools*, London, Routledge.

Carroll, S. and Walford, G. (1997) Parents' response to the school quasi-market, *Research Papers in Education*, Vol. 12, no. 1, pp. 3–26.

Clarke, J. and Newman, J. (1992) Managing to survive; dilemmas of changing organisational forms in the public sector, paper presented to the Social Policy Association Conference, Nottingham.

Cowell, D. (1984) *The Marketing of Services*, Oxford, Butterworth.

Davies, P. and Scribbins, K. (1985) *Marketing Further and Higher Education*, Harlow, Longman for FEU.

Evans, I. (1995) *Marketing for Schools*, London, Cassell.

FEFC (1995) *College Strategic Plans 1996–97 and Beyond, Circular 95/39*, Coventry, FEFC.

FEFC (1997) *Identifying and Addressing Needs: A Practical Guide*, Coventry, FEFC.

FEFC/NAO (1997) *Marketing in Further Education – A Good Practice Guide*, Coventry, FEFC.

Foskett, N.H. (1995) Marketing, management and schools: a study of a developing market culture in secondary schools, unpublished PhD thesis, University of Southampton.

Foskett, N.H. (1996) Conceptualising marketing in secondary schools – deconstructing an alien concept. In *Proceedings of the 'Markets in Education, Policy, Process and Practice' Symposium*, University of Southampton, Centre for Research in Education Marketing.

Foskett, N.H. and Hesketh, A.J. (1996) *Student Decision-Making and the Post-16 Market Place*, Leeds, Heist Publications.

Foskett, N.H. and Hesketh, A.J. (1997) Constructing choice in contiguous and parallel markets: institutional and school leavers' responses to the new post-16 market place, *Oxford Review of Education*, Vol. 23, no. 3, pp. 299–320.

Gewirtz, S., Ball, S. and Bowe, R. (1995) *Markets, Choice and Equity in Education*, Buckingham, Open University Press.

Glatter, R., Woods, P.A. and Bagley, C. (eds.) (1996) *Choice and Diversity in Schooling: Perspectives and Prospects*, London, Routledge.

Gray, L. (1991) *Marketing Education*, Milton Keynes, Open University Press.

Hanson, E.M. and Henry, W. (1992) Strategic marketing for educational systems, *School Organisation*, Vol. 12, no. 2, pp. 255–67.

Hargreaves, D. and Reynolds, D. (1989) *Educational Policies; Controversies and Critiques*, Lewes, Falmer Press.

Harvey, T. (1995) Stop worrying about the title – keep your eye on the new ball game, *Education Marketing*, Vol. 2, no. 2, p. 7.

James, C. and Phillips, P. (1995) The practice of educational marketing, *Schools' Educational Marketing and Administration*, Vol. 23, no. 2, pp. 12–14.

Kotler, P. and Fox, K. (1995) *Strategic Marketing for Educational Institutions* (2nd edn), New York, Prentice-Hall.

Martin, Y. (1995) What do parents want? *Management in Education*, Vol. 9, no. 1, pp. 12–14.

Minter, K. (1997) Marketing in the primary school, unpublished MA (Ed) thesis, University of Southampton.

Murgatroyd, S. and Morgan, C. (1993) *Total Quality Management and the School*, Buckingham, Open University Press.

O'Sullivan, C. and O'Sullivan, T. (1995) There's beauty in candlelight: relationship marketing in the non-profit sector. In *Proceedings, Annual Conference of the Marketing Education Group*, Bradford.

Payne, A., Christopher, M., Clark, M. and Peck, H. (1995) *Relationship Marketing for Competitive Advantage: Winning and Keeping Customers,* Oxford, Butterworth-Heinemann.

Pieda (for DfEE) (1995) *Labour Market Information for Further Education Colleges: A Handbook for Practitioners,* Manchester, Pieda.

Pieda (for DfEE) (1996) *Marketing Case Studies in Further Education Colleges,* Manchester, Pieda.

Scott, P. (1996) Markets in post-compulsory education. In *Proceedings of the 'Markets in Education, Policy, Process and Practice' Symposium,* University of Southampton, Centre for Research in Education Marketing.

Smith, D., Scott, P. and Lynch, J. (1995) *The Role of Marketing in the University and College Sector,* Leeds, Heist.

Stokes, D. (1996) Relationship marketing in primary schools. In *Proceedings of the 'Markets in Education, Policy, Process and Practice' Symposium,* University of Southampton, Centre for Research in Education Marketing.

5

AUTONOMY, CONSTRAINT AND THE STRATEGIC MANAGEMENT OF RESOURCES

Tim Simkins

INTRODUCTION

Over the past ten years the resource management context within which public sector schools and colleges are managed has changed radically. First, all institutions now have a high degree of autonomy in relation to the deployment of their resources. The vast majority of schools operate under schemes of local management or have grant-maintained status, while colleges and the former polytechnics have joined the older universities as fully incorporated bodies. These developments mean that resource decisions which were formerly taken elsewhere – mainly by local education authorities – are now taken by governing bodies and by institutional managers. Secondly, greater resource autonomy has been accompanied by increased 'marketisation' in all sectors and an encouragement for institutions to compete for clients.

The expectation of those designing these policies was that these arrangements would lead to enhanced quality and greater responsiveness in the educational experiences which are provided for pupils and students, higher standards in the outcomes which are produced and greater efficiency in the ways in which resources are used. The rationale for this was based on two assumptions which have critical implications for the management of strategy at institutional level. First, the improvement of efficiency, quality and standards is best achieved through a reliance on microlevel decision-making through which relevant decisions about resource deployment are located as close to the point of delivery as possible – that is to say, within institutions. Secondly, however, institutions need to be provided with frameworks of incentives which encourage them to pursue these desirable outcomes rather than others such as enhancing the quality of life for those who work in them. Increased competition provides one such framework, but it is not enough on its own: centrally driven quality assurance mechanisms such as inspection also have an important role to play.

THE FRAMEWORK OF FORMULA FUNDING

Although based apparently on similar assumptions, the resourcing mechanisms used in the schools sector and in further and higher education to facilitate these policy changes are significantly different. Both are based primarily on formula funding. However, while the funding formula for schools – both locally managed and grant-maintained – is designed primarily to encourage them to maintain and enhance their enrolment, much more complex formulae have been developed in further and higher education to enable their funding councils to pursue a number of policy objectives, in particular to manage growth, to increase efficiency (or, more specifically, to encourage high-cost institutions to reduce their unit costs) and to enhance quality which the councils operationalise in a variety of ways (Bradley, 1996).

The increasing power of formula funding within education and its use as a policy tool has two major strategic resource management implications for institutions. First, all are forced to develop strategies which seek to assure their income under the particular funding regime to which they are subject. Secondly, it pays all institutions to seek sources of income which are independent of their main funders: resource mobilisation becomes an increasingly important activity in enhancing the degree of strategic freedom which a school or college can exercise.

Before proceeding to explore the implications of these trends, one other element in the resource environment must be noted. The changes described above have taken place within a broader policy context of tight public expenditure control. The degree of financial constraint this has implied has varied over time, both between and within sectors, but its overall impact in association with financial autonomy and increased marketisation has been to place a much greater emphasis on the financial 'bottom line' in institutional strategy formulation.

RATIONALITY AND STRATEGIC RESOURCE MANAGEMENT

Strategic resource management can be viewed from a number of perspectives. The dominant one in the literature and in much of the policy discourse in this area is the so-called 'rational' perspective. Rational approaches are advocated widely by official bodies (Further Education Funding Council, 1992; National Audit Office, 1994; Ofsted, 1995a) and their use is frequently claimed to be a factor in securing the effectiveness of educational organisations (see, for example, Glover, 1997). Such approaches view strategic resource management in a number of complementary ways.

First, there is a strong emphasis on concepts such as 'efficiency', 'effectiveness' and 'value for money'. For example, Ofsted (1995a, p. 121) defines the efficient (*sic*) school as one which 'makes good use of all its available resources to achieve the best possible educational outcomes for all its pupils and in doing so provides excellent value for money'. The Further Education Funding Council, too, includes effectiveness and value for money among its key performance indicators (FEFC, 1997). The use of this terminology, however, is often not clear or consistent, and it is therefore helpful to keep in mind the fairly standard definitions of the 'three Es' provided by the Audit Commission (1985a):

1) *Economy*   The purchase of a given standard of good or service at lowest cost.
2) *Efficiency*   The achievement of given outcomes at least cost.
3) *Effectiveness*   The matching of results with objectives.

Arguments for the delegation of resource management responsibilities to schools and colleges emphasise, among other things, the potential for such delegation to enhance achievement of the three Es through giving those closest to the needs of the client the power to deploy resources in the most appropriate way. However, these potential benefits are not inevitable. They depend on how the tasks of resource management are carried out.

This brings us to the second dimension of the rational perspective: the emphasis given to clear structures and procedures for resource management. Figure 5.1 provides an idealised model of the resource management process. At its heart lies the *operational cycle* of resource management comprising five key activities: mobilisation, allocation, utilisation, control and review (Simkins and Lancaster, 1987; Simkins, 1997a). These activities take place over time in the form of one or more annual cycles (for example, those of budgeting and timetabling). Commonly these operational cycles dominate the resource management process. However, the rational perspective suggests that this is wrong: the operational cycle should be managed within the context of a *strategic cycle* through which, as Figure 5.1 indicates, the values and purposes of the organisation are translated into policies, priorities and plans which inform the operational cycle and which are used, in turn, to evaluate the impact of resource decisions.

The requirements for managing this strategic cycle give rise to the third dimension of the rational approach to resource management: the use of analysis to inform the process of choice. In part this is reflected in what Thomas and Martin (1996) call 'radical audit': the ability to think creatively and innovatively about the ways in which resources may be deployed in pursuit of an organisation's objectives. Radical audit is facilitated by a number of ways of thinking:

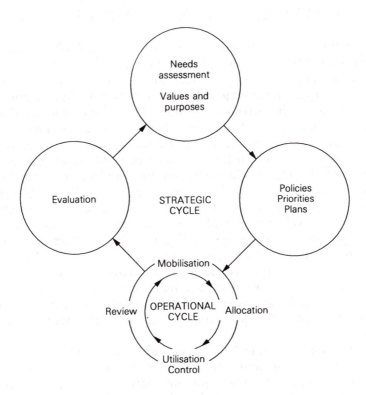

Figure 5.1 The resource management cycle

- *Organisation-wide thinking*   The ability to look at the overall pattern of resource deployment in relation to key purposes, priorities and challenges rather than simply to focus on particular aspects of expenditure or areas of activity.
- *Zero-base thinking*   The ability to question all aspects of current expenditure rather than simply to focus on changes at the margin, and to consider whether current activities could be better carried out in different ways or, indeed, whether they need to be carried out at all.
- *Longer-term thinking*   The ability to view choice not just within the constraints and pressures of the annual budgetary cycle, but in terms of a broader vision of where the organisation should be in three, five or even ten years' time, despite the uncertainties that such considerations involve.

Taken together these three emphases – on the 'three Es', systematic management processes and on the use of analysis – provide a strong prescriptive framework for those charged with the management of resources. Using some of these ideas, what has been the resource management experience of schools and colleges in recent years?

THE PURSUIT OF ECONOMY AND EFFICIENCY

Although the evidence is still limited, it seems that many schools and colleges have taken the opportunity provided by increased resource management powers to give particular attention to issues of economy and efficiency through reviewing patterns of resource deployment. In the schools sector this has involved attention being focused in three areas in particular (Simkins, 1994; Levacic, 1995): savings in areas such as premises and grounds maintenance and energy use; the employment of more support staff, both in the classroom (mainly teaching assistants in primary schools) and in administration, to complement or substitute for more expensive teaching staff (Mortimore *et al.*, 1994); and the employment of more staff, both teaching and support, on part-time or temporary contracts. There is less clear evidence about changing strategies in relation to the deployment of teaching staff. For the majority of schools, decisions in this area are probably still made on the basis of traditional judgements – about the desired pupil–teacher ratio and non-contact time for teachers in secondary schools and about maximum class sizes and the degree of tolerance for mixed-age classes in primary schools – with changes in traditionally preferred ratios occurring primarily in response to budgetary pressures.

The situation is rather different in postcompulsory education. The range of provision, both full time and part time, which has to be resourced is wide and varied. Furthermore, the non-compulsory nature of this sector means that the number of hours for which a student is expected to be in class is not a given and is, indeed, an important policy variable with both resource and educational implications. Consequently, in addition to choices in areas outside the teaching staff budget which were outlined above, colleges and universities also have a wider range of choices available to them about patterns of curriculum delivery and hence of staff deployment than do schools in general. That such choices will be taken seriously is ensured by the long tradition of quantifying key resource variables at institutional, departmental and course levels in further and higher education, and by the pressures within the relevant funding mechanisms for reductions in unit costs, especially for higher-cost institutions.

In postcompulsory education, therefore, the teaching staff budget and the staff–student ratio with its component parts – average class size, average lecturer hours and average student hours – are important foci for strategies which seek economy and efficiency in the use of resources. The Audit Commission (1985b; with Ofsted, 1993) has for many years drawn attention to differences in these variables, as well as in progression and completion rates, among colleges in the further education sector, while both the Further and Higher Education Funding Councils have published information demonstrating wide variations in unit costs among institutions. These data, together with the strong resource pressures on many institutions, have made the staffing budget a major focus for potential savings. One widely used strategy has been that of 'decremental drift' – adapting curriculum provision to a declining unit of resource through a steady upward drift in class sizes and lecturers' teaching hours and downward drift in contact hours. Beyond this, however, there have been increased pressures to enhance the 'productivity' of the teaching resource through changes in conditions of service (Hewitt and Crawford, 1997) and 'delayering' of management structures. As in the schools sector, however, it is unclear how far these strategies have been implemented in a truly *strategic* way which relates them systematically to institutional objectives and in particular to their consequences for educational outcomes.

BEYOND ECONOMY AND EFFICIENCY

Reasons for the emphasis on economy and efficiency in schools and colleges are not hard to find. First, given the difficulties associated with the measurement of effectiveness in education, strategies which focus on the changes in the deployment of inputs rather than on the enhancement of outputs are likely to be particularly attractive to resource managers since the choices available can be specified clearly in financial or other resource terms. Secondly – and of increasing importance for many institutions in all sectors – growing budgetary constraints place a premium on strategies which go beyond simply improving resource deployment and actually save money: again this focuses attention on the input side of the resource equation.

Nevertheless, viewed from a rational perspective such strategies clearly have their limitations. In particular they tend only to address questions of 'resource efficiency' (i.e. the minimisation of inputs), rather than true *economic* efficiency (i.e. maximising the relationship of outcomes, such as the quality of students' learning, to inputs), let alone to effectiveness (i.e. maximising the relationship between such outcomes and national and organisational goals).

This is not to say that effectiveness concerns have no place in strategic resource management in schools and colleges. In a general sense it is probably true that many resource decisions are based 'on professional judgements that the most beneficial learning outcomes would result from this particular use of resources' (Levacic, 1995, p. 155). Nevertheless, both Ofsted (1995b, p. 24) and the National Audit Office (1994, p. 17) have found reason to criticise schools for inadequately linking budgets to school development plans and for failing to develop mechanisms for assessing the cost-effectiveness of particular patterns of expenditure. Similar findings have emerged from recent academic studies (Levacic, 1995; Thomas and Martin, 1996; Bullock and Thomas, 1997). In postcompulsory education fewer public judgements are available about the quality of resource management strategies, but, for example, the Higher Education Funding Council has recently published a study which suggests that 'academic managers in HEIs are often unaware of the full costs of activities, and institutions generally lack a firm cost basis for decisions on resource allocation and management' (Joint Funding Councils, 1996, p. 6).

The literature on rational approaches suggests a number of ways forward in relation to these concerns, including activity-based costing (Mitchell, 1995), cost-effectiveness analysis (Levin, 1983) and 'benchmarking'. The last of these, through which organisations compare their performance in key areas with that of similar or competitor organisations in order to seek and understand areas of difference as a basis for improvement, seems to be receiving the most attention in education currently. In the schools' sector work has been undertaken in a number of areas, including resource inputs (DfEE, 1995a; Audit Commission, 1996; McAleese, 1996) and examination results (DfEE, 1995b), although little progress has been made to date in linking work on inputs and outcomes. In further education, the Audit Commission has explored differences among colleges in costs and in effectiveness, measured in terms both of completion rates and value added (Audit Commission/Ofsted, 1993, p. 58).

Analyses of these kinds can provide the basis for beginning to explore the difficult question of linking resource management to improved effectiveness. The challenge for the future is for schools and colleges to think more clearly about how particular strategies of resource deployment will impact on the learning outcomes of particular students. Some developments are taking place in this area: for example, the idea of targeting, i.e. 'identifying particular pupils or groups in order to focus attention, teaching resources and other support on them' is increasingly being advocated for schools (DfEE, 1996, p. 5). In part this is occurring in response to pressures from published performance indicators – for example, the targeting of those pupils who may just miss the 'magic' five A–C grades at GCSE. However, there is clearly a wide range of other possibilities both more and less contentious than this. For example, targeting strategies raise issues not just about effectiveness but also about a fourth 'E' which has almost disappeared from policy debate in recent years: namely, *equity* – the fair distribution of resources among individuals and groups. It is up to each school and college to determine exactly how these terms are to be interpreted in relation to the regulatory and resource constraints within which it operates. Such considerations raise important value questions which cast doubt on simplistic economic models of resource management (Simkins, 1994; 1995).

BEYOND RATIONALITY

An emphasis on efficiency and effectiveness, which has underpinned much of this chapter so far, tends to treat the strategic resource management process fairly simplisticly as a means of securing maximum outputs at minimum cost. Yet the underlying assumptions – that the prime (or even the sole) purpose of management is to achieve organisational purposes in the most efficient way, that such purposes are essentially non-problematic and that good-quality analysis will inevitably lead to better decision-making – ignore other important ways of viewing organisational life. Patterns and processes of resource management are much more than simply means for achieving ends. They have important *symbolic* implications, reflecting those things which are valued in the organisation both through the ways that difficult resource decisions are taken and through the resource allocation outcomes which result. Furthermore, since what is valued in a school or college, in terms both of processes and of goals and outcomes, may be contentious, resource management is also a *micro-political* process, providing an arena within which participants compete for the resources which will enable them to develop programmes of activity which embody their values, further their interests and help to provide legitimation for the activities in which they are engaged (Simkins, 1989).

Strategic resource management processes, therefore, need to be considered in relation to their behavioural consequences – which arise from the implicit or explicit rewards which they imply – and to the particular cultural assumptions about the organisation which they embody. One way of looking at this is in terms of the need for strategic resource management to balance a number of competing pressures. For example:

- The need to ensure *effectiveness* and *efficiency* in resource use at the level of the organisation as a whole, while ensuring *equity of treatment* for different areas of work and for individual students and student groups.
- The need to *prioritise and make difficult* choices where necessary, while *containing potential conflict* and maintaining a coalition of strategic support where resources are insufficient to meet the legitimate expectations of different areas of the organisation's work.
- The need to *respond flexibly* to changing environmental demands, while providing a *reasonably stable resource environment* to enable those responsible for undertaking the core activities of the institution, i.e. curricular and other provision for students, to work effectively.
- The need to encourage *innovation and responsiveness* among individual teachers and teams, while ensuring their *accountability* for their use of resources.
- The need to do all these things under continuing pressure of *limited time and information* and without consuming too many resources (especially staff time) in the resource management process itself.

Each of these tensions places pressures on the structures and processes through which resources are managed in an institution. These pressures will be increased when the external environment becomes more threatening as a result of the kinds of changes described at the beginning of this chapter. In these circumstances the question arises: are schools and colleges developing new approaches to resource management as they struggle to adapt to the more hostile world with which they are now faced? Research on these matters is still limited and fragmentary, but three possible trends can be identified.

First, the *role of senior managers* in making strategic resource decisions is probably being reinforced. Senior managers in most organisations recognise the potential of resource management decisions and processes to steer the behaviour of individuals and the direction of the organisation in ways which are relatively 'unobtrusive' (Cohen and March, 1974). Consequently it is not uncommon for them to retain fairly close control over these levers, even when considerable participation is permitted in other decision areas. It can be argued that current environmental trends are likely to reinforce such pressures for centralisation. On the one hand, senior managers will recognise the degree of formal accountability which they personally will have if the organisation's resources are seriously mismanaged. On the other, those at lower levels may prefer difficult resource decisions, and the potential blame attached to them, to be pushed upwards to those whom they see as being paid to take them.

Secondly, and related to the first point, there is growing evidence that some institutions are experiencing an increasing *distancing of senior managers from other staff*. For example, some writers on the consequences of local management of schools identify an increasing 'division of values and purposes' (Bowe and Ball, 1992, p. 58) between, on one hand, the 'corporatist' views of senior managers whose prime concern is with the school as a whole and its relationship with its external environment and, on the other hand, the more 'individualist' orientation of teachers whose prime concern is with the needs of individual pupils (Simkins, 1994). Similar analyses have been made in further education. For example, Lumby (1996, p. 336) describes the very strong tension which emerged for middle managers 'between a sense of being impelled by finance and a real struggle to retain student need as a basis for decisions', while another study, of the implementation of new contracts, contrasts the perspectives of senior managers 'who were very concerned with the survival of their colleges' with those of lecturers among whom 'there appeared to be little awareness or concern for the substantial financial pressures that were motivating the senior management' (Hewitt and Crawford, 1997, pp. 118–19, 125).

Thirdly, *the role of middle managers* seems to be being redefined in many educational organisations with inevitable consequences for resource management. For example, Levacic (1995) suggests that in secondary schools there may be some movement towards bidding systems, especially ones which require heads of department to be more accountable for their resource use through the establishment of departmental development plans, while in primary schools there may be some movement towards giving budgets to classroom teachers and establishing more explicit priorities which can be changed from year to year. In the further education sector, Carroll (1996) suggests that case-loading is being explored as a method through which individual lecturers and teams will be given responsibility for using the flexibility associated with a high degree of delegation of the staffing resource to deliver targets for recruitment, retention and student achievement derived from college's FEFC contracts. Such developments suggest that the increased distancing of senior managers and other staff described in the previous paragraph may, paradoxically, be accompanied by approaches to resource management which significantly reduce the degree of 'loose coupling' which has often been claimed as a key characteristic of many educational organisations.

Taken together, developments such as these suggest that external pressures may be pushing schools and colleges towards an increasingly 'managerialist' agenda (Newman and Clarke, 1994; Elliott and Crossley, 1997; Simkins, 1997b), at least as far as resource management is concerned, with an increasing centralisation of power over strategic choice being accompanied by greater delegation of responsibility for day-to-day resource management to middle managers accompanied by much stronger mechanisms of internal accountability.

It is important, however, not to overemphasise the general case for these trends. The empirical evidence is still relatively sparse, and a new government has introduced new agendas and priorities while retaining others. Furthermore, some studies suggest considerable variation among organisations in the ways in which the strategic management process operates. In particular, both schools (Sutton, 1994; Glover *et al.*, 1996a; 1996b) and colleges (Drodge and Cooper, 1997) seem to differ in the degree to which they adopt the kind of centralised and systematised approaches described above or retain more open and organic models. This leads us back to two central questions: what factors explain the variety of approaches which institutions take to the management of resources, and how far will the environmental changes described at the beginning of this chapter change the approaches which schools and colleges take in the future?

CONCLUSION

Over the past ten years the resource environment facing educational institutions in the UK has changed radically: schools and colleges have been given much greater autonomy over the ways in which they manage their resources, but alongside this they have been subjected to centrally driven funding mechanisms which have been used quite explicitly as major levers of central government policy. These developments have taken place within an environment of continuing pressure on levels of public expenditure. It has been suggested in this chapter that this context seems to have had the effect of encouraging institutions to develop resource management strategies which emphasise the management of inputs rather than outcomes – in other words, efficiency rather than effectiveness – and to evolve more 'managerialist' approaches to the structures and processes which they use for the management of resources.

Generalisations can be dangerous, however. Apart from the general resource environment facing all educational institutions, at least two other factors come in to play to influence the resource management approaches adopted by a particular school or college. One is the specific (as opposed to the general) environment which it faces. It seems clear, for example, that sectoral differences are important. Thus, whereas there seems little doubt that the severe funding pressures which are being placed on further education colleges are causing the efficiency objective to dominate all others and a 'hard' approach being taken to human resource management (Elliott and Hall, 1994), the government is establishing a climate in the schools sector – for example through its policies on target-setting and on teacher management – which is essentially 'effectiveness focused', albeit on the basis of an agenda which is tightly controlled from the centre.

Even within sectors, however, circumstances vary considerably among institutions. Bullock and Thomas (1997, p. 166) note, for example, that 'LM has affected planning, management and decision-making in schools, although the extent to which it has brought benefits seems to be affected by the financial position of the school and the management style of the headteacher'. This reflects the findings of earlier studies of 'winning' and 'losing' schools under LMS which suggested that losers are more likely to concentrate on 'efficiency' strategies than are winners, although this does not mean necessarily that the latter use the opportunity provided by an increase in resources to pursue explicit 'effectiveness' strategies. Much seems to depend on the headteacher's management style and the degree to which development planning is seen as a central element in school management (Simkins, 1994, p. 19).

This brings us to our final point. Effective strategic resource management concerns both ends and means. The ways in which resources are mobilised, allocated and used are a fundamental determinant of the quality and distribution of learning opportunities both within the educational system as a whole and within individual institutions. The processes used to make key decisions and the outcomes which result are major indicators of what, and who, is valued. This chapter has argued that environmental pressures have both raised the profile of resource management in schools and colleges and created pressures for particular kinds of managerial responses. Perhaps the key question for the next few years is how far, given these pressures, will those responsible for managing schools and colleges be able to develop approaches to resource management which ensure that educational purposes lead the resource management process and not the other way round.

REFERENCES

Audit Commission (1985a) *Audit Commission Handbook: A Guide to Economy, Efficiency and Effectiveness*, London, HMSO.
Audit Commission (1985b) *Obtaining Better Value from Further Education*, London, HMSO.
Audit Commission (1996) *Adding Up the Sums 4. Comparative Information for Schools 1995/96*, London, HMSO.
Audit Commission/Ofsted (1993) *Unfinished Business: Full-Time Educational Courses for 16–19 Year Olds*, London, HMSO.
Bowe, R. and Ball, S. (1992) *Reforming Education and Changing Schools: Case Studies in Policy Sociology*, London, Routledge.
Bradley, B. (1996) Who dares wins: intended and unintended consequences of the Further Education Funding Council methodology, *Educational Management and Administration*, Vol. 24, no. 4, pp. 379–88.
Bullock, A. and Thomas, H. (1997) *Schools at the Centre: a study of decentralisation*, London, Routledge.

Carroll, S. (1996) Caseloading. In *Developing FE (FEDA Reports)*, 1, 2.

Cohen, M.D. and March, J.G. (1974) *Leadership and Ambiguity: The American College President*, New York, McGraw-Hill.

Department for Education and Employment (1995a) *Benchmarking School Budgets*, London, DfEE.

Department for Education and Employment (1995b) *GCSE to GCE A/AS Value Added: Briefing for Schools and Colleges*, London, DfEE.

Department for Education and Employment (1996) *Setting Targets to Raise Standards: A Survey of Good Practice*, London, DfEE.

Drodge, D. and Cooper, N. (1997) Strategy and management in the further education sector. In Preedy, M., Glatter, R. and Levacic, R. (eds.) *Educational Management: Strategy, Quality and Resources*, Buckingham, Open University Press.

Elliott, G. and Crossley, M. (1997) Contested values in further education: findings from a case study of the management of change, *Educational Management and Administration*, Vol. 25, no. 1, pp. 79–92.

Elliott, G. and Hall, V. (1994) FE Inc.: business orientation in further education and the introduction of human resource management, *School Organisation*, Vol. 14, no. 1, pp. 3–10.

Further Education Funding Council (1992) *Circular 92/18: Requirements for College Strategic Plans*, Coventry, FEFC.

Further Education Funding Council (1997) *Measuring Achievement: Further Education College Performance Indicators 1994–95*, London, HMSO.

Glover, D. (1997) Resourcing education: linking budgeting to educational objectives. In Preedy, M., Glatter, R. and Levacic, R. (eds.) *Educational Management: Strategy, Quality and Resources*, Buckingham, Open University Press.

Glover, D., Levacic, R., Bennett, N. and Earley, P. (1996a) Leadership, planning and resource management in four very effective schools. Part I, *School Organisation*, Vol. 16, no. 2, pp. 135–48.

Glover, D., Levacic, R., Bennett, N. and Earley, P. (1996b) Leadership, planning and resource management in four very effective schools. Part II. Planning and performance, *School Organisation*, Vol. 16, no. 3, pp. 247–61.

Hewitt, P. and Crawford, M. (1997) Introducing new contracts: managing change in the context of an enterprise culture. In Levacic, R. and Glatter, R. (eds.) *Managing Change in Further Education, FEDA Report*, Vol. 1, no. 7, pp. 113–32.

Joint Funding Councils (1996) Management information for decision making: costing guidelines for higher education institutions (mimeo).

Levacic, R. (1995) *Local Management of Schools: Analysis and Practice*, Buckingham, Open University Press.

Levin, H.M. (1983) *Cost-Effectiveness: A Primer*, London, Sage.

Lumby, J. (1996) Curriculum change in further education, *Journal of Vocational Education and Training*, Vol. 48, no. 4, pp. 333–48.

McAleese, K. (1996) *Managing the Margins: A Benchmarking Approach to the School Budget*, London, Secondary Heads Association.

Mitchell, M. (1996), Activity-based costing in universities, *Public Money and Management*, Vol. 16, no. 1, pp. 51–7.

Mortimore, P., Mortimore, J. with Thomas, H. (1994) *Managing Associate Staff: Innovation in Primary and Secondary Schools*, London, Paul Chapman.

National Audit Office (1994) Appendix 3. Strategic planning and budgeting in grant-maintained schools. In *Value for Money at Grant-Maintained Schools: A Review of Performance*, London, HMSO.

Newman, J. and Clarke, J. (1994) Going about our business: the managerialisation of the public services. In Clarke, J., Cochrane, A. and McLaughlin, E. (eds.) *Managing Social Policy*, London, Sage.

Ofsted (1995a) *The Ofsted Handbook: Guidance on the Inspection of Secondary Schools*, London, HMSO.

Ofsted (1995b) *The Annual Report of Her Majesty's Chief Inspector of Schools*, London, HMSO.

Simkins, T. (1989) Budgeting as a political and organisational process in educational institutions. In Levacic, R. (ed.) *Financial Management in Education*, Buckingham, Open University Press.

Simkins, T. (1994) Efficiency, effectiveness and the local management of schools, *Journal of Education Policy*, Vol. 9, no. 1, pp. 15–33.

Simkins, T. (1995) The equity consequences of educational reform, *Educational Management and Administration*, Vol. 23, no. 4, pp. 221–32.

Simkins, T. (1997a) Managing resources. In Fidler, B., Russell, S. and Simkins, T. (eds.) *Choices for Self-Managing Schools: Autonomy and Accountability*, London, Paul Chapman.

Simkins, T. (1997b) Autonomy and accountability. In Fidler, B., Russell, S. and Simkins, T. (eds.) *Choices for Self-Managing Schools: Autonomy and Accountability*, London, Paul Chapman.

Simkins, T. and Lancaster, D. (1987) *Budgeting and Resource Allocation in Educational Institutions, Sheffield City Polytechnic Papers in Education Management* 35, Sheffield, Sheffield City Polytechnic.

Sutton, M. (1994) Sharing the purse strings, *Managing Schools Today*, Vol. 4, no. 7, pp. 14–16.

Thomas, H. and Martin, J. (1996) *Managing Resources for School Improvement: Creating a Cost-Effective School*, London, Routledge.

6

EFFECTIVE SCHOOL DEVELOPMENT PLANNING

Edith Jayne

HISTORY AND BACKGROUND

Some schools have been developing their curriculum, staff and systems in a systematic planning cycle for at least the past two decades. The Inner London Education Authority for instance advocated that all their schools should 'self-review' (ILEA, 1977) along set guidelines. A Schools Council project involving numbers of trial schools in varying local authorities in the early 1980s used a survey feedback technique in gathering data from school staff on the strengths and weaknesses of the school and their own teaching and their suggestions for areas to develop in the following year(s). This was eventually published in 1984 (and revised in 1988) and is known as GRIDS, i.e. Guidelines for the Review and Internal Development of Schools, in versions for all phases of schooling (primary, including special, and secondary). In some of the schools and LEAs where trialing of these materials and processes was being undertaken, some schools began development planning, so that one school in which a student on one of my courses documented this as her study, the school had undertaken four annual cycles by 1988, increasing their understanding of the processes, their sophistication and their specificity in setting criteria for implementation (what are now more commonly termed success criteria) with each cycle.

Other factors that influenced this development were varying government initiatives to stimulate school management training, initially focusing on headteachers through grant-aided courses beginning in the mid-1980s. The management in education courses increasingly available in higher education institutions, or through consortia of education authorities and higher education institutions, helped to promulgate a systematic and developmental approach to school development.

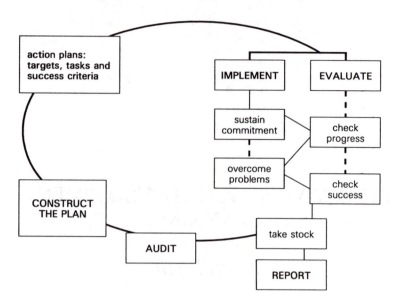

Figure 6.1   A model of an effective planning process
Source: Based on Hargreaves and Hopkins, 1990

Specific impetus came with the publication of the DES reports based on their sponsored School Development Plans Project (Hargreaves and Hopkins, 1990; 1991), copies of which were sent to all schools and to their chair of governors. This proposed a model of an effective planning process (see Figure 6.1). This cyclical process of audit, constructing the plan, agreeing and implementing the plan, and monitoring and evaluating the outcomes is to be followed in subsequent years with repeated cycles. Glover (1990) documented the process in an early case study at an Oxfordshire secondary school and Hutchinson (1993) related possible problems which one of his students, a Northern Irish primary headteacher, encountered in effecting school development through development planning efforts. Despite useful advice from pilot schemes (e.g. Holly and Southworth, 1989) and some LEA initiatives, development planning was still quite patchy nationally even after the Education Reform Act in 1988. Further guides were published, for example, Davies and Ellison (1992), Skelton *et al.* (1993), Hargreaves and Hopkins (1991; 1994), and education management journals featured articles on how to plan effectively for a school's development.

LOCAL HISTORIES/PRACTICES

While most schools by the early and mid-1990s were undergoing the development planning process, and there was some sharing of good practice in local networks often of such things as using spreadsheet packages for charting stages in a readable format, or ways of effectively engaging governing body support and understanding of the process, in individual schools there were widely varying experiences. In some schools development planning was seen as the head's 'managerialist' or 'issuing orders to the troops' agenda, in others it generated very useful discussions on setting aims and goals (or mission and vision statements) and a real attempt to involve the entire school community in the process of planning a school's development to improve constantly the teaching and learning on offer to the pupils.

Interestingly, little account was made of the learning and developmental aspects of the process by the guide writers or LEA personnel. It is really only by looking at series of case studies of schools that it becomes apparent that schools become better at this process over time and that many of the first attempts were either overly ambitious and therefore not achievable or sometimes too constrained in their focus to provide developmental opportunities for improving teaching and learning across the broad range of pupil's experiences (e.g. by focusing on only one curriculum area in a primary school or just on assessment procedures in a secondary school). However subsequent development plans in those schools tended to redress such imbalances and also involve increasing numbers of staff in their production. This will be discussed in more detail under the case studies later.

In different LEAs, there was a use of different names or terms – so, for example, Enfield favoured IDPs (institutional development plans), most LEAs asked for SDPs (school development plans), Devon asked its schools in the early 1990s to do school management plans. Guidance was given in varying degrees in different authorities (Bradford LEA, 1992, being a particularly 'popular' version in those LEAs that had not produced their own). Schools were often expected to submit their plans centrally but in the experience of the schools with which I have worked, they received no feedback on these or discussion on how the process could be improved in subsequent cycles.

These initiatives had varying impact on schools – it was not uncommon that if I were to ask staff of schools about their development plans (which we often did on our management courses) all but the most senior staff would have no knowledge of its contents. Arguably such (semi-private) plans could not serve as a spur to the school's development. What also seemed to have varied is the level of detail advocated in individual annual and three or five-year plans. The concept of strategic planning was, in many schools, embryonic. They may have been willing to produce five-year plans on request, but these were inflated versions of one-year plans rather than being future's-thinking orientated and about goals or directions for future development.

With the advent of ERA and the introduction of the National Curriculum and increasing setting of agendas for development by government initiatives, some schools became less disposed to do other than annual plans, although many adopted an 18-month cycle so that both the financial year (April–March) and the academic year (September–July) were spanned. In defence of schools it has to be said that rational long-term planning is exceptionally difficult when budgets for schools are set by LEAs annually (and frequently fluctuate) and when these budget figures are often unavailable until 30 days *after* the start of the financial year. Thus there may be an inherent tension between rational, strategic and long-term planning and the chaotic, non-rational short-term reality within which some current fiscal practice exists (see, e.g. Stacey, 1992, as quoted in Hargreaves, 1995; Mintzberg, 1994).

It could of course be argued that this is precisely why schools need a more flexible range of strategic and contingency planning techniques and strategies so that they can weather the political budgetary storms and mandated changes to curriculum or practice that were unforeseen in the previous year's thinking and planning processes.

Interestingly school development plans are still not a statutory requirement although, as they are expected by Ofsted in the framework for inspection, this is tantamount to their being obligatory.

CURRENT PRACTICE

Why do it – the purposes of development planning

Improving the quality of teaching and learning There are multiple reasons given, but the ultimate aim is to improve the quality of the learning and teaching in the school. This link with school effectiveness and improvement is posed by Holly and Southworth (1989); Burridge and Ribbins (1994); Hargreaves and Hopkins (1994); MacGilchrist *et al.* (1995); Hopkins and Lagerweij (1996). Other purposes mentioned are as follows.

That it rationalises and co-ordinates initiatives in schools and can act as a defence against innovation overload (Wallace, 1991).

That it can act as a spur to joint planning and shared decision-making and can enable the vision or mission to be translated into agreed action strategies Finance and resources can therefore be deployed to serve the curriculum and learning needs as defined by the school in its strategic and shorter-term development plans.

Early experiences in school development planning indicated that the school needed to plan simultaneously for development and change and for stability and continuity of previous development – that is simultaneously for new change and improvement and maintenance of previous change.

Hargreaves and Hopkins (1991, pp. 43–4) indicated that 'development planning involves two kinds of change: root innovations the base on which other, or branch innovations can be sustained'. They identify (*ibid.*) such strong roots as 'good management arrangements, a well designed staff development policy or a history of collaborative work among the school staff and with the school's partners'. This is quite a useful distinction using a systems metaphor and perspective to indicate that certain features of good management need to be operating (or the plan needs to encompass how these are to be encouraged) in order for effective innovation or development to begin.

Becoming a learning organisation More recently there has been a focus on the plan encompassing or generating a healthy school culture leading to the development of an effective learning organisation. The notion here is that the total organisation (teaching staff, auxiliary staff, management hierarchy, governors as well as clients, pupils or students) can and should consciously and interdependently learn and improve its processes of effective teaching and learning.

How to do it – process and content of SDPs

Writing about development planning in the 1980s assumed that it should be set into a framework of strategic management. This, in Johnson and Scholes' (1993) terms, would include strategic analysis (informed by the environmental scanning, analysis of culture and stakeholder expectations and of resources and strategic capability), strategic choice (informed by identifying strategic options, evaluating options and selecting strategy) and strategy implementation (managing strategic change, organisation structure and design and planning and allocating resources).

However, recent turbulence in geopolitics and market turbulence in organisations operating multinationally mean there is less reliance in the business community on long-range planning than was true in the 1980s. This along with the notion of chaos theory and the increasing uncontrollability of accurate futures planning in a postmodern age have had their effects on school management thinking. Thus 'forecasting – i.e. anticipating future states – and strategic planning – i.e. formulating an adaptive response' (Boiset, 1995, p. 31) may not always be the most effective strategy for school leaders in a turbulent environment. Boiset (*ibid.*, p. 36) goes on to describe 'strategic intent' as effective through a 'direct, intuitive understanding' by the leadership ('some would call it vision') which guides the organisation and all its members in the presence of turbulence or heavy turbulence in its environment. At least some leaders of schools would characterise their environments (including uncertain enrolments, externally imposed curricula, changing financial arrangements and formulae, etc.) as such. Thus planning is set into a framework of managerial information systems providing better data on which to plan strategically as well as to develop such 'strategic intent'.

In practice, therefore, if SDPs are asked to serve as co-ordinating and control mechanisms, then they will amalgamate separate plans regarding premises, buildings, and resources; staff development, in-service training, and appraisal and performance management; management development, training and succession planning; finance and budgeting; community relations, parents' and governors' development; and, crucially, curriculum development and planning regarding learning and teaching. Yet ideally

SDPs should be able to be presented succinctly and graphically and be understood by the various stakeholders and constituencies. Schools have tackled this in innovative ways by producing overviews as well as detailed plans, although Fullan's (1992) dictum that overly detailed planning may get in the way of development (or change, in the cases he was describing) does apply here.

Who does it?

The received wisdom is that development planning should involve all the school's stakeholders and the process itself may help to achieve a coherent vision and/or a corporate and productive or collegial culture. So, e.g. Biott *et al.* (1994, in Hargreaves and Hopkins, 1994, p. 81) found that 'where many or all of the staff had been involved in discussion about the school development plan the Headteacher regarded this in itself as beneficial; indeed this participation was seen as probably more important than the finished document and self-evidently a "good thing"'.

This is not inevitable, however, and micropolitical currents may also be evident as in a study by Newman and Pollard (1994) in the same book (Hargreaves and Hopkins, 1994) where a new head restructured posts and responsibilities with the perhaps predictable consequences of being supported by those who gained from her strategic plan and opposed by those who were 'losers' thereby.

As mentioned earlier, there is a developmental process to development planning: many early attempts are the province of the head or head and deputy or SMT and third, fourth and fifth annual cycles usually involve all staff, and middle managers have considerable input and monitoring and evaluation roles; often, too, governors are involved in a role wider than 'approving' the already developed plan(s). A few schools have also involved pupils but at this stage this is still a rarer development (see, e.g. Middlewood and Riley, 1995, p. 18 or Ruddock *et al.*, 1996). Scottish HMI (1992) and more recently MacBeath *et al.* for the NUT (1996) have examples of evaluation instruments for the full constituency of school stakeholders – pupils, parents, support staff, teachers and governors. The use of these in some schools has meant that there is indirect, and in some cases direct, input of a variety of views into the school development planning process.

MacGilchrist *et al.* (1995, pp. 120–1) describe the nine primary schools' SDPs in their detailed study as representing the following typology. Those with

- rhetorical plans (no ownership, little evaluation, little linking of different plans and budget);
- singular plans (devised by head alone – accountability led);
- co-operative plans (staff or SMT working together led by head, with some linkages of planning, e.g. finance and curriculum or staff development); and
- corporate plans (shared ownership, strong linkages, built-in evaluation, focus on learning).

The level of involvement increases in each of the four types. It is only in the last two types that there is a positive impact across the school and in classrooms with the corporate plan producing a significant impact on school development, teacher development and pupil learning.

An interesting dimension of development and strategic planning is the example of very small schools. While in a commonsense way it would appear to be easier to involve 'everyone' in schools with a very limited range of stakeholders, in practice this may not be the case. One of my students is the head of a two-teacher school, with three support staff. The major focus in such small establishments is often on survival (as the LEA has a policy on minimum numbers for viability/finance) and continuity. One or two families leaving have a proportionally greater effect and a member of staff leaving likewise may mean vital knowledge about the school or the curriculum is suddenly missing. On the one hand, such a scenario makes strategic planning all the more imperative; on the other, with so few possible planners/stakeholders it is actually difficult to do and the imperative of classroom teaching (the head having a 4½-day teaching load) means there is little time available for combined meetings of all staff and governors to undertake this. It may mean that it is harder in these circumstances to devise a 'corporate plan' (MacGilchrist *et al.*, 1995; see above) rather than its being easier to achieve.

THE CASE STUDIES

Two schools were looked at in close-up to flesh out details about the way in which schools come to learn about strategic and development planning and how they come to enact the process effectively in order to further the goals of improvement in pupils' learning. The first is a case study of a large first school for children of 4–8 years old; the second of a secondary school and community college spanning ages 11–18 as well as adult and continuing education. Evidence was collected differently in each case; in School A the author had worked as a consultant and trainer for three years, intermittently, and there were meeting agendas, some evaluation evidence and data collected from the management team (known as the steering group), several professional training days and four development plans available for study. There was also another interview with the head to bring the case study up to date. In the secondary school example, School B, data were in the form of one long interview with the headteacher and scrutiny of relevant documentary evidence. Thus the first case presents an evolutionary tale; the second a snapshot as seen from the leader's perspective.

School A

The first school is a large (five-form entry) institution in an urban environment. The school buildings were adapted for use by young children and during the time of the study were refurbished and a more suitable set of buildings added. This was a prominent feature of the first two SDPs as the building itself was felt to constrain the teaching and learning changes the school wished to undertake (and required much political endeavour by governors and friends of the school). A new head had been appointed in 1992 and introduced development planning as a joint process with the large staff. The school had a good local reputation and a stable staff profile though rather long serving even for the county (which is renowned for staff 'staying'). This factor also produced an unforeseen budget deficit to the new administration and governors, because salary costs had not been projected forward. There had been relatively little in the way of corporate planning among year groups or much sharing of classroom practices. The first development plan was written after staff development interviews with all staff by the new head, with the advice and counsel of the 'steering group' – an enlarged group of six to eight of the senior staff set up for this purpose. It used a cycle of audit (which had a subcycle of audit, statement of intent, review and planning and prioritising stages), action plan, implementation, review, planning and prioritising and the next cycle beginning again with audit. The steering group invested resources in itself – in consultancy and training in order to work together effectively, in team-building and to set coherent development goals and targets for the school. Varying survey–feedback techniques were used – diagnosing actual and preferred organisational culture (Harrison and Stokes, 1992), a self-assessment checklist (Sallis, 1992) and Coverdale's systematic approach framework for initially structuring the aims and purposes of the steering group as members saw it.

Professional training days were earmarked to work with staff on bottom-up approaches to sharing notions of good early years practice, ways of jointly planning rolling programmes of schemes of work, monitoring achievement across the year groups, catering for individual needs and differentiating work, etc. An early result of one such day was a policy for learning. The training days had a constituency of all staff – full and part time, teaching and associate staff – and the avowed aim was simultaneously to address the issue of the day (which varied) *and* to share practice, find a vocabulary for expressing aims and goals and to construct a joint vision and mission for the school. The 'pedagogy' was an empowering one with small-group work feeding into whole-staff work and a sharing of the chairing by members of the steering group or curriculum leaders as well as the head and the author as consultant and trainer. At the end of the first year there was a review of developments and some monitoring in relation to success criteria but these were fairly rudimentary and varied in sophistication depending on the experience and skills of the member of staff whose responsibility it had been. In the second cycle there was more active bidding for funds, priorities and more developed procedures for monitoring and evaluating developments. Some collaborative efforts with other schools were also incorporated, in at least one instance being part funded by an LEA initiative involving pupil self-assessment of work and setting of learning targets; these widened expertise of staff and brought in new ideas simultaneously.

The steering group returned to focus on its role (and those of others) in a more robust evaluation of developments for which they were responsible and devised a series of strategies for how it could discharge this responsibility. By this time there had been regular planning and strategy meetings in year groups and curriculum leaders had been into classrooms both to support developments and to evaluate progress, so there was some practice on which to draw. Moreover, mutual accountability had been accepted and this was an activity that was considered feasible by most although there were one or two members of staff who were still uncomfortable with this role. This was just one example where staff development and practice had to change and the culture of the school alter before the evaluation stage could be undertaken in any substantive way. It also fleshes out how the mechanics of development planning could have been imposed but not been successfully carried out to improve learning and teaching until there was a more corporate and collaborative culture in the school.

From the very beginning there was a strategic plan that was shared by the head, her deputy and the chair of governors to improve the physical site and conditions including the lunch-time dining arrangements and meal-time assistants' behaviour management of the children. In stages this became public and part of the development planning process and in turn was supported by parent groups who worked on creating environmental areas and more conducive play facilities for use at break and lunch-times. The building programme discussed earlier was also part of this strategic plan but took rather longer to accomplish than originally anticipated. A further development more recently will expand the age range of the school by adding a nursery unit.

The most recent development plan, corporately produced, has further refined the practices so that there is considerable detail of origins and reasons for the priorities identified (including evaluations of previous developments), clear targets, identified success criteria and evaluation strategies, who specifically is accountable for expenditure, monitoring and evaluation, and where this fits into the overall school aims and vision. Staff development, training, INSET, management development and succession planning all feature and there is a (loose) relationship with appraisal and appraisal targets. These are all set into the context of national and local priorities and the school's experience of an Ofsted inspection and its outcomes.

The school has used the development planning process as one of the means of changing the climate, ethos or culture of the school into a collaborative and mutually supportive one where pupil achievement is paramount supported by a rich brew of energetic staff development and mutual support. This was led by a highly experienced head who was willing to prepare the ground for development (akin to Hargreaves and Hopkins', 1991, 'root' rather than 'branch' developments) and to have a vision of where and how the school needed to develop but also the skill with which to bring about change slowly and deliberately so that the changes and innovations would 'grow' organically and be sustained by staff who understood, supported and could implement them.

School B

This school is a large secondary school in a town in a rural area though close to a city. The school is a large 11–18 comprehensive in an attractive setting but now rather cramped for classroom accommodation. It, too, had a 'settled' staff and a previous long-serving head. When the new head was appointed he, too, was faced with budget deficits and series of plans (for staff development, curriculum, etc.) which had not been combined into an overall strategic and coherent plan. The first few months were fact-finding and audit times for the senior management team including a large class-room visitation programme to get a 'feel' for the quality of the teaching and learning experiences on offer and where there were opportunities for development. SWOT analyses were undertaken to record the strengths, weaknesses, opportunities and threats at the time. There was then a period of consultation with departments and individual staff members before a development plan was drafted by the working group of the SMT. This then went back out to consultation and was in some cases amended or was retained but with a minority view presented alongside for governors and staff to see there had not necessarily been consensus on the issue(s). Governors were involved during a training weekend. The senior management team was responsible for the final production of the plan which was a three-year rolling programme (1995–98) and set the strategic intent for the school. It contains a vision statement and set of values, and development plans for curriculum pre- and post-16, the community, student, staff and governor development plans and implementation timetables. The head characterised the development plan as being primarily about the students' experience of teaching and learning. There were also structural changes made to strengthen the management structure – 23 departments were merged into a smaller number of faculties.

With the advent of the government initiative for specialist schools, the school (SMT led but with industrial and commercial sponsorship) bid for and obtained language college status. The reasons for this were to increase funding, to capitalise on an acknowledged strength of the school and to achieve a niche in the market-place. This produced another development plan for the years 1996–99. There is therefore an accelerated programme of staff development including modern languages and some considerable opening-up of opportunities for staff to take on initiatives on fixed-term enhanced salaries to get new programmes of study, or community or entre-preneurial initiatives, up and running. Because these changes happened in quite a short period of time, not all staff feel yet 'part' of this somewhat different school from the one they joined, but the school as a whole does project an image of future orientation and an internationalist, postmod-ernist outlook. There is therefore an agenda for the senior management in taking along all their staff to their new vision and mission.

Because the data for this summary were collected from a narrow range of sources (mainly an interview with the head and documentary evidence), it is difficult to evaluate the effectiveness of the development planning process. However, it is certainly a good example of a mainly top-down effort to change the culture of the school and to enhance the learning opportunities on offer to the students and the community through this process. The ability to follow an initiative that was not foreseen (language college status) was possible because the plan had involved a detailed strategic intent which allowed the flexibility to capitalise on something not known when the plan was devised.

The twin goals of finding a niche in the market-place that would attract students from outside the immediate catchment area and so increase enrolment and finances and to create a stimulating learning environment for staff and students alike, the so-called 'learning organisation' (Senge, 1990), were the driving forces.

The headteacher feels that the staff are now more able to contribute actively to the development and strategic planning process and is expecting it to be a more collaborative effort as reviews and evaluations occur and the plan is updated. The staff, the SMT and governors have all learned through this first phase and are now more able to develop the planning processes via the decision-making forums of the school – the faculties, subject groupings, pastoral elements, etc.

Both case studies exemplify new heads using the developmental planning processes to enhance the learning opportunities for the pupils or students and simultaneously to change the staff cultures to more nearly approximate the learning organisations that writers such as Senge (1993) feel are necessary for all organisations to be in the next century, and I would argue are particularly pertinent for schools which should be educative for all their members. Both the heads were interested in learning and ideas and were seen by their staff to be such. It appears to be particularly important for the leaders to model being a learner (publicly) and to set up or encourage learning opportunities and challenges for their staff.

Using the commonsense definition of 'strategic', both heads knew what they wanted to achieve, they were able to justify the direction (to their stakeholders) and were finding the best or appropriate ways of getting there.

CONCLUSION

Research and case-study evidence is accumulating that indicates that school effectiveness and improvement are enhanced with appropriate leadership, effective planning and resource management (Davies and Ellison, 1992; MacGilchrist *et al.*, 1995; Fidler, 1996; Glover *et al.*, 1996a; 1996b; MacGilchrist, 1996. However, these studies and the two cases described above do indicate that the school's planning processes may vary in degree of rationality, level of detail, specificity, etc., and be equally effective in outcome. Glover *et al.*, (1996b, p. 247) found that

there is a continuum between system-based and integrative culture forms of school development planning and resource allocation. We conclude that where the integrative culture is maintained with strongly shared values and flexibility of approach it can promote schools which are as effective as those following the rational planning model.

Teacher development and the creation of a learning and development culture within the school appear to be crucial. How this is likely to be achieved is outlined by Southworth (1994, in Burridge and Ribbins, 1994, p. 53) in his description of a learning school as one with the following five characteristics:

- the focus is on the pupils and their learning;
- individual teachers are encouraged to be continuing learners themselves;
- teachers and others who constitute the staff are encouraged to collaborate by learning with and from each other;
- the school . . . learns its way forward, i.e. the school as an organisation is a learning system . . . ;
- the Headteacher is the leading learner.

Development planning can in the ways outlined above contribute to school effectiveness and in this chapter examples of some of the varying possible routes have been charted in order to provide the developmental story/ stories to go alongside the 'how to do it' manuals.

Teachers and senior managers in schools are capable of engaging in the planning processes including strategic management and can engage in the debate about the future structure, content, and delivery of teaching and learning for the pupils and students they currently teach, as the case studies have shown. However, this is a relatively new activity for the teaching profession in the UK (and is only beginning elsewhere in Europe) and *therefore they need practice in doing it as well as engaging in robust evaluations of their efforts so that they can continue to learn about and improve these practices.*

Acknowledgement

With thanks to Jen Cartwright and Peter Upton.

REFERENCES

Biott, C., Easen, P. and Atkins, M. (1994) Written planning and school development: biding time or making time. In Hargreaves, D.H. (eds.) *Development Planning for School Improvement*, London, Cassell.

Boiset, M. (1995) Preparing for turbulence: the changing relationship between strategy and management development in the learning organization. In Garrett, B. (ed.) *Developing Strategic Thought*, London, McGraw-Hill.

Bradford LEA (1992) *School Development Planning Handbook*, Bradford, Bradford LEA.

Burridge, E. and Ribbins, P. (eds.) (1994) *Improving Education: Promoting Quality in Schools*, London, Cassell.

Davies, B. and Ellison, L. (1992) *School Development Planning*, Harlow, Longman.

DES (1989) *Planning for School Development: Advice to Governors, Headteachers and Teachers*, London, Department for Education and Science.

DES (1991) *Development Planning – A Practical Guide: Advice to Governors, Headteachers and Teachers*, London, Department for Education and Science.

Fidler, B. (1996) School development planning and strategic planning for school improvement. In Earley, P., Fidler, B. and Ouston, J. (eds.) *Improvement Through Inspection?* London, David Fulton.

Fullan, M. (1992) The New Meaning of Educational Change, London, Cassell.

Giles, C. (1995) Site-based planning and resource management: the role of the school development plan, *Educational Change and Development*, Vol. 15, no. 2, pp. 45–50.

Giles, C. (1997) *School Development Planning*, Plymouth, Northcote House Publishers.

Glover, D. (1990) Towards a school development plan: process and practice, *Educational Management and Administration*, Vol. 18, no. 3, pp. 22–6.

Glover, D., Levacic, R., Bennett, N. and Earley, P. (1996a) Leadership, planning and resource management in four very effective schools. Part I. Setting the scene, *School Organisation*, Vol. 16, no. 2, pp. 135–48.

Glover, D., Levacic, R., Bennett, N. and Earley, P. (1996b) Leadership, planning and resource management in four very effective schools. Part II. Planning and performance, *School Organisation*, Vol. 16, no. 3, pp. 247–61.

Hargreaves, D.H. (1995) Self-managing schools and development planning – chaos or control? *School Organisation*, Vol. 15, no. 3, pp. 215–27.

Hargreaves, D.H. and Hopkins, D. (1990) *Planning for School Development*, London, DES.

Hargreaves, D.H. and Hopkins, D. (1991) *The Empowered School: The Management and Practice of Development Planning*, London, Cassell.

Hargreaves, D.H. and Hopkins, D. (eds.) (1994) *Development Planning for School Improvement*, London, Cassell.

Harris, A., Jamieson, I. and Russ, J. (1996) *School Effectiveness and School Improvement*, London, Pitman.

Harrison, R. and Stokes, H. (1992) *Diagnosing Organisational Culture*, San Diego, Calif., Pfeiffer & Co.

HMI/Scottish Office (1992) *Using Ethos Indicators for Primary School/Secondary School Self-Evaluation*, Edinburgh, Scottish Office.

Holly, P. and Southworth, G. (1989) *The Developing School*, London, Falmer Press.

Hopkins, D. and Lagerweij, N. (1996) The school improvement knowledge base. In Reynolds, D. *et al.* (eds.) *Making Good Schools*, London, Routledge.

Hutchinson, B. (1993) The effective reflective school: visions and pipe dreams in development planning, *Educational Management and Administration*, Vol. 21, no. 1, pp. 4–18.

ILEA (1977) *Keeping the School under Review*, London, Inner London Education Authority.

Johnson, G. and Scholes, K. (1993) *Exploring Corporate Strategy* (3rd edn), Hemel Hemstead, Prentice-Hall.

MacBeath, J., Boyd, B., Rand, J. and Bell, S. (1996) *Schools Speak for Themselves: Towards a Framework for Self-Evaluation*, London, NUT.

MacGilchrist, B. (1996) Linking staff development and children's learning, *Educational Leadership*, Vol. 53, no. 6, pp. 72–5.

MacGilchrist, B., Mortimore P., Savage, J. and Beresford, C. (1995) *Planning Matters: The Impact of Development Planning in Primary Schools*, London, Paul Chapman.

Middlewood, D. and Riley, M. (1995) *Development Planning for Schools,* Leicester, University of Leicester.

Mintzberg, H. (1994) *The Rise and Fall of Strategic Planning*, London, Prentice-Hall.

Newman, E. and Pollard, A. (1994) Observing primary school change: through conflict to whole school collaboration? In Hargreaves, D.H. and Hopkins, D. (eds.) *Development Planning for School Improvement*, London, Cassell.

Reynolds, D., Bollen, R., Creemers, B., Hopkins, D., Stoll, L. and Lagerwij, N. (eds.)(1996) *Making Good Schools: Linking School Effectiveness and School Improvement*, London, Routledge.

Ruddock, J., Chaplain, R. and Wallace, G. (1996) *School Improvement – What Can Pupils Tell Us?* London, David Fulton.

Sallis, E. (1992) *TQM in Education*, London, Kogan Page.

Senge, P.M. (1990) *The Fifth Discipline*, New York, Doubleday.

Senge, P.M. (1993) Transforming the practice of management, *Human Resource Development Quarterly*, Vol. 4, no. 1, pp. 5–32.

Skelton, M., Reeves, G. and Playfoot, D. (1991) *Development Planning for Primary Schools*, Windsor, NFER/Nelson.

Wallace, M. (1991) Flexible planning: a key to the management of multiple innovations, *Education Management and Administration*, Vol. 19, no. 3, pp. 180–92.

7

STRATEGIC PLANNING IN FURTHER EDUCATION

Jacky Lumby

THE FURTHER EDUCATION CONTEXT

Prior to the incorporation of colleges in 1993, much of the strategic planning for further education was undertaken by local education authorities. Colleges' internal plans were founded on the basis of a relatively stable annual income, with little sense that the fate of the institution might depend on the quality of planning. Since 1993, colleges have found themselves in the position of undertaking planning which will determine the college's continued survival or otherwise in a highly competitive environment. Crisp (1991, p. 3) defines the process:

> Strategic planning is the set of activities designed to identify the appropriate future direction of a college, and includes specifying the steps necessary to move in that direction. Strategic management, on the other hand, is concerned with the total process of planning, implementing, monitoring and maintaining the strategy over a longer period.

Much of the current literature on strategy in further education focuses on the process of strategic planning. There is less available on the content, implementation and monitoring of plans. There has not yet been time since 1993 to assess satisfactorily the implementation of plans which have a 3–5-year timespan. Consequently, this chapter will focus mainly on the experience of colleges in undertaking strategic planning, and begin to explore some of the difficulties of implementation that are emerging.

DEFINITION OF TERMS

The language used in this area of activity varies. Colleges must produce strategic plans, which must contain an operating statement (FEFC, 1992). The operating statement (*ibid.*, p. 5) should identify:

- those components of a college's strategic objectives which are to be put into effect in the forthcoming sixteen months
- how each component is to be delivered and where responsibility for its delivery lies
- what resources are required and what monitoring and review of progress and delivery there will be.

There are obvious similarities between the operating statement as defined by the Further Education Funding Council (FEFC) and a generic business plan. However, different names are attached to plans at different levels both in further education and in business depending partly on the degree of operational detail which is provided: 'Strategic objectives . . . do not, in themselves, identify the action necessary to achieve them. They have first to be translated into more specific targets. This process is one which is increasingly being understood as *business planning* (Crisp, 1991, p. 26).

There is also a distinction drawn between a business plan and an action plan:

The business plan is like an action plan which converts the rather general, long-term objectives of strategy into specific, attainable goals in the short-term and identifies the steps necessary to achieve them. It is not a full action plan, which would spell out the precise steps to be taken, identify a timetable and assign responsibilities to named individuals and groups.

(Ibid., p. 27)

Colleges may use the terms, strategic plan, operating statement or plan, business plan and action plan in different ways. There is a common format for the first of these two, as suggested by the FEFC, but the ensuing more detailed plans, which translate strategic objectives into detailed guidance for action, may be described differently, perhaps merely attaching a different label, but possibly also indicating differences in underlying philosophy.

THE PURPOSE OF STRATEGIC PLANNING

Writing of business planning in education, Wheale (1991) identifies two purposes for such planning. The first is 'purely practical' enabling the business to be run 'as efficiently and effectively as possible'. The second purpose he designates as 'political' – that is, using the plan to satisfy the demands of various stakeholders including the funding bodies of the FEFC and the local Training and Enterprise Council (TEC).

Strategic planning is used to choose a path for the college in relation to the external environment, but may also simultaneously engineer internal change. Plans unsupported by organisational capability are unlikely to become anything more than a pile of paper. Limb (1992, p. 167) is quite explicit in her aim: 'The aim of the approach to strategic planning and management at Milton Keynes College was to build upon and enhance organizational capabilities.'

Strategic plans can therefore face outwards, in positioning the college in relation to the current and projected future environment, but also face inwards, in building commitment to the chosen path or mission, and the capabilities of individuals and the structure.

Much of the process and terminology in use is derived from generic strategic management in business and industry. Colleges face a very difficult task in straddling the business and public service boundary. It is clear that they face the same imperatives for survival as any business organisation. However, unlike businesses, and in common with other public services, generating income may be crucial, but it is not the only goal: 'The business of public service is not for competitive advantage but for social change' (Stewart, 1989, quoted in Wilkinson and Pedler, 1994, p. 203).

Moreover, colleges are not entirely free to make their own decisions. They are bounded by parameters set by legislation, the FEFC and TECs. As Austin (1994, p. 136) somewhat wryly states, 'Free standing independent businesses we are not'.

EXTERNAL FACTORS

Tristram (1996, p. 90) asserts that there is considerable debate within the further education sector as to 'whether colleges have sufficient independence to truly act strategically'. The perceived threats to the achievement of colleges' strategic plans are shown in Figure 7.1.

The ability to secure growth funding, competition from more generously funded sixth forms, discretionary awards from local authorities and legislation restricting the training of the unemployed, are all perceived as posing a risk to plans. Colleges may lobby for changes in all these, but ultimately have no alternative but to manage within the confines of systems which rest on local or national political decisions. The rise in colleges with insecure financial positions, 21 per cent in 1996 compared with 6 per cent in 1994 (FEFC, 1997), seems to suggest that the externally imposed financial regime has undermined the position of colleges to be managed successfully and achieve their plans. This is acknowledged by the FEFC which, in detailing the declining financial health of the sector, 'considers that the out-turn position for 1995–96 shows the effect of continued demands for efficiency gains from the sector' (*ibid.*, p. 2).

In formulating their strategic plans, colleges face competition from schools and private training organisations and must also respond to the complex factors impacting on consumer demand for education and training. At the same time as operating within this commercial environment, they are constrained by state control of their growth and the ways in which they may operate. Their strategic plans are therefore framed in an environment which is a hybrid of commercial and public sector constituents.

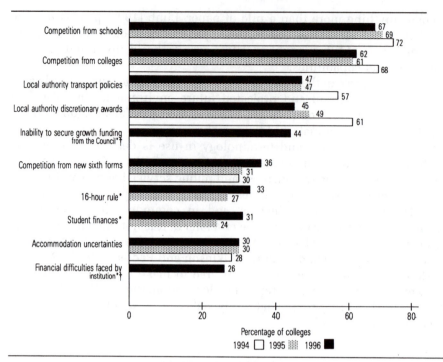

* *not identified as risks in 1994 analysis framework:* † *not identified as risks in 1995 analysis framework*
Source: colleges' strategic plans. July 1994, July 1995 and July 1996

Figure 7.1   Risk factors: college strategic plans
Source: FEFC *Circular 97/04*. Reproduced with permission of The Further Education Funding Council.

THE CONTEXT FOR STRATEGIC PLANNING

In 1992, the FEFC (p. 2), recognising 'that many colleges are relatively inexperienced in planning strategically', issued guidance on a framework for strategic planning. The process suggested used the mission statement as a basis for a 3–5-year plan, encompassing the key elements of numbers of students and their provision, human resources, physical resources and finance. It assumed an annual operating plan and an annual review of performance.

The FEFC (*ibid.*, pp. 3–4) also suggested that the plan itself should include:

- college mission
- needs analysis
- three-year strategic overview of objectives for student numbers and provision, and physical resources
- sensitivity analysis
- operating statement for the sixteen-month period commencing 1 April, to include the college's financial forecast

- numerical information to support the strategic objectives for students and provision.

The framework is decidedly rational in its approach, and eschews any reference to other approaches (see Chapter 1). Guidance in the strategic planning framework largely relates to the plan itself, rather than offering any support in terms of how the planning process is undertaken, or the plans implemented. Colleges were left to decide upon their own path to producing and implementing their plan. A review of colleges' strategic plans illustrates that colleges have largely followed the guidance of the FEFC in terms of the content of their strategic plan. The elements included in plans of colleges are shown in Figure 7.2.

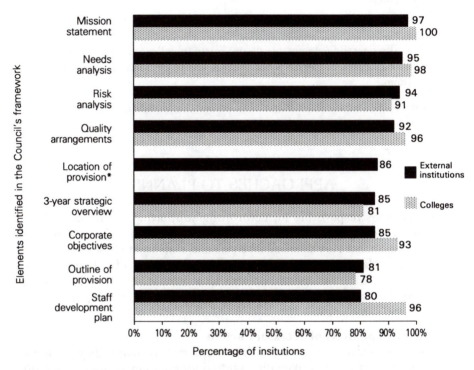

not included in the Council's framework for colleges

Source: external institutions' strategic plans, July 1995: 20 per cent sample of colleges' strategic plans, July 1994

Figure 7.2 Extent of colleges following the FEFC guidance
Source: FEFC 1996. Reproduced with permission of The Further Education Funding Council.

However, evidence collected to date shows that the process of arriving at the plan, and the effectiveness of its implementation have not been entirely successful for many colleges. The National Audit Office (1994, p. 29) visited 15 colleges and found:

In their 1993–96 plans, all of the colleges visited by the National Audit Office planned strategically for their academic activities. However, there were notable weaknesses in these plans, including:

- targets which were unrealistic or unrelated to the college mission or strategic aims;
- lack of costing or identification of resource requirements of objectives included in the plans; and
- lack of governing body involvement in discussion and approving plans.

Looking for progress, a year on, they discovered that weaknesses remained in 1994–97 plans and planning processes. Research carried out in ten colleges in England and Wales (FEDA, 1995, p. 44) concurred with the results of the National Audit Office's review:

Some college strategic plans lack strategy!

For example

- objectives describe current practice rather than new or specific developments
- faculty operating statements do not relate to college strategic objectives
- there is a lack of clarity about what needs to be done, how, when and by whom.

Colleges appear to have found the strategic planning process very problematic.

APPROACHES TO PLANNING

The agencies responsible for controlling/supporting further education all stress a rational approach to strategic planning. The FEFC planning framework demands a very detailed analysis and statement of measurable objectives. The National Audit Office's (1994) criticisms of colleges' strategic planning cite the failure to conform to a normative rational model. The Further Education Development Agency (1995, p. v, emphasis added) makes the same point:

Detailed analysis of necessary action
Some objectives prove difficult to implement because they have not been analysed and broken down into their component activities. *Only when this has been done* will it be possible to sequence and co-ordinate the various activities, and monitor the progress of implementation.

The emphasis appears to be on what Quinn (1993) refers to as 'awesome rationality', underpinned by a particular attitude which sees an imperative to control, and to be seen to be controlling, publicly funded bodies. Another theme pervading the evidence of what is happening in colleges is the attempt to identify and implement the appropriate degree of involvement of staff. As the FEDA's (1994) *Strategic Planning Handbook* puts it, 'Does the car park attendant need to think strategically?'. Colleges have found different answers to the question of how far to involve staff, reflecting a range of circumstance and belief. Principals have argued that there are reasons why a fully participative system simply will not work. In Australia, the same view has been expressed:

> I think out of 1000 full-time teachers and 2000 part-time – of all those, I could count on one hand how many would be interested [in participating in management planning] . . . We're going through a big restructuring at the moment, a changed culture, and most of the staff were recruited in the previous culture, and they haven't visited the future yet.
>
> (Peeke, 1994, p. 121)

Given the perceptions that consultation is too slow, that staff may be too busy, uninterested, sceptical of the whole process and determined to resist change, it is not surprising that some principals and senior management teams may argue against the involvement of a large number of staff. Others believe strongly that the involvement of all staff is not only practical but also paramount to the success of the whole process of planning and implementation:

> The majority of the full-time staff of Milton Keynes College are trained teachers with some industrial and commercial experience; planning skills form a part of their portfolio of competences. I believe it is professionally honest and managerially sensible to value, develop and promote the use of those abilities in determining the college's strategic plan.
>
> (Limb, 1992, p. 168)

One key choice appears to be that of deciding whether the strategic plan is an amalgam of subunit development plans or whether a central plan is created which programme areas/departments then translate into more localised planning. There is a tension between the need to create ownership by allowing subunits of the college to contribute their own strategic aims to a central plan, and the need for a whole-college approach, which would have to be mediated by one group, often senior management, at the risk of appearing remote and irrelevant to the mass of staff in the college. Comments on the strategic planning process in inspection reports show colleges working in both ways. For some a top-led draft plan is circulated to allow comment from all before it is finalised. The danger of this approach is that the plan becomes a public document which does not relate closely enough to operational plans developed by programme areas. The contrasting approach of gathering ideas and plans from programme areas and attempting to meld them into coherence risks contradictory and unholistic objectives. The FEDA (1995, p. 2) asks the question:

Is the plan

- a coherent strategic plan for the college as a whole

  or

- a collection of separate plans, produced by individual faculties, departments, programme areas?

The answer provided in fact suggested that the process may be cyclical, rather than two alternatives. Plans produced by subunits needed 'very little moderation' (*ibid.*) but only because they took sufficient account of a needs analysis and overall target-setting which had already taken place. However, the key issue of staff involvement is clearly critical in not only arriving at plans but also in raising the chances of their successful implementation.

THE CONTENT OF PLANS

The results of the dual pressure for a detailed rational approach and the involvement of staff may be seen in the plans themselves. A sample of just over 10 per cent of the plans of all general further education colleges in England was analysed to provide insights.

There were examples of plans which had a logical hierarchy of aims and objectives, each level relating strictly to that preceding it. In this way, some plans demonstrated a clear thinking progress from overall corporate aims to dependent objectives, each operationalised with specific responsibility, measurable targets and timescale. However, there were also many examples of plans where there were several sets of objectives, the relationship between each being unclear, a plethora of generalised aims and an inconsistency in attaching measurable performance criteria. The operational objectives did not always have any explicit relationship with the overall corporate aims and strategic objectives. A hypothesis needing further testing would be that there may be a relationship between the large number of unrelated sets of objectives in some plans, and the degree and nature of staff involvement.

Another problem appeared to be the inconsistency in the specificity of each level of aims/objectives. As Argenti (1992, p. 97) points out, a common problem is the confusion of objective and strategy. Saying how something is to be achieved is a strategy: 'The true corporate objective – whatever it is – will be strategy neutral.' The college plans often mixed strategy neutral and strategy decided statements at the same level of the plan. For example, the corporate aims might contain a number of general aims, such as meeting the educational and training needs of the community, and also statements indicating that choices for the achievement of aims had already been decided, for example, the achievement of Investors in People. It is not that choices as to how aims will be achieved do not need to be taken; rather it is that the mixing of strategy neutral and strategy decided aims seems to indicate a confusion of thinking, and a failure to establish the over-riding aims before deciding how they are to be achieved.

Argenti (*ibid.*) is also scathing of the general and homogeneous nature of many not-for-profit organisations' strategic aims. The generic literature on strategic planning stresses the need to make choices based on either costs, market or quality. As Peters (1989, p. 137) puts it, 'Don't just stand there, be something'. As colleges face the same market competition which is the foundation of theory in the management of businesses, there are expectations that they will equally find ways of distinguishing themselves from their rivals. However, the plans showed this generally not to be the case. There was great similarity between the aims chosen. They could be analysed under four headings:

- *Product*   (or learning).
- *Market*   (those target groups for which learning was to be provided).
- *Resources*   (acquisition and use of income and assets).
- *Capability*   (the strengthening of internal systems).

Of the plans scrutinised, 65 per cent had strategic aims in all these categories, often, despite differences in wording, very similar in intent. All the plans had aims of the 'market' category, though the specificity varied. Some colleges defined the recipients of their service very exactly as a catchment within a certain number of miles. One college was even more targeted in giving two strategic priorities, one of which was to meet the needs of only one disadvantaged area of a city. Other colleges described particular market segments in terms of the age, employment status or location of individuals. These plans were balanced by those which had an all-embracing view of the market, from targeting undefined 'all potential users', to those who planned to attract a local, national and international market.

The results of the analysis of the plans lead to the conclusions that the majority of college strategic aims are general in intent, usually stating the intention to improve the learning offered, to attract a comprehensive local market, to remain financially viable and to develop their staff and quality systems. In business terms, this may look very like the deplored 'stuck in the middle' position (Peters, 1989). However, colleges are not businesses and there may be room for both a distinctive market niche approach, demonstrated in some plans, which identified particular specialist markets for which colleges wished to tailor their organisation, and a less market segment or niche-based strategy, which aims to offer a comprehensive service to the local community.

In generic theory, the market need not be a distinguishing feature if the organisation can lead in reducing costs. While colleges were cost focused, it was not a distinguishing feature. As Bassett-Jones and Brewer (1997) argue, the emphasis on convergence, with all colleges to be paid the same unit fee in the near future, means that all colleges are inevitably cost focused. However, one might add that the probable continuing dependence of colleges on a unified payment structure, although focusing them into looking for internal efficiencies to reduce costs against income, also limits them considerably in using cost and price as distinguishing strategies.

It would seem that colleges are not always using the market or cost as strategic features to gain a competitive edge. However, the sector does demonstrate a wide range of strategies. Puffitt *et al.* (1992), writing of business planning in education, argue that there are infinite actions, but only ten basic strategies. Using this framework (Table 7.1), it can be seen that examples can be found of colleges using each of the ten strategies, with the exception of the fourth.

Table 7.1 Ten basic business planning strategies

Type of strategy	Example of college strategic aim
Additional resources (additional staff, staff skills, technology, etc.)	To obtain funds through grants and development projects
Increases in efficiency	A reduction from 74% to 65% in the percentage of staff costs against turnover
Increases in effectiveness	Specific curriculum weaknesses identified in the inspection report will be addressed
Rewards sought by employees are matched with the objectives the organisation seeks	No examples
Backward integration (secure greater control over the supply of resources)	Plan strategy as part of a local consortium of colleges
Forward integration (secure greater control over the need for the organisation's activities)	Form new and lasting relationships with local secondary schools
Market penetration (increase the organisation's market share)	To increase market share of school leavers from 20% to 30% over two years
Market extension (provide existing range of activity to new markets)	To expand the higher education provision in the college area through links with — university
Diversification (develop and provide new activities in new areas of need)	Seek opportunities for franchising non-advanced vocational courses to schools
Use of 'social influence processes' (ensure that some other organisation meets your objectives from its own resources)	Maximise contacts with employers to encourage investment in training and development

Source: Adapted from Puffitt *et al.*, 1992, pp. 73–5. Examples adapted from sample of college strategic plans.

The merging of the rewards sought by employees with the organisation's objectives was not an explicit objective, though it might be argued that strategic aims of offering staff development and increasing the opportunities for student learning do meet the expected rewards of professional teachers. However, with the probable arrival of performance-related pay for teachers as well as senior managers, the fourth of Puffit *et al.*'s ten strategies may become explicit in college plans in the near future.

The large number of objectives in the sample of plans (39 strategic aims was the highest individual number) raises another issue. Identifying essential strategic objectives, distinguished from merely desirable change, has proved very difficult. The National Audit Office (1994) suggested the need for a clear hierarchy of priorities. Identifying those critical objectives upon which continued survival and achievement of mission depend has eluded many colleges. This may be partly because strategic thinking is always in short supply (see Chapter 1) and partly because the format imposed by the FEFC directs attention to planned changes in the amount and areas of provision. The danger inherent is the encouragement merely to inflate or deflate existing objectives. However, some colleges have developed clearly prioritised aims and in their plans specify which one or two objectives take precedence over any others.

Other difficulties with establishing objectives may relate to understanding the relationship between objectives. For example, as FEDA (1995) point out, expansion of GNVQ in one area of the college may adversely affect recruitment to A-levels elsewhere. This example in itself demonstrates an incremental or decremental approach focusing on student numbers and areas of provision.

The strategic plan document itself is merely a piece of paper, but it represents the thoughts and intentions of those who have been involved in its creation. The actual format of the plan, its clarity and consistency, are important not just in terms of communicating the college's intention, but also as being in some way inextricably bound with the capability to implement it. Given the unrealistic and conflicting numbers of objectives in many of the plans in the sample, unlike the ubiquitous cry of more for less, in the case of strategic planning it would seem that less is more. Whether the demands of the FEFC in terms of the detail they require will allow colleges to develop plans of appropriate clarity and realism, it is too early to assess.

IMPLEMENTING PLANS

Once a strategic plan is established, with appropriate further business or action plans, the problem is then to implement the plans and achieve the strategy: 'Good intentions, good policies, good decisions must turn into effective actions . . . Effective organisations take it for granted that work isn't done by having a lovely plan' (Drucker, 1994, p. 109).

Although the major research attention to date has been on the process of planning, it is the implementation which is the more challenging task. As

Owen (1993, p. 143) asserts, 'Better a first-class implementation strategy for a second-class strategy than vice-versa'. Having acknowledged this, it is clear that planning and implementation cannot be neatly separated and seen as sequential. As FEDA (1995) reported, the success or otherwise of the implementation may have its roots in the way plans are produced.

The involvement of staff may be a part of the foundation of implementation, but it is not the only factor influencing the accomplishment of plans. FEDA (*ibid.*) reports a number of barriers, including:

* organisational structure making it difficult for people to work together;
* campuses spread apart, making communication and common approaches problematic;
* lack of resources or rewards to encourage staff to implement plans; and
* lack of awareness of the resource needed or lack of the resource itself.

Achievement of strategic plans involves ensuring that the structures in place allow people to work together strategically, across internal divisions, to achieve college-wide targets. It also involves the accurate use of resource to underpin plans and to motivate staff.

The normative approach to implementation (National Audit Office, 1994; FEDA, 1995) asserts that responsibility for achieving a measurable target must be assigned to a named individual, with explicit resources and timescale. However, as Cowham (1994, p. 279) discovered: 'A major issue for college mangers is to bridge and manage the "implementation gap" between the information and intentions as systematically stated in a plan, and the actual processes of staff and students learning and developing within an institution.'

Achieving any goal depends on more than clarity. The power base and capability of the person responsible underpin the capacity to achieve change (see Chapter 14). Implementation proceeds through the vehicle of monitoring, which may assess not only whether targets have been achieved but also how far structural changes, staff development and support from more senior staff may be needed to build the capacity to implement plans.

CONCLUSION

Most colleges are still relatively inexperienced in strategic planning and strategic management. The difficulties they have experienced in dealing with the processes of planning and implementation are not unique to further education. FEDA reminds us that there are many companies worldwide that have expended much energy on determining strategy, but cannot implement any of it (FEDA, 1995, p. ix). The central questions of who should be involved in planning, how the process should take place, how we achieve the structures necessary and motivate staff to implement plans, will receive different answers in each college. Not all colleges have, as yet, learned to use the process to their best advantage: 'For some colleges the strategic plan is descriptive rather than aspirational, noncommittal rather than challenging, and prepared in order to satisfy external stakeholders rather than as a shaping and co-ordinating mechanism for the development of the college' (FEDA, 1995, p. 11).

None of this is surprising given that colleges are inexperienced in a process which is acknowledged as very complex, and that externally imposed constraints have restricted the college's freedom of action. What is heartening is the achievement of many colleges who have evolved plans which are clear sighted and inspirational and continued to succeed despite a period of great turbulence and financial difficulty, giving some credence to the assertion that successful strategic planning has been achieved by some. Drodge and Cooper (1997, p. 47), in their case studies of three colleges, found a conviction that the new planning framework had led to 'the creation of a better structured, more consistent planning process and thus a more effective service'.

The framework imposed by the FEFC may have defined some part of colleges' actions, but it has evoked a response which goes beyond the bounds of the rational model implied, to continue to develop the complex art of managing the diverse community of students and staff in a way which has at least half an eye on the future.

REFERENCES

Argenti, J. (1992) *Practical Corporate Planning*, London, Routledge.

Austin, M. (1994) Conclusions. In Flint, C. and Austin, M. (eds.) *Going Further*, Bristol, The Staff College in association with the Association for Colleges.

Basset-Jones, N. and Brewer, R. (1997) Strategic Management and Competitive Advantage. In Levacic, R. and Glatter, R. (eds.) *Managing Change in Further Education, FEDA Report*, Vol. 1, no. 7, pp. 53–84.

Cowham, T. (1994) Strategic planning in the changing external context. In Crawford, M., Kydd, L. and Parker, S. (eds.) *Educational Management in Action*, London, Paul Chapman.

Crisp, P. (1991) *Strategic Planning and Management*, Blagdon, The Staff College.

Drodge, S. and Cooper, N. (1997) The management of strategic planning in further education colleges. In Levacic, R. and Glatter, R. (eds.) *Managing Change in Further Education, FEDA Report*, Vol. 1, no. 7, pp. 21–52.

Drucker, P.F. (1994) *Managing the Non-Profit Organization*, Oxford, Butterworth-Heinemann.

FEDA (1995) *Implementing College Strategic Plans*, London, FEDA.

FEFC (1992) *Circular 92/18, College Strategic Plans*, Coventry, FEFC.

FEFC (1996) *Circular 96/02, Analysis of Institutions' Strategic Planning Information for the Period 1995–96 to 1997–98*, Coventry, FEFC.

FEFC (1997) *Council News Number 39*, Coventry, FEFC.

FEU (1993) *Challenges for Colleges: Developing a Corporate Approach to Curriculum and Strategic Planning*, London, FEU.

FEU (1994) *Strategic Planning Handbook*, London, FEU.

Limb, A. (1992) Strategic planning: managing colleges into the next century. In Bennet, N., Crawford, M. and Riches, C. (eds.) *Managing Change in Education*, London, Paul Chapman.

National Audit Office (1994) *Managing to be Independent: Management and Financial Control in the Further Education Sector*, London, HMSO.

Owen, A.A. (1993) How to implement a strategy. In Mabey, C. and Mayon-White, B. (eds.) *Managing Change*, Milton Keynes, Open University Press.

Peeke, G. (1994) *Mission and Change*, Buckingham, SRHE and the Open University.

Peters, T. (1989) *Thriving on Chaos*, London, Pan.

Puffitt, R., Stoten, B. and Winkley, D. (1992) *Business Planning for Schools*, London, Longman.

Quinn, J.B. (1993) Managing strategic change. In Mabey, C. and Mayon-White, B. (eds.) *Managing Change*, Milton Keynes, Open University Press.

Thomas, H. (1996) Strategic planning. In Warner, D. and Palfreyman, D. (eds.) *Higher Education Management*, Buckingham, SRHE and the Open University.

Tristram, P. (1996) Developing strategic planning at Amersham and Wycombe College, dissertation presented for MBA at Leicester University.

Wheale, J. (1991) *Generating Income for Educational Institutions: A Business Planning Approach*, London, Kogan Page.

Wilkinson, D. and Pedler, M. (1994) Strategic thinking in public service. In Garratt, B. (ed.) *Developing Strategic Thought*, Maidenhead, McGraw-Hill.

Section C: strategic roles in action

8

WORKING TOGETHER: MANAGING STRATEGY COLLABORATIVELY

Carol Cardno

THE ROLE OF COLLABORATION IN EFFECTIVE STRATEGIC CHANGE

Strategic management is a key leadership task because one of its primary aims is change and improvement. It encompasses the identification of strategic initiatives, with an eye on the future but with feet firmly planted in the present in order to manage the implementation of plans which will keep the organisation on track. It is a dynamic and collaborative process requiring the active involvement of many people with and through whom a leader achieves strategic change. Hence, a fundamental challenge for educational leaders will always be the management of the participation of stakeholders in the organisation's planning of its priorities for success:

> The tasks of leadership for strategic planning are complex and many. Unless the organisation is very small, no single person or group can perform them all. Effective strategic planning is a collective phenomenon, typically involving sponsors, champions, facilitators, teams, task forces, and others in various ways at various times.
>
> (Bryson, 1995, p. 227)

THE SCOPE OF STRATEGIC MANAGEMENT IN EDUCATION

Planning has been identified as one of the facets of effective management since the earliest attempts to analyse and define the meaning of the term *management* (Drucker, 1955). In its widest sense, planning encompasses two management dimensions. One dimension is embedded in the present

105

and is concerned with current tasks and operations (operational planning). The other dimension is futuristic and is concerned with what will be different (strategic planning). Together, these dimensions constitute the arena in which strategic management is practised with and through others.

At the heart of strategic management is *strategic analysis* which provides the essential data to inform strategic decision-making. It requires an analysis of the internal and external environment in which an organisation operates and is based on identifying strengths and weaknesses, opportunities and threats with those best placed to assist in such analysis.

THE CHALLENGE OF WORKING TOGETHER

Strategic planning . . . is not a linear, lock-step process derived or implemented in an authoritarian manner. Nor is it intuitive or built on hunches or raw feelings. It involves the educational partners in defining and supporting the purposes and the missions, and it provides blueprints for results-oriented progress.

(Kaufman and Herman, 1991, p. xvii)

Managing the formulation and implementation of strategy involves collaboration with others. The following definition captures a particular view of collaboration: 'Collaboration is the term employed to express partnership, co-operation, agreement, consent and working in combination to accomplish institutional objectives' (Cardno, 1990, p. 1).

In this view, collaboration encompasses the values inherent in collegial organisational models. As Bush (1995, p. 52) states: 'Collegial models assume that organisations determine policy and make decisions through a process of discussion leading to consensus. Power is shared among some or all members of the organisation who are thought to have a mutual understanding about the objectives of the institution.'

At one end of the collegial approach continuum is a consensus model, a form of *pure collegiality*, in which every member of the organisation has an equal voice in determining policy. At the other end is a form of *restricted collegiality*, in which the leader shares power with a limited number of senior colleagues. A purely collegial model is not appropriate in the context of strategic management as not all stakeholders will need to or want to participate to the same extent. Nor is it appropriate for sharing to be limited to a senior management team as on occasion a wide range of others with interest and expertise needs to be drawn into the process.

The model of collaborative management for strategic change presented here falls midway along the collegiality continuum and is called *managed collaboration* because the leader is required to make several decisions about managing the collaborative process itself before engaging others in the partnership. Leadership decisions must be made about why it is necessary to collaborate in strategic management, about who should be involved, about how much they should be involved and about how teams and individuals can be effectively involved.

While decisions are not necessarily made in any ordered way, they are not made in isolation from one another. In practice, leaders alone or with their senior management teams make multiple decisions simultaneously, considering all relevant aspects (philosophical and pragmatic) and the implications of collaboration in strategic management, *before* they proceed to work with others. The next section of this chapter will address the manner in which leaders could set out to answer the questions associated with the four types of leadership decisions which need to be made in a collaborative approach to strategic management.

MAKING LEADERSHIP DECISIONS ABOUT COLLABORATION IN STRATEGIC MANAGEMENT

'Why' decisions

Leadership as stewardship of vision

Strategic thinking and the formulation of strategy are founded on the beliefs held by all those who have a stake in a particular educational organisation. The starting point for strategic planning is the articulation of a vision for an organisation and the principles which underpin it. Invariably the question arises as to *whose* vision guides the approach to strategic thinking.

School and college leaders are charged with responsibility for stating and actualising the organisation's vision. However, as Senge (1990, p. 352) puts it, the role of the leader is one of *stewardship*. Leaders may start by pursuing their own vision, but they should listen carefully and learn about others' visions until they begin to see their vision as part of something larger. Such leadership captures the notion of 'responsibility without possessiveness' in relation to the organisation's vision.

Fullan (1992) is also critical about the emphasis on personal vision in leadership literature. It has misled many a school and college leader to assume that the articulation of a strong individual vision, and the consequent drive to implement it, is critical to their success and credibility. He asserts (*ibid.*, p. 19):

> Principals are blinded by their own vision when they feel they must manipulate the teachers and the school culture to conform to it. . . . While principals can be instrumental in implementing particular innovations through direct monitoring and support, schools are not in the business of managing single innovations: they are in the business of contending with multiple innovations simultaneously. Rather than impose their individual visions, principals would do well to develop collaborative work cultures to help staff deal with all these innovations.

It is essential for leaders to *lead* the process of visioning, but effective leadership will encompass the inclusion of relevant stakeholders in determining the vision for which the leader assumes stewardship.

What is called for is the fostering of 'collective leadership' (Bryson, 1995, p. 219) so that many people contribute appropriately, and at different stages, as leaders and followers. The most valuable vehicle for achieving a collective approach is the team. In smaller schools and colleges only one or two teams might be involved. In larger organisations there will be several teams at different levels to be considered. How teams can engage in the strategic change process is a question addressed further on in this chapter.

Collaborative development of charters in New Zealand schools

The collaborative preparation of a school charter is government policy in New Zealand. Higher education organisations are also required to consult stakeholders in preparing the organisation's charter:

> In collaboration with the principal, the staff and the community, the board will be responsible for the preparation of the institution's charter within the overall national guidelines for education. The charter will define the purposes of the institution and the intended outcomes for students. It will also define the ways in which programmes will be designed to take account of:
>
> • the particular interests of students and potential students
> • the special skills and qualifications of the staff
> • the resources of the community
> • the particular wishes of the institution's community.
>
> (Government of New Zealand, 1988, pp. 3–4)

The basis for planning strategic change in the New Zealand context is regular review of the charter and its updating in conjunction with strategic initiatives which are determined at the governance level. As the chief executive of the board of trustees (the elective governing body), the principal must play a key role in acting on the board's behalf to manage the processes of charter review and strategic planning. The collaborative processes used must pay more than lip service to the notion of responsiveness to community wishes, yet must also be realistic and manageable.

To achieve the aim of meaningful and appropriate collaboration, leaders must know who are the key stakeholders in educational endeavour. They must be prepared to work in partnership with relevant stakeholder groups to confirm and amend the organisation's charter on a regular basis such as a three-year review span, to keep chartered objectives current and to mesh these with strategic initiatives which are drawn incrementally into annual plans from the organisation's 5–10-year strategic plan.

Figure 8.1 illustrates the hierarchy of planning, responsibility and accountability links that are intended to lead to co-ordinated strategic

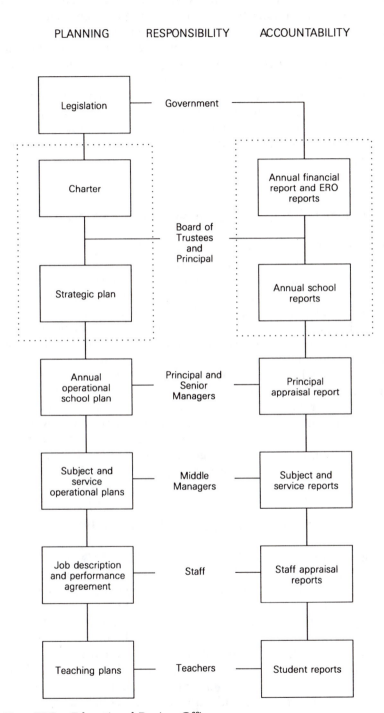

Note: ERO = Educational Review Office

Figure 8.1 Strategic management: planning and accountability links

management in New Zealand schools. In a managed strategic approach there are clear connections between planning and accountability at all levels. For example, when a school has decided to focus in the next five years on improving student access to computer technology in classrooms, then there should be a reflection of this goal in the principal's annual management plan, and the theme should be identifiable in departmental plans and in individual staff plans for professional development and for teaching. Initiatives at the individual teacher level, and in classrooms, may also directly influence school-wide plans through performance appraisal feedback processes which should impact on developmental planning (Cardno, 1996).

Sharing change management to secure ownership

Moss-Kanter (1983) asserts that any change is disturbing when it is done to us – but can be exhilarating when it is done by us – that is, when we are included in the momentum or excitement of change. Effective change management is a basic requirement of successful strategic management and, as Moss-Kanter (*ibid.*, pp. 241–2), says: 'Masters of change are also masters of the art of participation . . . Participation, it is clear, needs to be managed just as carefully as any other organisation system, and it creates new problems demanding attention in the course of solving others.'

The decisions which are made in relation to the long-term strategic priorities for an educational organisation impact hugely on those who will incrementally be required to act upon them by incorporating new goals into operational plans and then implementing them at all levels of the organisation. School and college leaders will need to determine how the participation of others will be managed so that the potential of collaborative decision-making is fully utilised and the pitfalls avoided.

Collaboration – potential and pitfalls

There is no doubt that a collaborative approach to strategic management can benefit the organisation and the participants in the planning processes because it can achieve a heightened sense of ownership and commitment. But this will only happen if one gets it right! If it goes wrong, it can be a setback to progress and can lead to alienation and a lowering of the sense of community endeavour which is so critical to the ongoing achievement of plans. At the governance–management interface the benefits of a collaborative approach include the development of skills in strategic thinking and planning, the creation of commitment to strategic decisions and a general unity about priorities and direction. The collaborative approach also has advantages at the organisation–departmental interface by increasing staff's knowledge of and commitment to the chosen direction of change. Balancing this are possible pitfalls, with governors developing unrealistic expectations of the degree to which they will participate and impinging on management autonomy. Middle managers can develop similar unrealistic expectations and also halt the collaborative approach by failing to involve their own team members.

'Who' decisions

Who are the stakeholders in strategic change?

Educational organisations need to recognise that paying attention to stakeholder concerns is crucial to success. The satisfaction of key stakeholders should be a paramount goal for leaders to aspire to. It is a goal that presents an immense challenge because of the diversity and complexity of the educational constituency. A first step in meeting this challenge is the identification of the organisation's stakeholders. Bryson's (1995, p. 27) definition is pertinent: 'A stakeholder is defined as any person, group, or organisation that can place a claim on an organisation's attention, resources, or output or is affected by that output.'

An educational organisation will have both external and internal stakeholders. External stakeholders may include potential employers of students, parents (of students – past, present and potential), various interest and lobby groups, professional and industrial associations, tax payers (the public), the ministry or state department of education, the local community (residential and business), feeder schools and further and higher education institutions. Internal stakeholders can include students, teachers, support staff, senior management, middle management and various interest groups.

Before any development or revision of the organisation's vision and statement of mission is undertaken, a stakeholder analysis should be at least initiated, if not completed. Once the range of groups with a stake in the organisation's success is identified then it is possible to consider the extent to which it is appropriate or essential to involve them in aspects of strategic management.

Who should be involved in planning?

The most commonly held erroneous assumption that is made about collaborative decision-making is that its intent is to involve everyone in every decision. This mistaken view, as Owens (1995, p. 195) cautions, is obviously neither practical nor desirable. In deciding who should participate at a particular point of strategic management, one can draw on three rules of thumb (the tests of *jurisdiction, relevance* and *expertise*), which combine the work of Edwin Bridges and Robert Owens, to identify aspects of planning in which it would be appropriate for particular stakeholders to participate. Although Bridges' (1967) model was concerned with determining when to involve teachers in curriculum-related decision-making, the principles on which it rests are transferable to stakeholder participation in strategic decisions.

Three tests to determine participation of stakeholders

Test one: the test of jurisdiction

Schools and colleges are organised on a hierarchical basis and mostly conform to a model in which the parameters of governance and management roles and responsibilities are defined and limited. Governors are charged with specific duties and a prescribed area of jurisdiction which is concerned with the setting and review of policy direction and 'big picture' or strategic planning. Senior managers are concerned with the implementation of policy and plans which enable strategic initiatives to be actualised incrementally or operationalised. Middle managers and their teams are charged with specific responsibilities and jurisdiction only over those decision-making areas which are assigned to them. At the very outset of determining who will be involved in aspects of strategic and operational planning, it is essential that the limits of jurisdiction are clarified. In spite of considerable interest or perceived personal stake in strategic change, it is possible that participants will not have jurisdiction to contribute to related decisions. Unfulfilled anticipation of participation in the making of strategic or operational decisions which are beyond their jurisdiction can lead to frustration at least as great as simple non-participation.

Rule of thumb: always involve those who have jurisdiction and clarify parameters in terms of official roles and responsibilities.

Test two: the test of relevance

When an individual's or group's personal stake in a decision is high, their interest in participation is also likely to be high. Issues that meet this test could be considered as ones in which the stakeholder group could participate, if they also meet the test of jurisdiction. Members of governing boards will have a high interest in shaping the future of the organisation and should always be involved in devising and revising strategic initiatives. At the level of operational plans, each member of a curriculum or service team will have a high interest because they will be expected to contribute to goal achievement. Their participation in planning and review activities is essential although they may not have participated directly at the level of management planning for organisation-wide initiatives. Team leaders, however, whose plans flow from organisation plans and contribute to them, will need to participate at this level because of their stake in meeting sections of organisational plans.

Rule of thumb: always involve those for whom the decision is highly relevant, i.e. they will be required to implement the decision and to be accountable for results and will, therefore, have a high interest in making it – but use the test in conjunction with judgement about their expertise to contribute to the decision.

Test three: the test of expertise

The test of relevance is closely linked to the test of expertise because it is not enough for the stakeholder to have an interest in the decision. If their participation is to be significant, then they must also be able to contribute effectively. The leader might well have to be selective in inviting stakeholder participation in particular aspects of strategic management to ensure that they meet both relevance and expertise criteria. On the other hand, where jurisdiction predetermines the right to participate, the leader might well have to accept the responsibility to heighten the level of expertise by providing opportunity to learn from experience or by arranging more formally for the prospective participant's professional development in that area.

Rule of thumb: involve those for whom the decision has high relevance selectively unless they have official jurisdiction, in which case expertise may need to be developed.

In the context of strategic management, two broad groups of stakeholders need to be considered when deciding who will be involved. At the level of strategy formulation and the associated review of an organisation's charter, the key stakeholders are the governors, the parents, the community, the students and the senior managers. At the operational level, the key stakeholders are the senior and middle managers and the staff.

'HOW MUCH' DECISIONS

How much collaboration is appropriate?

Linked very closely to the question of who should be considered as partners in planning decisions is the question of how much collaboration is appropriate once it has been decided that collaboration with a particular stakeholder group meets tests such as those of jurisdiction, relevance and expertise.

On one hand, too little collaboration results in decisions which may not be the best because vital perspectives and information have not been available to the decision-makers. It may also reduce the possibility of decisions being owned by those who will have to act on them. On the other hand, too much collaboration makes decision-making unwieldy and time-consuming, and creates overload for willing and unwilling participants.

Once the question of 'Who should be involved?' has been considered, it is necessary to ask to what degree it will be appropriate to involve them in order to capitalise on the potential benefits of collaborative practice and avoid the many pitfalls that attend this management style.

Categories of collaboration

Table 8.1 captures the notion that collaboration is a term with a very broad application. It can be applied to a minor or a major degree and the various degrees of collaboration fall into five categories. Each category is a valid form of collaboration because it increases the possibility for a diverse education community to understand and agree about the organisation's goals and then to co-operate and combine efforts so that they are achieved. Those who must manage planning have to make constant leadership decisions about the degree to which stakeholders are informed, consulted, engaged in discussion, invited to be involved, and participate either by right or because they have a valuable contribution to make.

Table 8.1 Categories of collaboration (the degree to which others might appropriately collaborate)

One: information	*Letting people know* what is happening by all available means and accepting feedback
Two: consultation	*Seeking response* or advice formally or informally from individuals and groups
Three: discussion	Presenting information and arranging forums to *facilitate debate,* which presents a plurality of views and serves to increase understanding and encourage questioning
Four: involvement	*Inviting people* to contribute to processes of planning, decision-making and review
Five: participation	*Taking a full part* in policy and strategic plan formulation (at governance and senior management levels) and policy, plan and programme implementation (at management and staff levels)

Because strategic management encompasses two dimensions – the long-term strategic change dimension and the short-term operational dimension – school and college leaders will have to consider the context of planning activity when they make decisions about which collaborative category to employ in a particular situation.

'HOW' DECISIONS

What techniques are appropriate for particular 'Categories of collaboration' (Table 8.1)?
How can teamwork be used to achieve effective collaboration?

Appropriate techniques

Leaders can employ a vast range of decision-making techniques for giving and gathering information, analysing, monitoring and reviewing in the course of strategic planning. Some of these techniques are useful with individuals, some are more appropriate for use with teams and others lend themselves to use with all stakeholders. Some appropriate techniques are briefly described in relation to the five categories of collaboration: information, consultation, discussion, involvement and participation, outlined in Table 8.1.

Techniques for informing and consulting categories of collaboration

There are numerous day-to-day opportunities for communication of strategic decisions and communication of opportunity for others to give feedback to managers about these decisions. Leaders must, however, consciously decide that it is priority to share information and consult others in the organisation when strategic issues are being considered. Many schools and colleges commonly use newsletters, meetings, discussion papers and techniques such as Ringi to consult.

Ringi technique   Ringi is a Japanese procedure which is an effective and fast means of consulting others. It involves circulation of a written document amongst selected individuals, groups or a wider audience, such as the whole staff to gather views and allow editing of the views of others. It enables a leader to gather information and perceptions quickly and the final version contributes a collective view, based on consultation with relevant parties, when an issue is discussed at a meeting. A version of Ringi, known as noticeboard Ringi, is used in many New Zealand schools. The principal or a team leader will outline an issue and an invitation to respond in a notice placed on the staff noticeboard. Staff write their responses on the notice provided. The most modern use of Ringi is via electronic communication. One person can initiate this by beginning an email debate or request for information or response via the Internet or intranet in an organisation. This has the advantage of opening up the issue widely and consulting others to get feedback in minutes rather than days or weeks.

Techniques for discussion category of collaboration

* Formal *meeting structures* that enable strategic information to flow up and down the system and are capable of demonstrating response to feedback also provide forums for discussion.

- Special meetings called to discuss specific or general strategic issues or to initiate strategic planning processes, e.g. a meeting of a range of stakeholders to conduct a *SWOT analysis.*
- Discussion can be facilitated with individuals or in groups by employing the *Delphi* or *nominal group techniques.*

The Delphi technique   This is a particularly useful technique when one is seeking contribution from individuals or groups, without bringing people together for a meeting. It is a form of discussion-at-a-distance. It extracts opinions, relevant information or judgements by asking people to communicate in written form to a leader. A set of statements is prepared by the leader (pertinent to strategic goals, analysis needs, initiatives, etc.) and is sent out in written form to relevant others. As input is received it is tabulated and then sent out again for further response and return. By receiving the second format of the document all readers are presented with the views of others and may wish to revise or confirm their own views accordingly. The leader takes responsibility to summarise the second set of responses showing key areas of agreement and disagreement and this is circulated to individuals and groups, and may be used as material for discussion at a subsequent meeting. The Delphi technique asks for expert judgements and shares those with all concerned. One of the chief advantages (in addition to this being a time-saving device) is that contribution is anonymous and often ensures objectivity.

The nominal group technique   This is a structured meeting which follows a prescribed format. It is orchestrated by a leader who provides members of a predetermined group with an opening statement to which response is invited. The group begins by responding to the statement individually, then sharing their response with one or two others and refining response to a collective statement before presenting the response to the whole team. Pashiardis (1993) describes the technique and its application and concludes that it enables groups to take into consideration the expertise and creativity of individual members as well as the wisdom of the group when an issue is opened up for debate.

Techniques for involvement and participation categories of collaboration

Employing teamwork to achieve strategic tasks   When leaders' decisions about 'who to involve' in strategic management processes point to the necessity to *include others* in strategic decision-making processes, via involving them in making a direct contribution to planning and review, or inviting them to participate fully in policy or plan formulation, they should consider the possibility of harnessing the potential of teamwork to achieve tasks related to strategic management.

Bryson (1995, p. 219) asserts that it is important to rely on teams in strategic planning:

> A strategic plan and intended strategies need the support of a critical coalition when they are adopted and during implementation. A wisely constructed strategic planning team can provide the basis for

such a coalition, and team members can do much of the work leading to forming the necessary coalition.

Leadership needs to take a particular form in relation to strategic planning. Bryson refers to the need to take on the role of champion – to spend time fostering the work of teams so that they can make an effective contribution to the process. There is no doubt that permanent teams can provide a vehicle for strategic thinking and planning. However, organisational norms and role perceptions may need to change to develop a commitment to strategic planning from team leaders and their teams.

West-Burnham (1994) suggests that

- job descriptions for those in leadership roles at all levels of the organisation should be reformulated to include responsibility for strategy;
- training in planning skills should be provided; and
- strategic goals and plans should become regular items on decision-making agendas to raise awareness and increase ownership.

An alternative to the involvement of permanent teams in strategic thinking and planning activities is suggested by Beare *et al.* (1992). They suggest the creation of taskforces or project teams. These are temporary teams brought into being to accomplish a particular task. The advantage of using short-life teams at the strategic planning level is that they can gather an enterprising group of people with the knowledge and skills to achieve a goal. They can also draw on further expertise and, as a team, champion major initiatives.

The leader of a school or college cannot, however, abrogate responsibility to champion the strategic planning cause even if the actual work is delegated to a project team. The leader is the necessary linchpin at the interface between a temporary team and the many permanent teams which will be responsible for operationalising strategic decisions. A leader will also rely on mature teams in the school, such as a senior management team, to support the championing of strategy and monitoring the operational plans at team level which contribute to achieving strategic goals.

Teams in schools and colleges will need support and professional development if their potential to contribute effectively to strategic management is to be realised. This is ultimately the responsibility of the leader who needs not only to model effective teamwork and decision-making strategies but also actively to provide the resources and development opportunities for teams to succeed in achieving the goals which contribute to effective strategic management. Leaders must support strategic teams by doing the following:

- Developing clear terms of reference for the team.
- Outlining the goal(s) to be achieved.
- Ensuring the team knows the limits of decision-making authority.
- Assisting the team in making leadership decisions for collaborative management.
- Providing the team with resources to do the job (training in decision-making techniques and finance to support the processes used).

LEADING THE MANAGEMENT OF STRATEGY

Fidler (1996, pp. 72–3) reminds us that leadership is a crucial ingredient of strategic management but that not all those in leadership positions can be expected to show appropriate leadership without some form of preparation and development. This is especially true in the context of schools and colleges where research shows that in contrast to chief executives in industry, educational leaders have until recently given lower priority to setting time aside for long-term strategic planning (Jenkins, 1991).

One way in which school and college leaders can improve their approach to, and success with, strategic management is to take time to make the fundamental leadership decisions about being collaborative in the processes they use to think and act strategically. Preparation for strategic decision-making requires a reflective and proactive approach rather than one which is reactive and crisis orientated. Leaders need to think carefully about what they know of successful processes and take time to reflect and check that they are on the right track every time there is a call for a leadership decision to be made about managing strategy collaboratively.

REFERENCES

Beare, H., Caldwell, B.J. and Millikan, R.H. (1992) *Creating an Excellent School,* London, Routledge.

Bridges, E.M. (1967) A model for shared decision-making in the school principalship, *Educational Administration Quarterly,* Vol. 3, no. 2, pp. 49–61.

Bryson, J.M. (1995) *Strategic Planning for Public and Nonprofit Organisations: A Guide to Strengthening and Sustaining Organisational Achievement,* San Francisco, Calif., Jossey-Bass.

Bush, T. (1995) *Theories of Educational Management,* London, Paul Chapman.

Cardno, C. (1990) *Collaborative Management in New Zealand Schools,* Auckland, Longman Paul.

Cardno, C. (1996) Professional development: an holistic approach, *New Zealand Journal of Educational Administration,* Vol. 11, no. 4, pp. 25–28.

Drucker, P. (1955) *The Practice of Management,* London, Heinemann.

Fidler, B. (1996) *Strategic Planning for School Improvement,* London, Pitman.

Fullan, M. (1992) Visions that blind, *Educational Leadership,* February, pp. 19–20.

Government of New Zealand (1988) *Tomorrow's Schools: The Reform of Education Administration in New Zealand,* Wellington, Government Printer.

Jenkins, H.O. (1991) *Getting It Right: A Handbook for Successful School Leadership,* Oxford, Blackwell Education.

Kaufman, R. and Herman, J. (1991) *Strategic Planning in Education,* Pittsburgh, Technomic Publishing.

Moss-Kanter, R. (1983) *The Change Masters: Corporate Entrepreneurs at Work*, London, Unwin Hyman.

Owens, R.G. (1995) *Organisational Behaviour in Education*, Boston, Allyn & Bacon.

Pashiardis, P. (1993) Group decision-making: the role of the principal, *International Journal of Educational Management*, Vol. 7, no. 2, pp. 8–11.

Senge, P. (1990) *The Fifth Discipline*, London, Random House.

West-Burnham, J. (1994) Strategy, policy and planning. In Bush, T. and West-Burnham, J. (eds.) *The Principles of Educational Management*, Harlow, Longman.

9

THE STRATEGIC ROLE OF GOVERNORS IN SCHOOL IMPROVEMENT

Michael Creese

INTRODUCTION

> The main aim of the governing body is to maintain and **improve** its
> school's standards of education.
>
> (Audit Commission/Ofsted, 1995, p. 4, emphasis added)

Concern about the effectiveness of the nation's schools have been
expressed for a number of years, the present debate having its roots in
Prime Minister Callaghan's speech at Ruskin College in 1976. More
recently, the emphasis has shifted from drawing up lists of the characteristics of an effective school to a consideration of how schools might be
helped to improve – of how to raise standards in the classroom. However,
governors have usually seen their primary role as providing advice and
support (Kogan *et al.*, 1984; Curtis, 1994) and have often failed to address
in any meaningful way the main business of their schools – which is teaching and learning – and have rarely discussed strategic issues. When Earley
(1994) invited governors to list the features of an effective governing body,
among those mentioned most frequently were giving time to the school,
supporting the school, staff and pupils and sharing tasks among the governors. However, as Corrick (1996) points out, the features considered most
desirable are notable for their passivity and there is no mention within the
list of strategy or school improvement.

There is a tendency for governors to become very involved in the
minutiae of matters concerning finance and the premises – matters with
which they feel familiar and comfortable: 'Minor matters and a dense mass
of routine business are permitted to dominate meetings and to drive out
discussion of strategic issues' (*ibid.*, p. 94). Earley (1994) suggests that
governors often have a fairly limited view of their role in school improvement, seeing themselves principally as facilitating the work of the profes-

sionals and they are reluctant to monitor the performance of headteachers or principals (Packwood, 1984; Pascal, 1987). The headteacher/principal may be reluctant to allow governors to impinge upon what is seen as the preserve of the professionals (Huckman, 1994). Governors, because of their lack of knowledge, may feel inhibited about questioning the judgements of the professionals or they may be blinded by educational jargon. For whatever reason, many governing bodies have found it difficult in the past to make any meaningful contribution to improvement in their schools or colleges.

This chapter considers the contribution which governors can make to improvement in their institutions. A discussion of the strategic role of the governing body is followed by consideration of what is meant by 'improvement' in this context. Examples, drawn from research currently in progress, are then introduced to show how some governing bodies are involving themselves in three particular activities which lead towards school improvement: planning, policy-making and monitoring. The governing bodies in these schools are attempting to take a strategic overview and to help their teacher partners to develop strategies for improvement. Following this, some more general issues concerning the involvement of governors in improvement are addressed including a discussion of some of the factors which reduce the effectiveness of governing bodies.

THE STRATEGIC ROLE OF THE GOVERNING BODY

Fidler (1996) suggests that strategy as related to schools has four distinctive features:

- A consideration of the long term.
- Planning for the future of the school in an integrated way.
- Taking account of future trends outside the school.
- Taking account of the resources available.

Strategic thinking is proactive rather than reactive; governors thinking in this way will have a long-term vision, shared with the staff, for the future of the institution of which they are a part: 'The most important management task of the governing body is to take ownership of the vision of the future of the college' (Monk, 1992, p. 15). Corrick (1996) argues that such thinking demands high levels of skill, knowledge and confidence on the part of the governors. They must be able to detach themselves from immediate concerns while possessing a sound knowledge of the range of options which are open to them.

Governors often give little consideration to cost-effectiveness or 'value for money', yet it is important that the limited resources available to schools are used to maximum effect. All Ofsted reports on schools contain a reference to the inspector's view of the education provided by the school in those terms. Thomas and Martin (1996) suggest that governors need a source of information independent of the head and staff if they are to enter properly into a dialogue of accountability about educational needs and the allocation of resources, though it is not clear where this information is to come from if Ofsted inspections become less frequent and if LEAs are unable or unwilling to offer help in this area. It seems unlikely that there will be any major increase in the funding available to schools, at least in the immediate future, and this makes it all the more important that governors should consider very carefully all the options open to them before making decisions and evaluate equally carefully the impact of those decisions upon pupil outcomes.

Just as the *Guide for College Governors* (FEFC, 1994) defines the main aim of the governing body of an FE college as agreeing policies and strategies and monitoring progress in implementing them, so the responsibilities of school governing bodies listed in *School Governors: A Guide to the Law* include 'helping to establish (with the head) the aims and policies of the school, and *how the standards of education can be improved*' (DFE, 1994, p. 15, emphasis added). The role of the governing body as set out in a broadsheet entitled *Governing Bodies and Effective Schools* refers to governors providing a strategic view, monitoring and evaluating the school's effectiveness and helping to decide the school's strategy for improvement (BIS/DFE/Ofsted, 1995, p. 2). Corrick (1996, p. 45) encapsulates these statements when he defines the principal duties of governing bodies in six key words: 'ethos, strategy, monitoring, school improvement, co-operation and accountability'.

Increasing accountability was one of the key themes running through the Conservative government's educational policy in the 1980s and early 1990s (DFE/WO, 1992). Parents were provided with more information about the schools in their area and, in theory at least, were given greater freedom of choice when selecting schools for their children. Following the Taylor Report (1977), the membership of governing bodies was broadened to include parents and representatives of the local community. That document (*ibid.*, p. 6) saw governors as having a responsibility for every aspect of the life and work of their schools: 'There should be no area of the school's activities in respect of which the governing body should have no responsibility nor on which the head and staff should be accountable only to themselves or the LEA.'

Governors are themselves accountable to parents through their annual report to – and meeting with – parents, and Ofsted reports of school inspections include comment on the work of the governing body.

IMPROVEMENT IN SCHOOLS

In the booklet *Improving Schools*, published by Ofsted (1994, p. 6), school improvement is defined as the ways in which schools

- raise standards;
- enhance quality;
- increase efficiency;

- achieve greater success in promoting pupils' spiritual, moral, social and cultural development; in a word the ethos of the school.

Hopkins *et al.* (1996, p. 1) take a slightly wider view, regarding school improvement as 'enhancing student outcomes *as well as* strengthening the school's capacity for managing improving initiatives'. Taking these two definitions together, governors might help to raise standards through their contribution to the monitoring and review programme in their school, by putting in place energy-saving schemes or by using their management experience to help the institution to manage change better. Because the governors are operating at one remove from the classroom, it may not always be easy to demonstrate a direct link between the decisions made by governors and pupil outcomes. Corrick (1996, p. 144) suggests that 'it is inherently more likely that governors can influence the strategy of a school rather than make a direct impact on the details of professional practice'.

However, governors may also contribute to the development of a commitment to improvement within the school. Hopkins *et al.* (1996, p. 25) draw attention to the conditions necessary for school improvement. These, they suggest, are:

- a commitment to staff development;
- practical efforts to involve staff, students and the community in school policies and decision making;
- leadership styles which develop a shared vision within the team;
- effective co-ordination strategies;
- serious attention to the benefits of enquiry and reflection;
- a commitment to collaborative planning activity.

The contribution made by governors to the climate for improvement may actually be as significant as any direct impact which they have upon standards. Thus governors who place a high priority on staff (and governor) training, who seek to encourage staff, student and community involvement or who regularly set aside time in their meetings to review progress are contributing to school or college improvement just as much as those who involve themselves more directly. Where governing bodies are actively concerned with the priorities and targets which the school or college sets itself and the quality of education which it provides, the governors recognise that they need the right information in order to be able to monitor the performance of their institution (Audit Commission/Ofsted, 1995). There has to be a high level of mutual trust between governors and staff if weaknesses within the organisation are to be dealt with frankly and openly.

SOME PRACTICAL EXAMPLES OF THE INVOLVEMENT OF SCHOOL GOVERNORS IN STRATEGIC ACTIVITIES

This part of the chapter draws upon the findings of a research project currently being undertaken into the role of governors in school improvement. The strategic role of a governing body, geared towards improving the effectiveness of the institution, includes the following key activities, to be conducted in partnership with the head/principal and the staff:

- Planning for the future.
- Deciding on policies.
- Monitoring progress.

Governors' involvement in planning

Inspection evidence shows that where governing bodies have been fully involved in their school's planning they have better informed and more effective oversight of the work of the school.

(Ofsted, 1994, p. 12)

The head and chair of one particular junior school had been concerned for some time about the format of their school development plan (SDP) and how it was produced – the 'ownership' of the document. They had a belief that it was important for staff and governors to be involved in the planning process rather than just to receive a finished document. The practice had been for the head to prepare the first draft of the plan, following consultation with the staff. This draft was then presented for discussion to a group of governors. In the year in question, the plan was distributed at the governors' meeting rather than in advance because of a shortage of time. Some of the governors made adverse comments on the draft and the head, while understanding the criticisms at a rational level, felt painfully and personally affronted by them. The chair was concerned about the effect of these comments on the head at a difficult time and so took over the first draft and presented a revised plan to the next meeting of the full governing body. Because the head didn't appear to 'own' this version, the governors 'felt they could wade in and have a real go' and there was a very full discussion of the ideas embodied in the plan.

The head and chair believe that the questioning process is all important:

Previously we've been asking the wrong questions (head).
  The questions you ask, shape what happens (chair).
  Ask not – 'Have you got any ideas?' but rather – 'What are the needs of the school?' How will this make a difference to the children's learning? (head).

They feel that sharing the task with the rest of the governors has enabled them to move towards a framework within which they feel more comfortable so that both staff and governors can contribute more easily. Governors have since told the chair that they felt that they had their hands on the plan and that looking at the basic document had been much more enriching. The SDP is a working document for both governors and staff and is frequently referred to:

Our current SDP is the best we've had. Last year's was more airy-fairy and the one before that was too bland (governor).

X [a governor who is a senior manager with a multinational retail chain] has given a new approach and helped us to sharpen up our success criteria (teacher-governor).

In a secondary school, the governors, following a critical report on the school by HMI, were faced with the need to produce an action plan in a very short space of time. Seven areas of the work of the school were identified by HMI as in need of urgent attention. At a meeting held very soon after the presentation of the HMI report, the governors were made aware of their responsibilities; key tasks for action were identified and a brief, applicable to all task groups, was also prepared. A task group, consisting of a governor, a senior member of staff and other members of staff as appropriate, was set up for each of the key targets. As the vice-chair noted in a diary which she kept at this time: 'We are seeing partnership in action.' In order to keep everybody informed, the minutes of all task group meetings were posted in the staffroom. The task groups were required to recommend ways forward, particularly in relation to classroom practice, consistency of implementation and the professional development needs of staff. Each group was responsible for the production of their section of the draft action plan. There was a very positive response from both staff and governors to this crisis: 'It is forcing us all to examine ourselves as never before' (vice-chair of governors).

Governors' involvement in policy-making

Following difficulties between them over the wording and content of policy documents the staff and governors of one junior school have evolved a new way of working together. Initially the first drafts of policies on different aspects of the work of the school were produced, as they are in many schools, by individual members of staff or small groups of teachers. Following consultation with a wider group of teachers and the headteacher, the amended policy was then presented to the governors for their approval. This caused some difficulties for the staff who saw, in some cases at least, their policies being significantly altered by the governors. In the case of the draft policy for one major subject area, the governors questioned the content, layout and wording of the document:

> Governors didn't appear to appreciate the amount of work which had gone into the writing of the policy or the professional expertise of the teachers who have to operate the policy (teacher).
> One can accept someone saying 'I'm not clear about what you are saying' but not someone saying 'This is what you meant to say – say it this way' (teacher).

The staff do however recognise that input from governors can be beneficial: 'There have been times when questions on a policy have made staff think. Governors have been instrumental in making subtle changes' (teacher).
Following these experiences it was decided to amend the policy-making

process in order to avoid these confrontations in which the teachers saw their professionalism being questioned:

> It's a learning process; each side has to be tactful. It means both sides learning (teacher).
>
> We have to be wary of the dividing line – one can easily cause an upset (governor).

Under the new system, the process starts with a presentation on the subject by the subject co-ordinator to the full governing body at one of their termly 'special focus' meetings. The aim of the presentation is to make the governors aware of the general background before the policy is drafted or revised. Frequently a governor is linked to the subject area under discussion and he or she will be involved in the detailed drafting and consultation with other members of staff which then follows. In order to ensure consistency, the governors have produced a framework for the writing of policy documents. This lists the points to be covered such as aims and objectives, the teaching and learning strategies which will be used, the arrangements for monitoring, assessment and recording, etc. The final draft policy then goes for final scrutiny to the editing group which consists of the subject co-ordinator, the governor concerned and the two deputy headteachers.

Creese and Bradley (1997) found that the policies on the same issue might be handled in different ways in different schools and they also became aware that a particular governing body would not necessarily handle apparently similar issues in the same way. In one school, discussion by the staff of pupil behaviour had led to a draft policy being written by the head and presented to the governors. A heated discussion followed, with the governors voicing opinions which differed from those of the staff and this led to changes in the final version of the policy document. The same issue had arisen in another school through the wish of the deputy head to review the school's policy. A working party had been set up which had governor and pupil involvement from the beginning. However, when dealing with the sex education policy, the governors of this school accepted without demur the draft policy prepared by the staff after a presentation illustrating the proposed approach to the topic.

Governors' involvement in monitoring and evaluation

> The governing body has a responsibility for monitoring and evaluating the school's effectiveness.
>
> (BIS/DFE/Ofsted, 1995, p. 2)

Governors' involvement in monitoring the standards of education provided in their school is an important link in the chain of accountability. However, the manner in which governing bodies choose to address this aspect of their role will vary from school to school. Schools are different and governing bodies are different. What works well for one governing body in one school will not necessarily be appropriate for another governing body in another school. Some governors will, with the agreement of the staff, adopt a very 'hands-on' approach and be personally involved in the monitoring process. In other schools, the governors, having ensured that suitable strategies for monitoring pupil performance are in place, will rely upon reports from the headteacher and staff to assure themselves that all is well.

In one secondary school, the governors linked to its faculties are involved in the regular cycle of internal inspections of the work of those faculties which are part of the school's quality assurance programme. The inspections last for three days and are carried out by a team consisting of three members of the senior management team of the school – including the SMT member linked to that faculty, the head of another faculty, the link-governor and an external subject specialist adviser/inspector. Internal inspections were introduced originally as a way of preparing staff for a forthcoming Ofsted inspection and they are modelled very closely on the Ofsted procedure using material from the Ofsted handbook including the lesson observation pro-forma. Data are gathered by lesson observation, interviews with each member of staff within the faculty and the examination of documentation provided by the faculty as well as samples of pupils' work, and the governor shares in all these activities. The staff accept, and indeed welcome, the involvement of a governor in the inspection process believing that they benefit from the increased awareness and experience gained by members of the inspection team, including the governor.

In another secondary school the members of the senior management team became aware that they were perhaps not as knowledgeable about what was happening in classrooms as they should have been. They linked themselves to departments as line managers and they instituted the practice of seeing every teacher teaching at least six times a year. The governors oversee this aspect of the work of the SMT: 'The governor watches me in the line-manager role, observing lessons, looking at samples of pupils' work and giving feedback to the head of department' (deputy head).

This was a deliberate decision by the governors and they see this as an effective way of actively monitoring the work of the school. The staff accept the right of governors to ask questions: 'There are times when practice needs to be questioned' (teacher-governor).

That acceptance, however, is based upon a feeling of partnership and trust:

> Staff now accept governors as part of the common team – they have been supportive in every way (teacher-governor).
> Staff don't feel threatened – the governors aren't abrasive (teacher-governor).

One of the criticisms made by HMI of a junior school identified as in need of special measures was that there was insufficient monitoring and evaluation and that there were no success criteria. The governors were shocked by the unfavourable report on their school; they had accepted the then head's assurances that all was well: 'I didn't know what I didn't know' (chair of governors).

The governors are now prepared to ask much more searching questions and they have set up a monitoring group consisting of the chair, head, two other teachers (including the teacher-governor) and two other governors (including the vice-chair). The new headteacher has instituted annual testing of pupils and the results of these tests and proposals for future action are discussed in detail by this group.

SOME GENERAL ISSUES ARISING FROM THE RESEARCH EVIDENCE

Improvements in the school's practice suggested by the governing body will not always be on the grand scale and, as previously indicated, governors' contribution to a climate for improvement may be more significant than their direct impact on classroom practice. In the schools being studied, governors have shown their commitment to staff – and governor – development by their own attendance at courses (sometimes with staff) and by their encouragement of teachers in their professional development – in one secondary school a significant proportion of the staff are following an MBA course. Collaborative planning is a strong feature of these schools and instances of the wish of governors to involve parents and pupils in school policy and decision-making include the chair's willingness to attend meetings of the school council in a junior school and the active involvement of a parent-governor in a newly formed parents' group in a secondary school. Governors and staff together spend time reflecting on their progress through their study of the reports on faculty or departmental reviews, through an evaluation of the effectiveness of the annual parent-governors' meeting or through regular discussion on progress towards the targets set out in the school's action plan.

The BIS/DFE/Ofsted document (1995) includes the following amongst the features of an effective governing body:

• Knowing the school well.
• Enjoying a good relationship with the headteacher (and staff).
• Working as a team.
• Taking the training and development of its own members seriously.

If governors are to become involved in formulating strategy for their schools and colleges, then a good knowledge of the institution is an absolute prerequisite. Only then will the staff have confidence in the decisions which are being made:

> Getting governors into school and involving them really gets them on board. If they are knowledgeable about the school then they are much more likely to make sound decisions (deputy head of a secondary school).
>
> You want to give the head as much support as possible. You can

only do that from a position of strength; you can't do it if you don't know the school (vice-chair of governors of a junior school).

Governors who visit their schools and colleges frequently are also contributing to the enhancement of the partnership between staff and governors. As one primary school teacher put it: 'You can't form a relationship with people you never meet.'

Governors and teachers both rate frequent and close contact between them as the most important factor in fostering a good relationship (Creese, 1995). A true partnership between staff and governors with good communication between them and based upon openness, trust and mutual respect is an essential foundation stone for the involvement of governors in institutional improvement. Joint working groups of governors and staff are an excellent way of bringing the two sides together and developing the sense of partnership.

Several of the governing bodies involved in the research study have chosen to undertake team-building activities of one kind or another. These sessions provide an opportunity to develop shared aims and values. In one secondary school a recently retired head now working as a consultant led team-building sessions for the governing body:

He has helped the governing body to work together and helped the staff to see how we could include governors more (teacher-governor).

He made us look at ourselves and gave us confidence; he put the job of the governing body into perspective (teacher-governor).

He focused the governing body much more on the issues (governor).

The same governing body has now established an induction programme for its new governors.

FACTORS AFFECTING THE EFFECTIVENESS OF THE GOVERNING BODY

If governors are going to help their schools and colleges to improve, then they need to be enabled to ask the right questions of the staff. This requires, first, that governors should know their institution and, secondly, that there should be a sense of partnership between staff and governors. The professionals have then to be prepared to prompt the lay governors to ask the questions. Governors involved in monitoring exercises need to be well briefed if they and the institution are to obtain maximum benefit from the time invested. Questioning of one's professionalism – by even the friendliest of critics – can be very threatening and tact is required from both sides. Governors have to steer a delicate middle course between interfering with the head's/principal's day-to-day management of the institution while at the same time being able to ask challenging questions without provoking confrontation.

A difficulty, particularly for some schools, is the rapidly changing membership of the governing body. Schools need to recruit a group of committed governors, willing and able to devote time to the school. These governors need an understanding of educational issues (which has implications for governor training) and the confidence and drive to address these issues. They also need the personal and social skills to be able to work in partnership with the head and staff. School governors serve a four-year term of office and it often takes them a year or two to come to know their school. If few of the governors elect to serve for a second term there is a lack of experience within the governing body and too much effort has to be devoted to the induction of the new members.

Another difficulty for governors which emerges from every study undertaken of their work is the limited time which they have available to devote to governance (e.g. Creese, 1994). In a study conducted in the eight schools (*ibid.*), the governors were devoting a considerable amount of time to their schools but the majority of this time was spent in meetings either of the full governing body or its subgroups. These meetings did not, in general, involve teachers other than the headteacher and the teacher-governor(s). Most governors are busy people, often working full time and it may well be that they need to review carefully the way in which they spend the time which they are able to devote to school governance.

One of the most significant changes in the working practice of governing bodies since the Education Acts 1986 and 1988 has been their use of subgroups, whether committees with delegated powers or working parties without. Graystone (1996) suggests that a governing body should devote around 50 per cent of its work to strategic decision-making and only 20 per cent to operational matters. Proper use of subgroups, together with well organised meetings of the full governing body with appropriate agendas – with the most important items tabled early on – offers governing bodies a way of achieving this target.

CONCLUSION

There is a clear expectation that governors will be involved in school improvement and yet, at present, many are not. One has to ask the question, 'If governors are not about improvement, then what, precisely, is their function?' As one governor expressed it: 'We [the governors] have to believe that we can make a difference.'

Governing bodies and individual governors should ask themselves, 'What have I/we contributed over the past year to the improvement of the education of the young people in the school?' Sadly, in some cases the answer will be 'Not a lot', in spite of a considerable investment of time and effort on the part of the governors. However, governors are accountable to parents and to the wider community for what happens in their schools and for improvement in the standard and quality of education provided and they cannot afford to be satisfied with the status quo.

If governing bodies are to contribute effectively to improvement, then they need to be very clear about their purpose and to concentrate their efforts, perhaps more sharply than many do at present. Some governors, perhaps particularly those from a business background, are aware of the need for governing bodies to sharpen their focus: 'We need to be better at targeting the really big issues and giving ourselves time to discuss them. We need to be better in terms of the process; in the way in which we tackle issues' (governor). Headteachers and teachers will have to help the governors to highlight these key issues and to provide sufficient and appropriate background information so that governors are able to discuss them from an informed standpoint. When governors' discussions are no longer restricted to mundane matters and if the governors feel that they are not side lined when the real issues are discussed, then they will come to realise that they have a very real role to play in school improvement.

Acknowledgements

The financial support of BT, the Post Office, Unilever and the University of Cambridge School of Education in funding research into governors and school improvement is acknowledged with gratitude. Without the unstinting generosity and co-operation – sometimes at times of considerable stress – of the governors, headteachers and other members of staff in the schools concerned the research would have been impossible.

REFERENCES

Audit Commission/Ofsted (1995) *Lessons in Teamwork: How School Governing Bodies can Become more Effective,* London, HMSO.

BIS/DFE/Ofsted (1995) *Governing Bodies and Effective Schools*, London, Banking Information Service/Department for Education/Office for Standards in Education, DFE.

Corrick, M. (1996) Effective governing bodies, effective schools?" In Earley, P., Fidler, B. and Ouston, J. (eds.) *Improvement through Inspection?* London, David Fulton.

Creese, M. (1994) Governor–teacher relationships following the 1986 and 1988 Education Acts, unpublished PhD thesis.

Creese, M. (1995) A multi-site study into governor–teacher relationships in eight schools. In Wallace, G. (ed.) *School, Markets and Management,* Bournemouth, Hyde Publications.

Creese, M. and Bradley, H. (1997) A report on a pilot project to study ways in which governing bodies contribute to school improvement, *School Management and Leadership,* Vol. 17, no. 1, pp. 37–8.

Curtis, A. (1994) Effectiveness and efficiency: governors' views from south Oxfordshire. In Thody, A. (ed.) *School Governors: Leaders or Followers?* London, Longman.

DFE (1994) *School Governors: A Guide to the Law,* London, HMSO.

DFE/WO (1992) *Choice and Diversity,* London, HMSO.

DfEE (1996) *Guidance on Good Governance,* London, Department for Education and Employment.

Earley, P. (1994) *School Governing Bodies: Making Progress?* Slough, NFER.

FEFC (1994) *Guide for College Governors,* London, HMSO.

Fidler, B. (1996) School development planning and strategic planning for school improvement. In Earley, P., Fidler, B. and Ouston, J. (eds.) *Improvement through Inspection,* London, David Fulton.

Graystone, J. (1996) Efficient, but can you prove it? *The Times Higher Education Supplement,* 29 November.

Hopkins, D., West, M. and Ainscow, M. (1996) *Improving the Quality of Education for All,* London, David Fulton.

Huckman, L. (1994) Developing roles and relationships in primary school governance. In Thody, A. (ed.) *School Governors: Leaders or Followers?* Harlow, Longman.

Kogan, M., Johnson, D., Whitaker, T. and Packwood, T. (1984) *School Governing Bodies,* London, Heinemann.

Monk, C. (1992) College governance – the management responsibility. In Limb, A. *et al.* (eds.) *The Road to Incorporation,* Bristol, The Staff College and the Association of Colleges for Further and Higher Education.

Ofsted (1994) *Improving Schools,* London, HMSO.

Packwood, T. (1984) Models of governing bodies. In Glatter, R. (ed.) *Understanding School Management,* Milton Keynes, Open University Press.

Pascal, C. (1987) Democratised primary school government: conflicts and dichotomies. In Southworth, G. (ed.) *Readings in Primary School Management,* Lewes, Falmer Press.

Taylor Report (1977) *A New Partnership for our Schools,* London, HMSO.

Thomas, H. and Martin, J. (1996) *Managing Resources for School Improvement: Creating a Cost-Effective School,* London, Routledge.

10

STRATEGIC LEADERSHIP IN EDUCATION: BECOMING, BEING, DOING

Valerie Hall

INTRODUCTION

Skilful and imaginative leadership is central to managing strategy implementation in schools and colleges. Whatever else is disputed about this highly complex field of activity, the role of leadership in its successful achievement is unequivocal. A primary purpose of this chapter is to explore what it might mean to lead strategically (as well as lead strategy), and what those who are 'strategic leaders' must be and do. I will argue that the successful implementation of strategy depends on, among other things, the qualities, knowledge and skills of the individuals responsible for leading colleagues and others on the difficult journey of school improvement. Without rejecting the value of systems approaches to management with their emphasis on its rational and technical characteristics, this chapter aims to demonstrate the importance of the relationship between personal leadership style, creative thinking and management skills in leading schools and colleges to success.

While the centrality of leadership is indisputable, there is a bigger question mark over who the leaders are. On the one hand are teachers' increasing calls for and acceptance of a leadership role in achieving goals in the context of their own spheres of responsibility. On the other hand, research suggests an ever-growing divide between 'leaders' and 'followers' as a result of the transformation in education management arising from self-governance. In schools, as Wallace and Hall's (1994) research shows, the creation of a senior management team can lead to a schism between senior managers and others as a result of the cohesiveness that is created by senior managers' decisions to work as a team. In further education, as Elliott's (1996) research shows, there is evidence of a pedagogic culture amongst FE lecturers which conflicts with the strong managerialist culture represented by the senior managers. In both cases the divide is exacerbated by those aspects of self-governance that identify headteachers and principals (with governors) as having ultimate responsibility for human, financial and other resource decisions. This aspect of new managerialism inevitably encourages 'them–us' attitudes which operate against the collaborative institutional development which is essential for effective learning. One of the challenges for strategic leaders is to lead in ways that break down barriers rather than create them. At the same time, the Teacher Training Agency's prescriptions for a professional qualification for headship stress strategic direction and development of the school as a key area of headship. Having created a strategic plan heads must, the TTA claims, 'ensure that all those involved in the school are committed to its aims, motivated to achieve them and involved in meeting long, medium and short-term objectives and targets' to secure the educational success of the school (Teacher Training Agency, 1997, p. 6). Responsibility for securing this necessary commitment is firmly placed by the TTA in the hands of the designated leaders.

Given this official acknowledgement of the central leadership role of senior staff, and the next chapter's focus on middle managers, I will concentrate here on heads, principals and senior staff. In spite of the differences across phases and sectors, many issues regarding strategic leadership are common to them all. The implementation of school and college strategic plans has to be managed, monitored and reviewed. Progress towards achieving the plan needs to be supported by shared values manifest in senior staff's 'symbolic leadership behaviour' or the ways in which leaders attempt to manage the meanings of their organisations (Sergiovanni, 1991). Changes to structures may be necessary to accommodate the demands of the plan. Where these impact on existing functions and roles and create new or changed ones, leaders will have to tread carefully in order to ensure staff stay with them. They have a responsibility for establishing effective systems for achieving strategic objectives, and ensuring their smooth running. Leadership styles can have a powerful effect on the way attempts to implement the strategic plan are perceived and responded to by staff. Strategies are required within strategies, together with the capacity to sustain a 'helicopter view' of the changing landscape. Successful implementation is only possible if all staff are involved, including part-time and support staff. The staffing implications of the agreed strategies have to be identified and the effects of their actions monitored. Finally, leaders will have control of the resources required to implement the plan effectively. Unless these are deployed appropriately and fairly, they will become a barrier rather than a springboard to successful implementation. In spite of different contexts (environment, students, staff, structures, etc.) these implementation issues represent similar challenges to leaders in each phase and sector.

BEING A STRATEGIC LEADER

In the remainder of this chapter I will consider what is required to achieve these different implementation tasks successfully in schools and colleges, drawing on examples from research and practitioner accounts. At the heart of the description of strategic leadership that follows is Hodgkinson's (1992) conception of leadership as 'a moral art'. Within this conception, leadership and management are inseparable and leading a school or college involves translating philosophy into action. Fidler (1996), on the other hand, associates the leadership role with the genesis of strategy rather than its implementation. He defines strategic leadership (*ibid.*, p. xxi) as 'those processes of bringing about change by inspiring others to follow' and management as 'processes for implementing the change'. Whichever view is preferred, it is clear that guiding staff, students, governors and others along the road from philosophy to action cannot be done by rulebooks alone. The ability to think not only strategically but also creatively is a crucial part of the leader's repertoire for translating a vision for the school into policies from which decisions can be made, plans formed and a culture of quality or continuous improvement created and sustained.

This examination of strategic leadership, therefore, takes leadership and management to be mutually reinforcing within a conception of leadership that is diffused rather than hierarchical. As I have suggested, research and informed discussion demonstrate that leadership makes a difference to strategy implementation. It also shows how the skills required are both generic and context specific, within and between phases and sectors. It can be argued, for example, that the kind of 'moral' leadership that Hodgkinson advocates is generic across educational sectors. Similarly leaders in all contexts must have the ability to read and adjust to the context. On the other hand, individuals and the organisations they lead operate within a framework of constraints, demands and choices that inhibit or liberate their actions. As Middlewood shows in Chapter 1, the context of strategic management in education is complex and varies between schools and colleges, large and small institutions. The capacity of leaders to make a difference will depend on their interpretation of and responses to these constraints and demands and their ability to transform them by making choices and being proactive. Goldring (1997, p. 291) argues that educational leaders must know how to 'span boundaries' in order to promote information and resource control. At the same time as they negotiate the constraints of the environment, they must capitalise on the many opportunities it provides for making choices.

The choices will relate to their own beliefs, values, actions and leadership style, and the support they give others as autonomous individuals. Different contexts present different leadership challenges for implementing strategy and require different responses. In turbulent, unpredictable times the room for manoeuvre at institutional level is constrained, however much decentralised budgetary arrangements appear to allow scope. Wallace and McMahon's (1994) study of planning for change in multiracial primary schools shows the considerable variety in headteachers' responses to the requirement of school development planning. Describing the heads as 'key orchestrators of the management of planning and implementation', the authors show how they had continuously to adapt strategies and tactics as a result of unanticipated events and new requirements. One head, for example, was trying to implement plans in the context of concerns about the long-term viability of the school. This was reflected in the steady decline in the school roll, which had implications for the school's budget, particularly since the site was large and expensive to run (*ibid.*, p. 160). In another school, the head's copy of the development plan was stolen and the document ceased to be the basis for guiding the school's development planning and implementation. Neither set of circumstances had been envisaged when the plan was first put into action.

This turbulence and continual need to respond to unanticipated events do not make the lot of the designated leaders in schools and colleges currently a happy one. Challenges to positional authority combined with pessimism about schools' and colleges' capacities to withstand externally imposed change appear to encourage some leaders to make a strategic withdrawal. When they stand their ground and fight, as research in both primary and secondary schools shows many to do (Grace, 1995; Hall, 1996; Webb and Vulliamy, 1996), their performance may be judged differently according to whether they are 'leader-managers' or 'leader-resistors'. The former welcome recent educational reforms as opportunities to transform their organisations, even if it means accepting the values that accompany them. The term 'leader-manager' does not refer to the integration of leadership and management that Hodgkinson is talking of, but to the acceptance of the principles of new managerialism. The resistors refuse to embrace antipathetic values, preferring to challenge what they see as an attack on educational values. From the point of view of students, whose educational fates are at stake in the political battleground, the successful leader-manager may appear more appropriate for their needs. Whether this style paves the way for successful schooling in the future is a question which is beyond the scope of this chapter. Much depends on the content of the strategies which leaders are required to lead and the choices they make in how they implement them.

It may be, and certainly is from a critical perspective on new managerialism (Smyth, 1989), that the actions of the leader who acts strategically now in the interests of his or her school may work against a longer-term strategy for the improvement of educational opportunity for all. In the mean time, it is today's leaders who must have the knowledge and skills to implement the strategies that guide their institution's development. Attacking what he describes as 'Kentucky fried schooling' (in which schools compete and market themselves only as licensed franchises, selling remarkably similar products to their customers), Hargreaves (1995) provides suggestions for restructuring that include strategies that go far beyond traditional models. He argues (*ibid.*, p. 147):

> We need to build more time and incentives for professional learning into the system, to create more opportunities for teachers to connect with each other in the classroom as well as in the staffroom, and to foster the kind of visionary leadership that includes staff collaboratively in the change process instead of imposing change managerially on them.

So far, I have concentrated on what is required to be a strategic leader and argued that effective strategic leadership is about making choices about how to lead in the context of ever-changing demands and constraints. Paying attention to what leaders need to be to implement strategy successfully shifts the focus from their skills and actions to their beliefs and qualities. Equally important is their attention to the structures within which strategic decisions are made and implemented; or to what Kotter quoted in Telford (1996, p. 59) describes as 'aligning people – communicating the direction by words and deeds to all those whose cooperation may be needed so as to influence the creation of teams and coalitions that understand the vision and the strategies and accept their validity'.

Most studies of change efforts in education consider the ways heads use management structures to create their own schools. The structures they support are taken as evidence of their values, whether deriving from predominantly bureaucratic or collegial conceptions of educational organisations (Bush, 1997, p. 48). Wallace and McMahon's (1994) study shows that restructuring staff's activities around teams, for example, is not without its difficulties. One headteacher occasionally postponed management team meetings because she found them unproductive. A change to the structure was not enough to promote the new ways of working needed to implement the plans. She also needed to pay attention to culture and the demands of continuity and change. On the other hand, as Stoll and Fink (1996, p. 129) show in their analysis of school improvement efforts in Canadian schools, 'restructuring means a total, critical reexamination of our use of time and space, roles and relationships, with a view to adopting new structures which enhance the learning of all pupils and abandoning those structures which are unproductive and obsolete'. To allow time for teachers to work together to implement strategy, they propose redesigned timetables and school years, more use of technology, flexible schedules, teams of teachers rather than conventional departmental and subject organisations. They discuss space as structure which can be manipulated to extend beyond the usual boundaries of the school. They include as an example a teacher responsible for science wanting a two-day study of rivers. If volunteers from the community are used to supervise, then the remaining teachers have two days to plan collaboratively (*ibid.*, p. 131). Still more radically, they ask whether the re-examination of current roles and structures might not lead to the abandonment and reformulation of some, including the principal's.

All these are ways of realigning people to implement the school's agreed strategic plans. Leaders who aim to bring about this alignment must first have deep-seated beliefs about the intrinsic value of their own purposes. As Bhindi and Duignan (1996) have proposed in their 'Visionary paradigm' for leadership in 2020:

Organisations are not solely concerned with outcomes, processes and resources. They are also concerned with the human spirit and their values and relationships. Authentic leaders breathe the life force into the workplace and keep the people feeling energised and focused. As stewards and guides they build people and their self-esteem. They derive their credibility from personal integrity and 'walking' their values.

My own study of six effective headteachers (Hall, 1996) showed what this kind of leadership looks like in action. There I refer to leaders who 'walk their talk' and seek through the consistency and integrity of their actions to model the behaviours they consider desirable for achieving the school's goals. Limb (1994, p. 228) uses similar terms to describe her own approach to leading a large further education college through major changes. She says (*ibid.*): 'In essence the head of the college must not only promote the values and oversee their implementation, but must embody them in his or her own practice. The principal of a college based on a commitment to individual learning must be committed to a learning approach to all his or her management functions.' This approach reflects Stoll and Fink's call for a reconceptualisation of leadership that focuses on the 'human side of education'. Their attack on the limitations of technocratic models of educational leadership (so popular in the 1980s) leads to their advocacy of 'invitational leadership' as the appropriate style for tomorrow's schools. Within this model, leadership is about 'communicating invitations to individuals and groups with whom leaders interact in order to build and act on a shared and evolving vision of enhanced educational experiences for pupils' (*ibid.*, p. 109). To invite others, they claim, 'leaders must first invite themselves, physically, intellectually, socially, emotionally, spiritually' (*ibid.*, p. 111).

In Chapter 1, Middlewood refers to the need for leaders to combine strategic thinking and the ability to make intelligent guesses about the future with a capacity for operational management thinking that addresses the process of managing improvement. Hall *et al.* (1997) use Gareth Morgan's concept of 'Imaginisation' to link creative approaches to leading and managing with strategic action. Morgan (1993, p. 10) describes 'Imaginisation' as about:

- improving our abilities to see and understand situations in new ways
- finding new images for ways of organising
- the creation of shared understandings
- personal empowerment
- developing capacities for continuous self-organisation.

The authors then provide an example of a headteacher whose artistic and intuitive imaginisation of the future school was given concrete expression in the new buildings, the creation of which provided the opportunity for other stakeholders in the school to contribute to and share this vision.

Many of the structures advocated for successful implementation of strategy involve collaboration. Some (e.g. Hargreaves, 1994) have challenged its unquestioning acceptance as an appropriate strategy for almost every task. Yet in the context of senior management teams, Wallace and Hall's (1994) research shows that headteachers choosing to share leadership in this way have identified a highly creative approach to tackling the demands of implementing multiple change. The authors argue that a team approach to managing secondary schools is a 'high gain, high pain' strategy for senior staff (particularly heads) to adopt. The pay-off of this risky strategy is synergy where the team together achieves more than the aggregate of what its individual members would do as individuals. The decision to work with and through a team rests with the headteacher. They alone have the authority to create the conditions for other senior staff to participate in fulfilling a shared role in managing the school. Wallace and Hall's study shows the critical part each of the six heads played in creating the SMT and promoting a shared culture of teamwork. The heads were also potentially the most vulnerable if teamwork failed. As SMT leader they were accountable and failure would dent their rather than their colleagues' credibility in the eyes of governors and other staff. In spite of the strains of teamwork, the authors argue that working as a team can make a difference to the working conditions of SMT members, to the range of factors taken into account in making decisions about school-wide policies, and to the degree of co-ordination in managing the school. They conclude (*ibid.*, p. 194):

> Teamwork among senior staff may well not be a necessary condition for school effectiveness, but we are willing to hazard the guess that heads without the support of teamwork among senior staff are likely to have even greater difficulty in promoting synergy across the school in the current climate than those who are successful in going for a team approach.

The appropriateness of teamwork as an approach to strategic planning and implementation is confirmed in Bolam *et al.*'s (1993) study of effective management in schools. Their detailed example of an effective secondary headteacher shows how he used team structures as a way of delegating and empowering others. His organisational structure included a senior management team and, at year level, a team of two (year leader and partner). As a result, colleagues enjoyed a high degree of autonomy (for example, in curriculum delivery and control over resources), though coupled with responsibility.

Telford (1996) draws on her research into schools in Australia to argue for collaborative leadership as the most certain way of ensuring the vision of the school is realised. She proposes a model of collaborative leadership based on Bolman and Deal's (1991) four frames of reference: structural elements; human resource elements; political elements; and symbolic elements. She uses this framework to analyse what leaders actually do in a school to promote and sustain a collaborative culture. She identifies 'artistry' as an additional key ingredient of successful school leadership. Such artistry is required to apply the recipe, to read the idiosyncrasies of each leadership context and the know-how to manoeuvre, manipulate and exploit the four frames: structures, people, politics and symbols.

This discussion of collaboration as central to achieving a school or college's main purposes has inevitably shifted the focus to the leader's attitude towards and capacity for managing strategic change. On the one hand such a capacity can be represented in terms of knowledge about what is involved and skills in managing the different phases of change. Yet as Fullan (1993) argues in his new paradigm of change, every person is a change agent and personal mindset and mastery are the ultimate protections against being the passive tools for others' change efforts. Seeing change through is much harder than launching it. Fung (1992, p. 223) has compared managing an educational innovation to leading an exploratory adventure rather than guiding a package tour. The disposition as well as the skills of the adventure leader are very different from the package tour guide. They include, above all, a capacity to be flexible and resilient in the face of uncertainty. The same is true of implementing strategic plans. As Wallace and McMahon (1994, p. 177) discovered in their research into primary schools' attempts to manage school development planning:

> Development planning was a palliative, but no panacea for dealing with multiple changes. The assumption of relative environmental stability proved false in so far as factors promoting turbulence led to spasmodically shifting circumstances which, in turn, forced other priorities to be addressed, with consequent adjustment of priorities within the development plan.

LEADING SKILFULLY: FROM PLANS TO ACTION

So far I have talked of the qualities and predispositions required for leading strategy successfully and some structural changes that might be necessary for new styles of working. In this section I will look at the skills needed for effective action. A case has been made here, and in Chapter 2 by Foreman, for the centrality of vision and the leader's role in creating a vision for the organisation. Yet the art of leading and managing is not a clinical process. The apparently neat linear progression from philosophy to vision, mission, goals and targets is rarely experienced as a logical progression. Caldwell and Spinks' (1988) version of the self-managing school captured educators' attention by proposing an attractive, pragmatic method of policy-making and planning that make it appear manageable. Less easily identified and acquired are the skills or competencies that allow leaders to 'ride the waves of change', as the school or college juggles its short, medium and long-term targets.

Among these is the skill of communicating the vision for the school, something which Bolam and colleagues' (1993) study suggests does not always happen, even among otherwise 'good' leaders. They conclude (*ibid.*, p. 37) that in many of the schools visited, the majority of teachers interviewed had had to deduce or infer what the vision might be (e.g. by noting what aspects their headteacher would enthuse about, draw to their attention or possibly allocate resources to, or what from among their own practice won praise). The strategic actions that led to devising the plan have not been transformed into shorter-term tactics to communicate and implement it.

Central to implementing strategy is the ability to manage people, to take them as willing companions on a journey during which, as Fung's 'adventure tour' analogy suggests, they learn through experience of travel. Managing through teams is only one way of bringing out the best in people. Managing people for strategic success (which outside education would more commonly be called strategic human resource management or HRM) depends on asking how people can help formulate and accomplish the strategies and what support for motivation and development they need. Within a strategic human resource management framework, the leader must attempt to address organisational and individual needs together so that meeting individual needs complements rather than clashes with meeting the school's or college's needs. Elsewhere (Hall, 1997) I have examined the potential of different HRM strategies for liberating or constraining staff performance. These include how staff are recruited, selected, developed, reviewed and rewarded. The staffing implications of each objective within the strategic plan need to be thought through. Who is going to lead different parts of the implementation strategy? Do they have the necessary authority and skills? Will any resource consequences of implementing the plan have a negative effect on staff motivation? Will pressures on staff time undermine their ability and willingness to engage in changes required in implementing the strategy? Have the staff development implications of implementing the plan been identified and resources allocated to enable them to be met?

Getting the structures of responsibility right is just a first step in managing people effectively for strategy implementation. Evans (1996) describes the dilemmas faced by her own head in drawing up a document describing new roles and responsibilities. The dilemma lay in making it acceptable to the existing culture and using it as an instrument for shaping and developing that culture. She says (*ibid.*, p. 227):

> Some criticisms were easily dealt with, e.g. those concerning the tone. 'A teacher with no responsibilities above . . . ' was reworded, a structure diagram of non-teaching staff was added, and 'autocracy' was re-ordered within a list of forms of involvement in decision-making in order to lower the profile of potentially the most contentious approach.

Other concerns were that it read like an essay, was too long and the language was too sophisticated. Doubts were expressed whether staff would read it at all and a highly simplified version produced. A further step down the implementation line, Lewis (1994, p. 256) describes his own actions in bringing about cultural change in a college:

> The senior management set about developing incentives and new procedures which encouraged people to buy into the strategy and to reward success. This was accompanied by a large scale redistribution of resources to the new priorities. Inevitably these changes challenged vested interests and as a result a sense of alienation and resentment developed among some staff.

This led to the implementation strategy described earlier: ridding the organisation of rigid organisation structures and replacing them with a form of matrix organisation involving delegation of responsibility and project-focused management teams. In Lewis' view, the success of the implementation rested upon the efforts of the managers to win the college staff's support. As Elliott (1996) found in his study of an FE college, the main resistance was from academic staff who prioritised their individual teaching commitments above identifying with the success of the college as a whole. In contrast, support staff more readily recognised the necessity for the college to change and were willing to identify ways in which they could help. This no doubt reflected the care taken by the college leadership to involve them from the start in discussions about the new strategy, a tactic which is not always so evident in schools undergoing change.

In this respect, Lewis and his colleagues were using strategies for bringing out the best in staff that Blase and Kirby (1992) have associated in their research with effective principals: the power of praise, influencing by expecting and by involving, granting professional autonomy, leading by standing behind, gentle nudging, positive use of formal authority, providing mirrors to the possible. Although they concentrate on teaching staff, the same approaches are crucial in working with associate staff, governors and parents if strategies are to be successful. Managing people means taking account of and valuing equally all the people in the enterprise. Lewis used an external consultant to run a development project in the college aimed at developing management and staff to act as 'enterprising people'. A forerunner of Investors in People (whose aims it replicates), it contributed to the creation of the business-like management culture that the principal deemed necessary for implementing new strategies. Highlighting the centrality of the leader's role in implementing change, Bolam *et al.* (1993) provide a negative portrait of a head who failed significantly on the interpersonal dimension. He became defensive and even aggressive if challenged publicly, was unable to admit to being wrong, failed to smooth ruffled feathers or sooth wounded pride and did not praise staff for their efforts or achievements (*ibid.*, p. 32). In contrast, an effective head in the same study was described by one teacher as follows: 'I think he is a good leader because he sorts out what he wants to do, he rallies round his troops . . . he delegates well, he's informed and enthusiastic – so you trust him, and he's very supportive' (*ibid.*, p. 102).

These examples show how managing people for strategic success also means knowing how to help people overcome their resistance to change. It requires leaders to be competent in the planning and administrative process, dealing with people, professional and technical knowledge and personal skills. These are the competency areas identified by Jirasinghe and Lyons (1996, p. 96). The fourth area of competence proposed by Jirasinghe and Lyons is 'managing the political environment', including political ability and skills in persuading and negotiating. For them, strategic leadership means being politically adept and able to generate support amongst stakeholders for the school or college. As well as skills in persuading and negotiating, they must be able to manage conflict in a way that achieves positive outcomes. In his account of transferring a further education college to incorporated status, Togher (1994) shows just how painful the process of 'getting to yes' can be. He comments on the 'still naive belief amongst many senior managers in education that radical change can and should be painless' (*ibid.*, p. 268). In his example, the change involved a new organisational structure for the college at the same time as the implementation of a new staff contract. He attributes the success of his strategy for implementation in the face of considerable union opposition to the following (*ibid.*, p. 275):

> The central reason for the overall success of our strategy was that it was meticulously planned and took account of advice from our solicitors and the CEF. It was communicated exhaustively, with commitment and patience by the whole of the corporation board, and the college executive, within an adequate time frame. We did not falter but continued to implement the strategy even when circumstances did not look favourable. We prepared for a sustained process of change and the sheer inevitability has won more and more staff over as time has moved on.

His account has the flavour of a military campaign on a field of battle but provides a vivid example of a hard-edged approach to managing people to achieve strategic goals. In his view, 'It is the principal and chief executive who must lead change and be prepared to handle the strategic management of the problems that will arise' (*ibid.*, p. 268).

The political context he describes for managing change resembles that described by Hoyle (1986) and Ball (1987) in their versions of schools as micropolitical battlegrounds. The emphasis is on winning not losing, with the dangers that such a solution can bring for longer-term relationships in the organisation. In some contexts, as Togher's account shows, it is a necessary strategy and may need to be combined with the more collaborative approaches that I described earlier. Blase and Anderson (1995) bring the debate about the politics of strategic leadership in schools up to date with their account of the outcomes of their research into micropolitics in schools. In their view, the real world of schools is also a political world in which power and influence, bargaining and negotiation, assertion and protection hold sway. Effective principals are those who are able to influence teacher behaviour through their leadership style (using 'power over', 'power through' and 'power with' as appropriate). They show how any micropolitical strategy can be manipulative or authentic, a departure from those views of micropolitics as malignant (and predominantly masculine) processes. While advocating democratic, empowering leadership, they acknowledge the dilemma of creating 'power-with' organisations that can thrive in a 'power over' world. The examples given throughout this chapter demonstrate the limits of leadership approaches based on making others do what they do not want to do.

My own study of six women headteachers found that they preferred to use power to empower, based on their beliefs and values about collaborating. When this did not work they reverted reluctantly and rarely to a less preferred but more directive form of power. This sometimes meant putting values about goals (e.g. quality teaching) above values about people (e.g. about supporting, not sanctioning). My conclusion was that their reinterpretation of what it means to be political in schools constitutes a challenge to those who claim that organisations can be understood only in terms of politics, and that organisational actors, to be successful, must learn to play political games of a particular kind (Hall, 1996, p. 161).

To implement strategy, highly honed skills of dealing with conflict and resistance are required but the desired outcomes are 'win-win' and not 'win-lose'. Potentially, micropolitical behaviour is in conflict with collaboration, yet both are necessary, as the Lewis and Togher examples cited earlier suggest, if plans for change are to be realised.

The examples of collaboration discussed earlier all point to the perceived value of involving staff in decision-making. Here the leader must choose whether to share some or all of the decision-making, consult or retain exclusive responsibility. He or she must distinguish between strategic and tactical decisions, i.e. those which have long-term consequences such as staffing and structures; and those which require more immediate responses with shorter-term consequences. If decision-making is to be shared then staff need support in developing their decision-making skills, including recognising what constitutes a high-quality decision. Changes to the organisation's structures along the lines indicated earlier will generate the formal decision-making machinery. This, however, will only be as good as the decision-making skills of those involved and the strength of their desire to be involved. Stoll and Fink (1996, p. 67) advise that it is neither manageable nor a good use of teachers' time for every one to be involved in all the decisions arising from development plans. In their view, it is not the shared decision-making *per se* that is significant but, rather, the feeling of control that ensues.

Yet the emphasis throughout this chapter has been on collaboration as a preferred mode for leading the implementation of strategy. Bolam *et al.*'s (1993) study of effective management in schools found that responses about decision-making processes were influenced less by the structure of committee and staff meetings than by staff opinions as to the genuineness of the consultation process. Many were unhappy with the degree to which their canvassed views were actually taken into account. The authors cite (*ibid.*, p. 51) as a typical example: 'Consultation exists in theory, but little regard seems to be taken of staff views. Discussions are often hurried, and then at a later meeting it is said, "this was agreed at a previous meeting" when in fact no decision had been reached.' The authors identify as factors contributing to staff's satisfaction with the decision-making process: when their views are taken into account; when they are clear about which groups and individuals were responsible for taking particular decisions; if, having been consulted, they obtained feedback about the decision that was made; and if they felt there was some flexibility in the process (*ibid.*, pp. 52–3).

Since many decisions are taken, in the eyes of staff, within senior management teams, the quality of decision-making within the teams becomes crucial. Wallace and Hall's study illustrates the advantages of team approaches to decision-making, in spite of its complexity and time requirements. They quote (1994, p. 59) the deputy of one team:

> By using a team, however small or large, you cut out arbitrary decisions, whimsical decisions, impulsive decisions, decisions based on a whole host of background reasons . . . that introduces an element of accountability. You are in a sense called upon by the team to justify yourself, or you can be.

Wallace and Hall found that sharing decisions relating to the responsibilities of individual members meant the heads and other SMT members were accountable to the team, so reducing the likelihood of decisions of poor quality. Since the implementation of most decisions depends on the efforts of other staff, feedback was encouraged and changes to decisions made in the light of it. The implementation of decisions was usually led by the SMT members responsible for the area in question, who shared the task of ensuring decisions were properly communicated and their implementation monitored.

SUMMARY AND CONCLUSIONS

I began the chapter by highlighting the centrality of leadership for successful strategy implementation. It is not enough for leaders to have the vision, sell it and then move on, leaving others to translate it into action. Implementation of the strategic plan needs continual monitoring and evaluation by those with the creative ability to understand where diversions may be appropriate and how obstacles can be surmounted. Strategic plans should be, after all, liberating and not constraining. As Wallace (1991) has cogently argued, flexible planning must be the order of the day. Leaders need to combine a moral purpose with a willingness to be collaborative and promote collaboration amongst colleagues, whether through teamwork or extending the boundaries of participation in decision-making. They need skills in communicating (both of vision and with people); in matching people to strategic objectives and reorganising structures and roles appropriately; in supporting colleagues' development so that they feel confident in fulfilling expectations of their contribution to the achievement of strategic goals; and in managing conflict and negotiating positive outcomes. It would appear that, even within a context of increasing diffusion of leadership responsibilities, leaders still have to be and act as superwomen and men, if they are to make the plan become a reality.

REFERENCES

Ball, S. (1987) *The Micropolitics of the School*, London, Methuen.

Bhindi, N. and Duignan, P. (1996) *Leadership 2020: a visionary paradigm*, paper presented at Commonwealth Council for Educational Administration International Conference, Kuala Lumpur.

Blase, J. and Anderson, G. (1995) *The Micropolitics of Educational Leadership: From Control to Empowerment,* London, Cassell.

Blase, J. and Kirby, P (1992) *Bringing out the Best in Teachers,* Newbury Park, Calif., Corwin Press.

Bolman, L.G. and Deal, T.E. (1991) *Reframing Organisations,* San Francisco, Calif., Jossey-Bass.

Bolam, R., McMahon, A., Pocklington, K. and Weindling, D. (1993) *Effective Management in Schools,* London, HMSO.

Bush, T. (1997) Management structures. In Bush, T. and Middlewood, D. (eds.) *Managing People in Education,* London, Paul Chapman.

Caldwell, B. and Spinks, J. (1988) *The Self-Managing School,* Lewes, Falmer Press.

Elliott, G. (1996) *Crisis and Change in Vocational Education and Training,* London, Jessica Kingsley.

Evans, B. (1996) A strategic plan for a comprehensive school. In Fidler, B., (ed.) *Strategic Planning for School Improvement,* London, Pitman.

Fidler, B. (1996) *Strategic Planning for School Improvement,* London, Pitman.

Fullan, M. (1993) *Change Forces: Probing the Depth of Educational Reform,* London, Falmer Press.

Fung, A. (1992) Management of educational innovation. The case of computer-aided administration, unpublished PhD dissertation, University of London, Institute of Education.

Goldring, E. (1997) Educational leadership: schools, environments and boundary spanning. In Preedy, M. *et al.* (eds.) *Educational Management Strategy, Quality and Resources,* Buckingham, Open University Press.

Gorringe, R. and Toogood, P. (eds.) (1994) *Changing the Culture of a College, Coombe Lodge Report,* Vol. 24, no. 3, Blagdon, The Staff College.

Grace, G. (1995) *School Leadership: Beyond Education Management.* An Essay in Policy Scholarship, Lewes, Falmer Press.

Hall, V. (1996) *Dancing on the Ceiling: A Study of Women Managers in Education,* London, Paul Chapman.

Hall, V. (1997) Management roles in education. In Bush, T. and Middlewood, D. (eds.) *Managing People in Education,* London, Paul Chapman.

Hall, V., Cromey-Hawke, N. and Oldroyd, D. (1997) *Management Self-Development: A School-Based Distance Learning Programme,* Bristol, University of Bristol, NDCEMP.

Hargreaves, A. (1994) *Changing Teachers, Changing Times: Teachers' Work and Culture in the Post-Modern Age,* London, Cassell.

Hargreaves, A. (1995) Kentucky fried schooling, *The Times Educational Supplement,* 31 March.

Hodgkinson, C. (1992) *Educational Leadership: The Moral Art,* Albany, NY, State University of New York Press.

Hoyle, E. (1986) *The Politics of School Management,* London, Hodder & Stoughton.

Jirasinghe, D. and Lyons, G. (1996) *The Competent Head: A Job Analysis of Heads' Tasks and Personality Factors,* London, Falmer Press.

Kotter, J.P. (1990) *A Force for Change: How Leadership Differs from Management,* London and New York: The Free Press.

Lewis, N. (1994) Re-engineering the culture of a college. In Gorringe, R. and Toogood, P. (eds.) *Changing the Culture of a College, Coombe Lodge Report,* Vol. 24, no. 3.

Limb, A. (1994) Inspiring a shared vision. In Gorringe, R. and Toogood, P. (eds.) *Changing the Culture of a College, Coombe Lodge Report,* Vol. 24, no. 3, pp. 225–33.

Morgan, G. (1993) *Imaginisation: The Art of Creative Management,* London, Sage.

Sergiovanni, T. (1991) *The Principalship: a reflective practice perspective,* Boston, Allyn & Bacon.

Smyth, J. (ed.) (1989) *Critical Perspectives on Educational Leadership,* London, Falmer Press.

Stoll, L. and Fink, D. (1996) *Changing Our Schools,* Buckingham, Open University Press.

Teacher Training Agency (1997) *National Professional Qualification for Headteachers,* London, TTA.

Telford, H. (1996) *Transforming Schools through Collaborative Leadership,* London, Falmer Press.

Togher, J. (1994) Incorporation at City of Bath College. In Gorringe, R. and Toogood, P. (eds.) *Changing the Culture of a College, Coombe Lodge Report,* Vol. 24, no. 3.

Wallace, M. (1991) Flexible planning: a key to the management of multiple innovations, *Educational Management and Administration,* Vol. 19, no. 3, pp. 180–92.

Wallace, M. and Hall, V. (1994) *Inside the SMT: Teamwork in Secondary School Management,* London, Paul Chapman.

Wallace, M. and McMahon, A. (1994) *Planning for Change in Turbulent Times,* London, Cassell.

Webb, R. and Vulliamy, G. (1996) *Roles and Responsibilities in the Primary School: Changing Demands, Changing Practices,* Buckingham, Open University Press.

11

MIDDLE MANAGEMENT – THE KEY
TO ORGANISATIONAL SUCCESS?

Peter Earley

MANAGEMENT, STRATEGY AND MIDDLE MANAGERS

This chapter examines the part middle managers can play in matters of strategy and strategic management. It does this by outlining, in broad terms, current conceptions of the middle manager's role in both primary and secondary schools and in the further education sector. Relevant research and inspection findings as well as recent writings on middle management are drawn upon to demonstrate that the role is predominantly defined and enacted in terms of subject or curriculum management. Middle managers above all are curriculum and programme managers who, as such, have a major responsibility for the implementation of organisational aims and objectives as expressed in school and college policies and strategic plans. This does not mean that middle managers have no role in strategy and strategic management. Strategy is unlikely, however, to be seen as central although the contribution of middle managers – indeed that of all staff – to whole-school or college decision-making is becoming increasingly important for organisational success in an ever-changing educational environment where resources are at a premium and market forces play an increasing role.

NOTIONS OF STRATEGIC MANAGEMENT

In broad terms, the notion of 'strategy' has been seen as responding to external trends and being concerned with the long-term future of an organisation – with planning for a successful future. As Weindling (1997, p. 220) notes: 'The business literature uses a variety of terms such as "strategic management", "strategic planning" and "strategic thinking", but in essence, strategy is the process by which members of the organisation envision its future and develop the necessary procedures to achieve that future.'

Clearly such activities, reflecting as they do the importance of a vision or future state for the whole organisation, are largely seen as being a key responsibility of senior staff, particularly the headteacher, principal or chief executive. This does not mean, however, that middle managers and other staff will not be able to contribute to strategic thinking; there will be a need to make use of all the resources at the organisation's disposal. School and college staff, regardless of level or grade, are likely to be perceived by organisational leaders as an important source of information about the external world and its likely impact, particularly on their areas of responsibility or expertise. In the secondary school sector, for example, effective middle managers have been seen as contributing to whole-school issues, keeping senior staff informed of developments as they affect their subject and the school, and to have a role in decision-making at both department and school levels (Earley and Fletcher-Campbell, 1992). Their main role, however – both as delineated in job descriptions and as carried out in practice – has tended to focus predominantly on matters closer to the 'chalk face'. Traditionally, the prime concern of middle managers has been with the successful implementation of the organisation's strategy rather than with its creation.

NOTIONS OF MIDDLE MANAGEMENT

The definition of middle management itself, however, is not unproblematic. All teachers and lecturers are managers in that they are responsible for the management of pupils (or students) and resources, and the management of the learning process. Only some, however, have responsibility for the work of other adults – the key factor in any definition of management. Management, at senior or middle management level, is about getting things done by working with and through other people and it is likely to consist of a combination of activities such as planning, organising, resourcing, controlling, evaluating and leading.

The concept of middle management is explored in detail by Bennett (1995, p. 137) who states that the very notion

> assumes a hierarchy of status in the organisation, with those in senior positions providing leadership and direction and those in middle ranking positions having responsibility for spreading understanding of the leadership and support for that direction so that everyone works to the same objectives.

So while leaders will make decisions and decide policies they will have much less influence on how things actually work out in practice. Bennett notes (*ibid.*, p. 18): '[Leaders] need assistants who can transmit the vision on through the organisation, articulate it in practical terms, and work with their colleagues to turn it into reality. This is a key role for that group commonly referred to as "middle managers".'

It would be incorrect, however, to see middle manager's role solely in these terms as they also have a pivotal role in passing ideas and information 'up the line' to organisational leaders. Senior managers will rely heavily on middle managers to keep them informed of what is going on at the 'chalk face' and to alert them to problems and opportunities. The ability to take on a wider organisational perspective and not be restricted to a departmental or sectional viewpoint, as noted above, was highly valued and encouraged by senior staff. Middle managers as key brokers within organisations are, therefore, potential agents of change through their ability to control and influence the flow of information. An organisation's success is also likely to depend heavily on the degree to which middle managers and their teams 'share the goals and intentions of the bosses and will work loyally towards their achievement' (*ibid.,* p. 29). This, of course, may not always be the case and can be a creative force for organisational change.

STRATEGY AND LEVELS OF INVOLVEMENT

It has become increasingly apparent that for organisations to survive in an increasingly turbulent and changing environment, issues of strategy can no longer simply be seen as the exclusive preserve of senior staff. For strategy to be successfully implemented, staff at all levels in an organisation increasingly need to be involved in decision-making and policy formulation – albeit to varying degrees – and be encouraged to develop a sense of ownership and share the organisation's mission. As Peters (1988), writing within a business context, remarked a decade ago: 'The essence of strategy is the creation of organisational capabilities that will allow us to react opportunistically to whatever happens. In the fully developed organisation, the front line person should be capable of being involved in strategy making.'

Middle managers working with their teams are very much in the front line but capability, in itself, does not necessarily mean involvement in strategic matters or organisation decision-making. Levels of involvement are likely to vary according to a number of factors, including the nature of the organisation and the attitude or predisposition of staff. Much is likely to depend on such factors as the structure of the organisation (is it hierarchical or relatively flat, for example?), the management style of senior staff (is it predominantly participative or directive?) and the culture of the organisation (how are things done and what are the expectations of each other?). Are all staff – but particularly those with management responsibilities – encouraged or expected to be involved in policy formulation and whole-school or college decision-making? Strategic planning must become embedded in the culture of the organisation if all staff are to work together in the same direction towards common goals. An individual's willingness or desire to become involved in such matters will also need to be taken into account and these in turn are likely to be shaped by the culture of the organisation or subunit (e.g. department, section, course team, year group) and, most importantly, the time and opportunities that are created for such activities to occur.

Jones and O'Sullivan (1997) argue that recent trends in the business world, such as the general move to flatter organisational hierarchies with devolved responsibilities and a concern for process rather than structure, have meant that the ability of middle managers to think strategically is crucial. They state (*ibid.*, p. 96):

> In such a scenario, the capacity for strategic thinking has to reside throughout an organisation, although it is true that those in the more senior positions will have this as a, if not the, major part of their role whereas middle managers' strategic thinking will properly focus on development in their area of expertise with some appreciation of the general environmental and professional context.

The strategic role of middle managers has recently been re-emphasised in the corporate world. Floyd and Wooldridge's *The Strategic Middle Manager* (1996) – a study of 250 managers in 25 organisations in the USA – stresses the importance of middle management involvement in the formulation of new strategies as well as in the implementation of existing strategies. They identify four strategic roles for middle managers: championing innovative initiatives, facilitating adaptability to new behaviour, synthesising information (both within and outside the organisation) and implementing strategy. In their view the performance of these roles has a direct bearing on a company's overall ability to pursue its strategies and maintain its competitive advantage.

Middle managers' prime focus in any organisation, however, is likely to be on short-term tactical planning and operations management rather than the wider strategic vision for the organisation as a whole, although, as essentially curriculum managers, they will be expected to play an important role in policy development at both section or subject level (broadly defined) and at whole-school or college level. Involvement in the production and implementation of institutional development plans and strategic plans will also be important but planning processes will be undertaken, for the most part, at the level of the section or unit – the department, the curriculum area or the course team. These plans will be expected to fit in or dovetail with those of the organisation as a whole. Planning at unit or section level is more likely to be the case in larger organisations (e.g. secondary schools, colleges) where a greater degree of responsibility has been devolved to departments, faculties and course teams, and, increasingly, cost centres created.

CONCEPTUALISATIONS OF THE MIDDLE MANAGER'S ROLE

In order to explore further middle managers' participation in matters of strategy and related areas, their roles and responsibilities in both the statutory (primary and secondary schools) and non-statutory (further education) sectors are briefly outlined. Various models or conceptualisations of middle managers' roles have been developed over the years, both for primary schools (e.g. West, 1995) and secondary schools (e.g. Edwards, 1985; Earley and Fletcher-Campbell, 1992), whilst those for FE colleges are more difficult to find or, post incorporation, out of date (e.g. Janes, 1989; Credland, 1993). An examination of 'subject leader' standards for middle managers from both statutory phases follows. These are part of a set of national standards or role expectations being developed by the Teacher Training Agency in England and Wales. Finally, a brief description of the middle manager's role in the further education sector, post incorporation, is presented.

MIDDLE MANAGEMENT IN SCHOOLS – NATIONAL STANDARDS FOR SUBJECT LEADERS

For some primary school practitioners the very notion of middle management continues to be problematic (see, for example, the various views in Bennett, 1995), whereas in the secondary school sector the term middle manager is commonplace and has a relatively long history. If middle managers are defined as all staff who have a responsibility for the work of fellow professionals, then should most primary school teachers be included as, since the introduction of the National Curriculum, many have at least one subject or curricular responsibility? Or should the term be restricted to only those staff who have a wider role within the whole school, such as head of key stage or year group?

In the description of the role (for both primary and secondary schools) offered by the Teacher Training Agency, the term 'subject leader' is preferred to either middle manager or curriculum co-ordinator. As part of a much wider initiative to establish a professional development framework for teachers and to define standards of performance within the profession at a number of key points, the TTA issued in late 1996 a set of draft national standards which will underpin a national qualification for subject leaders. (These were revised in the light of a consultation exercise (TTA, 1997) but are still in a draft form.) It is intended that the qualification will be 'based on clear standards for those who have the key role of subject leadership and management in primary and secondary schools' (TTA, 1996, p. 1).

The TTA (1997, p. 2) defines the core purpose for subject leadership as 'to provide professional leadership for a subject to secure high quality teaching and effective use of resources, and ensure improved standards of achievement'.

It goes on (*ibid.*, emphasis added) to state that:

> A subject leader must provide leadership and direction for the subject and ensure that it is managed and organised to meet school and subject aims and objectives. While the headteacher and governors carry overall responsibility for school improvement, a subject leader

has responsibility for the subject curriculum and for establishing high standards of teaching and learning in their subject *as well as playing a major role in the development of school policy.*

Most importantly, it is assumed that subject leaders work within a school-wide context, are able to identify subject needs but recognise these have to be weighed against the overall needs of the school. The key areas of subject leadership and management are set out in detail under the four headings of

- strategic direction and development of the subject;
- teaching and learning;
- leading and managing staff; and
- development and deployment of people and resources.

Each of these areas is further defined and subdivided into a number of component parts. For example, in the first key area – the one which is of most relevance to this chapter – it is the subject leader's task to 'develop a strategic view, within the context of the school's aims and policies, which guides subject policies, plans, targets and practices' (*ibid.*, p. 7).

MIDDLE MANAGEMENT IN THE FE COLLEGE

The literature on the middle manager's role in further education is not extensive and, in the light of the fact that many colleges have changed their management structures since incorporation in 1992 (NAO, 1994), there is a clear need to update the earlier work of the Further Education Staff College (Janes, 1989). Such research and inquiry would help to gain a better understanding of current notions of middle management in the sector since incorporation in 1993.

There is much current interest in the sector in management training and development. The Further Education Development Agency (FEDA), in recognition of the key role of quality management in college effectiveness, has recently conducted a major survey of management development needs (Fletcher, 1997) and announced a management development and training initiative with routes for senior, middle and first-line managers (*The Times Educational Supplement*, 25 April 1997). In addition, the Association of Colleges are promoting university-based middle management training programmes (*ibid.*, 27 March 1997). Colleges interested in management training and development have tended, perhaps because of their close links with training and enterprise councils, to look to the generic management standards of the Management Charter Initiative or their FE variant as developed by the FE staff college or individual colleges. There have, however, been no recent attempts to conceptualise the middle manager's role in the 'new FE'. This may be due to the difficulty of generalisation when practice is so varied and complex (NAO, 1994), and where many colleges are continuing to restructure (*The Times Educational Supplement*, 25 April 1997).

Communication with FEDA personnel (Peeke, 1997) elicited the following thoughts on the typical role of the middle manager in FE. The role was seen as consisting of seven main activities:

- Servicing the college bureaucracy – attending committees, providing data on such matters as student enrolment, retention and achievement, reading circulars and following procedures.
- Leading curriculum development in terms of preparing validation and review documents and leading curriculum development activity.
- Quality assurance activities – chairing course committees, writing reports, sitting on validations.
- External liaison with employers, parents, schools, higher education institutes, examination bodies, etc.
- Managing people – recruitment, appraisal, staff development, dealing with personal problems and anxieties, complaints and special pleading; securing the trust and confidence of one's colleagues.
- Managing resources – timetabling, room allocation, budgets.
- Development activity or academic leadership – new courses, new markets, new products/services, new income streams; projects such as modularisation, the introduction of flexible learning.

In addition to the above it should be noted that middle managers in FE teach for 10–12 hours per week. (The teaching load of an FE middle manager compares favourably with that of, for example, a secondary school faculty or department head who may teach for 65–90 per cent of a timetable and very favourably with primary schools where most co-ordinators are allocated little or no non-contact time.)

All the above are primarily operational in character rather than strategic. Middle managers' role in relation to strategy was seen as varying from college to college (Peeke, 1997) and it is to the research evidence on school and college middle managers' role that attention is now given.

MIDDLE MANAGERS AND STRATEGIC ISSUES

In the first instance, middle managers are expected to think and act strategically in relation to their own area of responsibility. But they have an important part to play, particularly in relation to offering advice, information and intelligence, and perhaps above all, thinking strategically about what is in the best long-term interests for the future of the organisation as a whole. From the organisation's viewpoint, the effective middle manager is one who is able to take into account the long-term interests of the whole school or college rather than the more immediate interests of his or her subject or curriculum area. Studies of the actual practice of middle management show that this is not always the case; indeed, research points to the considerable discrepancy that exists between what actually takes place 'on the ground' and that outlined in job descriptions and role definitions. It is to the research literature that attention is now given.

It must be stated at the outset that there are very few studies that are based on what middle managers actually do, compared to those that report what middle managers (or others) claim they do or (more commonly) should do. The few observational studies that have been conducted demonstrate that the work of middle managers – like their senior counterparts – tends to be characterised by fragmentation and involves them in a myriad of interactions with both pupils and staff. Routine administration and crisis management seem to be the norm with middle managers having little time for strategic thinking and planning, either within the department or across the school as a whole (Earley and Fletcher-Campbell, 1992). Also, of course, it should not be forgotten that middle managers spend the bulk of their time teaching.

In the NFER study, which included shadowing and observation of practice, middle managers were often criticised by senior school staff for their rather limited or subject-bound perspectives. Involvement in whole-school decision-making was seen as highly desirable. Although this level of involvement was seen as desirable for heads of department it was reported to be an essential attribute for heads of faculty. Staff, from their perspective, liked to be consulted about major issues and welcomed the opportunity to put forward ideas and suggestions.

In general, however, the NFER research found that many teachers felt they had little say in whole-school decision-making and particularly objected to being consulted after a course of action had been decided on. Senior managers were seen as having responsibility and the right to make decisions but 'pseudo-democracy' was something to be avoided and could contribute to low staff morale. Staff looked for genuine opportunities to participate in decisions about school issues but much did depend on the significance of the issue under discussion, the level of commitment required and teachers' own views about their preferred level of involvement.

Brown and Rutherford (1996) in their research study, which included the shadowing of eight heads of department, report a similar tendency for senior managers to look for the wider perspective. They note (*ibid.*, p. 9) the comments of a deputy who remarked of an otherwise effective department head:

> He makes little contribution to the management of the school. He does not discuss the wider issues of where the school is going with the senior management team and so lacks a 'whole-school' perspective. He is too tied up in his own department, perhaps because the role of the head of department has expanded so much over the last few years . . . Nevertheless he should make a wider contribution to the school.

With the above in mind, it is interesting to note Glover's (1994, quoted in Bennett, 1995, p. 118) conclusions after an analysis of secondary school inspection reports. He found that the inspectors' key issues for action and main findings 'repeatedly make statements suggesting that "middle management" is cut off from whole-school decisions, particularly those concerned with longer-term planning, even when faculty and department planning is deemed "effective"'.

The contributions middle managers are likely to make to whole-school decisions will be affected by a variety of factors: those specific to the organisation, its structure and culture, and those related more to the individual and the degree to which the role is perceived in strategic and whole-school terms. Certainly the research evidence from the secondary sector suggests that there is still some way to go before many middle managers define their role largely in management terms. The NFER report, for example, suggested that it was time for middle managers in schools to reconceptualise the role away from seeing themselves as 'senior subject teachers' towards that of a manager and subject leader with responsibilities for people as well as resources and programmes. Strategic management and an interest in whole-school issues was seen as part of that broader conceptualisation.

If this is the situation for secondary schools – and recent Ofsted inspection reports suggest that although there have been changes, the middle manager's role has still to be developed in many secondary schools (Ofsted, 1997) – then it is hardly surprising that evidence from the primary sector shows a similar pattern. As noted earlier, there is often limited or no non-contact time for middle managers in primary schools to perform their co-ordinating and management functions even if they wished to do so.

A summary of recent Ofsted findings on subject co-ordination in primary schools (Ofsted, 1996), for example, states that essential though the role is, there are few schools in which the management of all the subjects is effective. It continues (*ibid.*, p. 34):

> In Key Stage 1, the quality of management of subjects is weak overall in over a quarter of schools; for individual subjects, this figure ranges from one-fifth to well over one-third. In Key Stage 2 the situation is worse: it is weak overall in almost one-third of schools, and in individual subjects from a quarter to well over two-fifths.

Clearly, many subject or curriculum co-ordinators in primary schools have difficulty, due to limited time and/or a reluctance to see themselves in this way, in performing the role of curriculum manager with whole-school responsibilities for other staff and subject areas. The monitoring role in particular is seen as the responsibility of the headteacher and not that of one's professional peers or colleagues (Webb and Vulliamy, 1996). However, it is not a simple matter of saying primary school staff are therefore unlikely to be involved – in a broad sense – in strategic matters, particularly as these affect the long-term future of the organisation. The smaller size and collegiality of the primary school has usually meant that headteachers who wished to consult staff were able to do so relatively easily, although the culture of the primary school has been found to be an important factor in determining levels of involvement in whole-school decision-making (Nias *et al.*, 1989). Research suggests that recent educational reforms in relation to the curriculum and its assessment may have created more teamwork within primary schools (through, for example, joint planning) whilst also, paradoxically, setting up possible divisions through the establishment of senior management teams (Wallace and Huckman, 1996), and less direct consultation as many heads attempt to 'protect' staff from matters that take the teachers away from their main focus – the classroom. Similarly, models of leadership currently being promulgated point to the importance of the strong, directive head having a clear vision of the future direction of the school. The involvement of staff in the creation and implementation of that vision may be seen as less important (Webb and Vulliamy, 1996).

Empirical evidence or research on the middle manager's role as practised in the further education sector is noticeable by its absence. Peeke (1997) states that in his experience many middle managers will be involved in helping to shape college strategic plans, primarily by developing their own department plan and commenting on drafts of the whole institutional plan. But the degree of involvement is likely to vary from college to college often reflecting the management style of the principal or chief executive. Peeke (*ibid.*) notes that middle managers may also

> participate in college 'away days' and similar types of conclave where they contribute to brainstorming about the future direction of the college . . . Many in middle management in college will complain about the lack of involvement in strategic issues and the lack of consultation over important areas like the composition of budgets, estates management, and strategic partnerships with HEIs, other colleges, TECs and employers.

He concludes (*ibid.*) by stating that 'In these days of "delayering" many middle managers spend much of their time watching their backs and defending their achievements, however modest'.

There is, however, a growing body of research and writing within the sector which examines senior management practices, some of which focuses on strategic matters (e.g. Cowham, 1994). This is perhaps partly a reflection of the fact that since incorporation each FE college has been obliged to provide the funding council with a copy of its strategic plan using, if it wishes, the guidance provided for the construction of such plans (FEFC, 1996). Following this requirement a growing body of literature has been produced aimed at college senior management and governors. Case studies of colleges and summaries of the relevant literature provide advice and offer examples of good practice in corporate decision-making, strategic planning and visioning (e.g. Crisp, 1991; Limb, 1992; FEU, 1993; NAO, 1994). The body of empirical work focusing on middle managers' role in all this is noticeable by its absence although reference to the importance of involving middle managers and other staff in key decisions is frequently noted (e.g. FEU, 1993; Dearing, 1994).

An interesting small-scale study of the processes of strategic planning in FE was carried out by Drodge and Cooper (1997). The FEFC perceives strategic planning as having a pivotal role in college management, seeing the plan as 'the culmination of a process, within college, of analysis, testing, discussion, negotiation, persuasion and finally, agreement on the fundamental purpose and direction of the college' (*ibid.*, p. 206). The researchers wished to examine the reality of these strategic planning processes in three colleges.

Drodge and Cooper found that all three FE colleges in their research adopted a structured approach to planning but essential differences emerged in the management of the strategic planning process, particularly in the role of leadership and vision; the approach to planning (directive or participative); and the relationship between strategic planning, values and organisational culture.

For vision to develop into strategy, 'it must be effectively articulated, communicated and shared, and the role of the chief executive in providing vision and leadership to the strategic planning process as a whole was of significance in all the colleges' (*ibid.*, p. 210). The degree of devolution and participation in planning was found to vary between the colleges and, in one, 'middle managers were significantly involved in, and had the ability to influence, the planning process' (*ibid.*, p. 211). In one college a more directive, managerialist, planning process was found with major responsibility resting with senior staff. In another, wide staff involvement had been promoted with a focus on cross-college planning so that 'those working in smaller cross-college teams were able to see their part in the whole and put forward ideas which could influence the planning process' (*ibid.*, p. 213). The change to a more participative approach to strategic planning at this college was generally welcomed by staff although there was some cynicism about these attempts at wider staff involvement in planning processes. In a rapidly changing environment gaining commitment to change through staff involvement was imperative. There is some evidence, however, that the overall style of management in the post-corporation college has become more 'directive' (Burton, 1994) or 'macho' (Earley, 1994).

MIDDLE MANAGERS AND ORGANISATIONAL SUCCESS

Middle managers have long been recognised as crucial to an organisation's success. Schools and colleges are no different from other organisations in this respect but it is only comparatively recently that the importance of middle management has attracted the attention of policy-makers and educational researchers. This is perhaps surprising given that middle managers are uniquely placed to have a major impact on the organisation and the quality of its teaching and learning.

The NFER research into middle managers suggested that they were the driving force behind the organisation and the key to improving the quality of teaching and learning. Frequent references were made in the research to middle managers as 'king-pins', 'the boiler house', 'the engine room' or 'the hub of the school' and Her Majesty's Inspectorate have gone as far as to say that schools 'rely more for their success on the dynamism and leadership qualities of the head of department than on any other factor' (HMI, 1984, p. 8). However, despite its obvious importance, inspection evidence from schools and colleges has consistently shown that the leadership role of middle managers continues to be variable (Ofsted, 1997) and although examples of good practice can be found, as a group, middle managers are less effective than they could be (Jones and O'Sullivan, 1997).

There is a growing body of evidence from studies within the school effectiveness research paradigm which points specifically to the key role of middle managers in school improvement. The first such study – a detailed quantitative study of a small number of multiracial comprehensive schools in England – found that rates of pupil progress differed widely within the same secondary school between subject areas. Different departments were shown to have achieved substantially different results with children who were comparable in terms of background and attainment at an earlier time (Smith and Tomlinson, 1989). Significantly, the researchers suggested that explanations of school success, at least as measured in terms of pupil attainment, could not be confined to managerial or organisational factors that involved the whole school, but had to take account of management and leadership at the department level.

More recently, in the most detailed study to date, a team of school effectiveness researchers from the University of London's Institute of Education has made similar claims (Sammons *et al.*, 1997). Both this study and one based at the University of Bath (which also made use of 'value added' data) have delineated some of the key characteristics associated with effective secondary school departments (Harris *et al.*, 1995), whilst Turner (1996) in a useful review of the secondary school literature offers suggestions on ways in which middle managers can influence effective teaching and learning outcomes.

Recognition of the key strategic value of an organisation's middle managers is of more recent origin. Their precise contribution to strategic management will depend upon a number of factors and although strategy is traditionally considered to be the preserve or main responsibility of senior staff, it would be an unwise headteacher, chief executive or senior management team who thought they had a monopoly of wisdom! Effective middle managers can and do contribute to strategic matters.

CONCLUSION

The function of middle management in schools and colleges is crucial and is likely to increase in importance over the next few years. This increasing significance is reflected in the recent growth of research and writing on middle management (e.g. Blandford, 1996; Gold, 1997; Leask and Terrell, 1997; Sammons *et al.*, 1997), along with the development of training programmes and qualifications focusing specifically on this group of managers. It is generally recognised that there is an urgent need for training, particularly in such areas as staff motivation, problem-solving, team-building, planning and resource management. With restructuring and the general move towards flatter management structures, the pressure at the middle manager level for attitudinal change and the need for a range of new skills are critical issues in quality improvement for both schools and colleges.

Those organisations that define strategy only or predominantly in terms of senior management responsibilities are unlikely to be making the best use of the resources at their disposal. It is generally recognised to be important to encourage all staff to be involved, either through consultation or direct participation, in the creation of strategic and operational plans. Different mechanisms and processes for involving staff and governors are likely to be found. Staff will also decide on their preferred level of involvement in the process and this will be affected, as earlier discussed, by a number of organisational and individual factors.

The delegation of resources and the growth of decision-making powers, through local management of schools and the incorporation of colleges, have meant organisations, more than ever before, need to plan strategically and to think in strategic terms. Strategic planning enables organisations to develop and act in a proactive manner. Rapid change and uncertainty in the environment make it ever more difficult to predict future external trends. With such a scenario in mind for schools and colleges, strategic management and planning increasingly become everybody's responsibility. A central theme of this chapter has been to show that school and college middle managers are in a key position to help shape the future direction and continued success of their organisations.

REFERENCES

Bennett, N. (1995) *Managing Professional Teachers: Middle Management in Primary and Secondary Schools*, London, Paul Chapman.

Blandford, S. (1996) *Middle Management in Schools*, London, Pitman.

Brown, M. and Rutherford, D. (1996) Leadership for school improvement: the changing role of the head of department, paper presented to the BEMAS Research Conference, Cambridge, March.

Burton, S. (1994) *Factors Affecting Quality in the New FE: Principals' Views*, Blagdon, The Staff College.

Cowham, T. (1994) Strategic planning in the changing external context. In Crawford, M., Kydd, L. and Parker, S. (eds.) *Educational Management in Action: A Collection of Case Studies*, London, Paul Chapman.

Credland, I. (1993) *A Study in Organisational Change, Henley College, Coventry, Coombe Lodge Reports*, Blagdon, FESC.

Crisp, P. (1991) *Strategic Planning and Management*, Blagdon, The Staff College.

Dearing, R. (1994) *Strategic Planning in FE: The Impact of Incorporation*, Blagdon, The Staff College.

Drodge, S. and Cooper, N. (1997) Strategy and management in the further education sector. In Preedy, M., Glatter, R. and Levacic, R. (eds.) *Educational Management: Strategy, Quality and Resources*, Buckingham, Open University Press.

Earley, P. (1994) *Lecturers' Workloads and Factors Affecting Stress Levels: A Research Report*, London, NATFHE/NFER.

Earley, P. and Fletcher-Campbell, F. (1992) *The Time to Manage? Department and Faculty Heads at Work*, London, Routledge.

Edwards, R. (1985) Departmental organisation and management. In Edwards, R. and Bennett, D. (eds.) *Schools in Action*, Cardiff, Welsh Office.

Fletcher, M. (1997) *Management Development Survey*, Blagdon, FEDA.

Floyd, S. and Wooldridge, B. (1996) *The Strategic Middle Manager*, New York, Jossey-Bass.

Further Education Funding Council (1996) *Strategic plans 1997–98 to 1999–2000, Circular 96/34*, Coventry, FEFC.

Further Education Unit (1993) *Challenges for Colleges: Developing a Corporate Approach to Curriculum and Strategic Planning*, London, FEU.

Gold, A. (1998) *Principles in Practice: Head of Department*, London, Cassell.

Harris, A., Jamieson, I. and Russ, J. (1995) A study of 'effective' departments in secondary schools, *School Organisation*, Vol. 15, no. 3, pp. 283–99.

Her Majesty's Inspectorate (1984) *Departmental Organisation in Secondary Schools, HMI (Wales) Occasional Paper*, Cardiff, Welsh Office.

Janes, F. (ed.) (1989) *Managing Flexible College Structures (Parts 1 and 2), Coombe Lodge Reports*, Blagdon, FESC.

Jones, J. and O'Sullivan, F. (1997) Energising middle management. In Tomlinson, H. (ed.) *Managing Continuing Professional Development in Schools*, London, Paul Chapman.

Leask, M. and Terrell, I. (1997) *Development Planning and School Improvement for Middle Managers*, London, Kogan Page.

Limb, A. (1992) Strategic planning: managing colleges into the next century. In Bennett, N., Crawford, M. and Riches, C. (eds.) *Managing Change in Education*, London, Paul Chapman.

National Audit Office (1994) *Managing to be Independent: Management and Financial Control in the Further Education Sector*, London, HMSO.

Nias, J., Southworth, G. and Yeomans, R. (1989) *Staff Relationships in the Primary School: A Study of Organisational Cultures*, London, Cassell.

Ofsted (1996) *Subjects and Standards: Issues for School Development Arising from Ofsted Inspection Findings 1994–5, Key Stages 1 and 2*, London, Ofsted.

Ofsted (1997) *Annual Report of Her Majesty's Chief Inspector of Schools*, London, Ofsted.

Peeke, G. (1997) Role of middle managers in FE, personal communication (email), 31 July.

Peters, T. (1988) *Thriving on Chaos: A Handbook for Management Revolution*, London, Macmillan.

Sammons, P., Thomas, S. and Mortimore, P. (1997) *Forging Links: Effective Schools: Effective Departments*, London, Paul Chapman.

Smith, D. and Tomlinson, S. (1989) *The School Effect: A Study of Multiracial Comprehensives*, Exeter, Policy Studies Institute.

Teacher Training Agency (1996) *Draft Standards for Subject Leaders,* London, Teacher Training Agency.

Teacher Training Agency (1997) *National Standards for Subject Leaders,* London, Teacher Training Agency.

Turner, C. (1996) The roles and tasks of a subject head of department in secondary schools: a neglected area of research? *School Organisation,* Vol. 16, no. 2, pp. 203–17.

Wallace, M. and Huckman, L. (1996) Senior management teams in large primary schools: a headteacher's solution to the complexities of post-reform management? *School Organisation,* Vol. 16, no. 3, pp. 309–23.

Webb, R. and Vulliamy, G. (1996) A deluge of directives: conflict between collegiality and managerialism in the post-ERA primary school, *British Educational Research Journal,* Vol. 22, no. 4, pp. 441–58.

Weindling, D. (1997) Strategic planning in schools: some practical techniques. In Preedy, M., Glatter, R. and Levacic, R. (eds.) *Educational Management: Strategy, Quality and Resources,* Buckingham, Open University Press.

West, N. (1995) *Middle Management in the Primary School,* London, David Fulton.

Section D: reviewing strategic effectiveness

12

MANAGING MONITORING AND EVALUATION

Brian Hardie

THE CONTEXT OF EVALUATION

The need for effective management to include monitoring and evaluation as a basic component is well established, both in the business and, more recently perhaps, in the educational world. It is therefore clear that strategic management needs to address how its process and the changes engendered are reviewed, so that effectiveness or otherwise can be assessed. Given that strategic plans and their implementation are recent innovations in education (see Middlewood and Lumby, Preface), there is relatively little actual evidence available, so it is all the more important that an understanding and application of monitoring and evaluation are integrated into strategic management processes. Education has been relatively slow at applying these processes to its management. HMI (1994) found that evaluation was weakly developed in 80 per cent of schools. They found that vision and ethos were developed in 80 per cent of schools, priorities and planning in 75 per cent, implementation in 60 per cent, but evaluation and review were a strength in only 20 per cent of schools.

Given that business and industry have had a longer period of engagement with strategic management, it is not surprising that there is far more generic literature linking evaluation and strategy. This chapter tries to adapt some of the models of evaluation originating outside education to appropriate usage in schools and colleges, and explores the reasons for undertaking evaluation, what aspects of a school or college's strategic management process and its outcomes could be evaluated, and the methods by which evaluation can be undertaken. The use of evaluation to select appropriate strategies and to assess progress to achieve them are both considered. The chapter concludes that only by inclusiveness, by involving staff and their understanding in the process, will monitoring and evaluation be effective.

WHAT IS MEANT BY MONITORING AND EVALUATION?

Monitoring and evaluation are sometimes used as if they were synonymous, or alternatively the description of a single process. However, there are differences: monitoring offers an answer to the question 'How *are* we getting on?', whereas evaluation offers an answer to the question 'How *did* we get on?'

Monitoring

Monitoring is about making adjustments to the plan, both small and large, during the implementation process. Monitoring may thus be seen as a continuous process, which may or may not involve the collection of data. It involves looking and checking without necessarily making value judgements or taking any action.

Evaluation

In addition to this monitoring process, it is necessary to have a periodic evaluation which is more in-depth, thoughtful and considered, to find out the answers to the questions:

• Did we do what we set out to do?
• If not, why not?

Evaluation may draw on information gathered through monitoring, or assembled at the point of evaluation. Although it does not have to, it normally takes place at the end of a 'cycle' in order to see if the educational organisation is achieving what it set out to achieve and if not, why not, as part of a 'feedback loop' to compare strategy formulation and implementation with the results. Where intention and results do not match, corrective action can take place. The model given by Gronlund (1981) brings together the possible elements of evaluation, quantitative, qualitative and value judgements, in the following way:

EVALUATION

IS

QUANTITATIVE DESCRIPTIONS
(Measurement)

AND/OR

QUALITATIVE DESCRIPTIONS
(Non-measurement)

PLUS

VALUE JUDGEMENTS

This understanding of evaluation comprising quantitative and qualitative descriptions and value judgements underpins this chapter. Evaluation is seen as an activity which involves thought, reflection and analysis.

THE PURPOSE OF EVALUATION

One obvious reason evaluation is needed (Stoner and Freeman, 1992) is to check on progress and correct mistakes. But evaluation also serves other purposes. It helps managers take account of changes and their effects on the organisation's progress. Given the pace of change in recent years, this aspect of evaluation has grown steadily more important. Some of the factors which exert most influence on progress are the changing nature of expectations from central government, the importance of 'value added', changes in workers' and organisational cultures, and the increasing need for delegation and teamwork within organisations (Ohame, 1988; Steingraber, 1990).

Change is an inevitable part of any organisation's environment. Government regulations are passed or amended, new materials and technologies, such as the use of computers, emerge. By helping managers to detect changes that are affecting their organisation, for example its position in the league tables, evaluation aids them in managing the resulting threats or opportunities.

The increasing expectations of schools and colleges also imply a need for evaluation. An ever-growing speed of response is the expected standard of the present time, but also personalisation: 'In the 21st century, you need to personalise things more to make them more reflective of individual needs' (Morohoshi, in Stoner and Freeman, 1992, p. 602). The idea of making a school or college reflective of the individual's needs may be one on which the school or college prides itself, but finds quite difficult to achieve in practice. Effective evaluation is essential to developing speed and a personalised approach, since it allows managers to monitor quality, speed of delivery and change, and most important of all, whether customers, such as students and parents, are getting what they want, when they want it (Stoner and Freeman, 1992).

A further trend towards participative management increases the need to delegate authority and encourage employees to work together as teams. This is certainly true for schools and colleges where 'teams do make a difference' (West-Burnham, 1992), but this does not reduce the manager's ultimate responsibility, of course. Rather, it changes the nature of the evaluation process. Under an autocratic system, the manager would specify both the standards for performance and the methods for achieving them. Under a participative system, managers communicate the standards, but then let employees, either as individuals or as teams, use their own creativity to decide how to solve certain work problems. This would seem to be desirable in schools and colleges, where professional autonomy exists. The evaluation process enables the manager to monitor employees' progress without hampering their creativity or involvement with the work. Evaluation then is important, not just because it can provide answers to the questions surrounding progress towards aims, but because the process itself can empower and motivate staff to engage with the organisation's strategic aims.

Nixon (1992) provides examples of evaluation in action used to alert, challenge and stabilise in secondary and primary schools. In one secondary school, a staff survey by questionnaire was used to assess how far an understanding of economic and industrial issues was integrated into the curriculum. Discovering that only staff in specialist areas such as business and information technology seemed to show much awareness, the member of staff concerned was able to use the process as a catalyst to alert others to the necessity for review of practice and the possible need for training, but also to celebrate and share successful practice.

The English department of a secondary school used paired observation of their teaching to assess how far their commitment to mixed-ability teaching was achieving the aim of developing each pupil to his or her full potential. A series of individual and small-group interviews with pupils led to discoveries which challenged some of the assumptions that English staff had been making about how far they were fostering independent learning.

Nixon's third example is of a primary school which asked all staff to comment on the equal opportunities policy and to note any lessons or event they had been involved in which demonstrated the school's commitment in this area. Virtually the entire staff responded, and the school was able to feel that its commitment and practice in this area made the policy a reality. The school was stabilised on course.

In all three cases, strategic aims, to integrate understanding of industrial and economic issues, to develop the full potential of all pupils and to achieve equality of opportunity, had been underpinned by the targeted use of evaluation.

Approaching evaluation

Hardie (1995) suggests that an evaluation needs to be

- comprehensive,
- systematic,
- objective,
- periodic,
- reliable.

Comprehensiveness relates to the extent of the evaluation or audit, when it covers the whole of the organisation, or a part of it, and not just those areas which are causing concern. The same rigour that is brought to any research process may build confidence in the reliability of the information gathered, though, of course, time constraints may limit the possible. This implies that evidence is collected systematically and not on an *ad hoc* basis. All these elements can be integrated within an evaluation plan, which may well be part of the school development plan. An objective and rigorous process, harnessing the commitment and skills of governors, parents and others from outside the school, undertaken as a regular, repeated, periodic activity can draw the community together to focus on and judge progress towards critical strategic aims and to review direction.

EVALUATING STRATEGY

This section considers how evaluation can contribute to the selection of strategies from the options available to the organisation. There are a number of initial questions concerning the process of evaluation of strategy. Where does the responsibility lie? Is it the principal on his or her own? Is it the principal together with the senior management team? What is the place of the governors? What others might be involved in the evaluation? Should a team be developed as suggested by Hardie (1995)?

This leads to questions about resources. Evaluation does require resources, the main one being time. Whatever decision is made about the people to be involved, there will be resource implications which require planning, not only for the resources which are needed but also to allow for the constraints which a lack of resources imposes. The resources required may be equipment, back-up facilities, paper for the reports, duplicating and other reprographic equipment, wordprocessors and perhaps more important when considering resources, their availability when they are needed. Such issues may be very important, particularly for smaller schools. What equipment could save time, the greatest of all the resources which are likely to be needed? It may be interesting to add up the resources, including time, at the end of the whole evaluation and to compare them with those costs that were anticipated at the beginning.

Moving on to the process of selecting strategies, Johnson and Scholes (1993) suggest the strategic evaluation criteria of suitability, feasibility, acceptability as benchmarks against which organisations might judge the merits of particular strategic options. These criteria may conflict with each other, and evaluation usually requires sensible judgements on how the differing requirements should be weighed against each other. The criteria may be used for the evaluation of strategies and, in addition, they may also be used at the formulation stage.

One of the prime purposes of strategic analysis is to gain a clear understanding of the organisation and the environment in which it is operating, suitability. A simple summary of this situation might include a SWOT analysis which includes the strengths, weaknesses, opportunities and threats which face the organisation and any expectations which are an important influence on strategic choice. Suitability is a criterion for assessing the extent to which a proposed strategy 'fits' the situation identified in the strategic analysis and how it would sustain or improve the organisation. Tilles (1963) referred to this as consistency. Suitability can also be thought of as a 'first round' evaluation of strategies.

Johnson and Scholes (1993) further suggest a series of questions to evaluate strategic options:

1) Does the strategy exploit the school or college strengths? Are there opportunities where, for example, there has been the building of new housing, so helping to establish the school or college in new growth sectors such as opening a nursery unit or expanding the sixth form?

2) How far does the strategy overcome the difficulties identified in the strategic analysis? Can a resource weakness be overcome by increasing the number of students? Are there threats from increased recruiting by a nearby school or college or the opening of a new road or bus service?

3) Does the strategy adopted fit in with the organisation's main purposes, the education of young people?

An evaluation of the feasibility of any strategy is concerned, say Johnson and Scholes (*ibid.*), with whether it can be implemented successfully. The scale of the proposed changes needs to be achievable in resource terms. This assessment will already have started during the identification of options and continued through the process of planning the details of implementation. At the evaluation stage there are a number of fundamental questions to be asked when assessing feasibility. For example:

- Can the strategy be funded?
- Is the organisation capable of performing to the required level?
- Can the necessary market position be achieved?
- Will the necessary marketing skills be available?
- Will the reactions of students or parents be manageable?
- How will the organisation ensure that the required skills at both managerial and operative level are available?
- Will the technology (both product and process) be available to compete effectively?
- Can the necessary materials be obtained?

Considering stakeholders

Alongside suitability and feasibility is the third criterion, acceptability. This can be a difficult area, since acceptability is strongly related to people's expectations, and therefore the issue of 'acceptable to whom?' requires careful thought. Consideration of the likely impact of any strategy may assess whether any proposed changes will match the expectations within the organisation, from teachers, students and others and the effect on internal and external relationships.

Johnson and Scholes (1993) consider that the way in which stakeholders' 'line up' is dependent on the specific situation or the strategy being evaluated. Clearly a new strategy is unlikely to be the ideal choice of all stakeholders. The evaluation of stakeholder expectations is therefore critical. Stakeholders in the school or college's environment are often very concerned about corporate activities and performance. Each has its own set of criteria to determine how well the corporation is performing. These criteria typically deal with the direct and indirect impact of corporate activities on stakeholder interests. Freeman (1984) proposed that top management needs to 'keep score' with these stakeholders and that it should establish one or more simple measures for each stakeholder category. This idea has been adapted to educational stakeholders in Table 12.1.

Table 12.1   A sample scorecard for 'keeping score' with stakeholders

Stakeholder category	Possible short-term measures	Possible long-term measures
Students	Numbers of students on roll	Trends in student numbers
Parents	Numbers of parents at parents' evenings Number of complaints	Satisfaction surveys
Governors	Views from governors' meetings	Numbers of people wishing to be governors
Colleagues	Views from staff meetings	Turnover of staff
Staff	Number of internal appointments	Numbers of 'potential' staff applying for posts
Sponsors	Equipment provided	Numbers of new sponsors coming forward
HE institutions	Numbers moving on to HE	Variety of HE institutions used
Employers	Number of pupils getting a job	Numbers of employers available for work experience
Feeder schools	Number of meetings with staff Numbers of pupils from a school	Outcomes of this co-operation Number of feeder schools
Community	Use of facilities Number of meetings Number of 'hostile' meetings	Provision of new joint facilities Number of changes in policy as a result of these meetings
Local government (LEA)	Number of changes made to the school	Number of changes made to all schools
National government	Number of new pieces of legislation that affect the school	Number of new pieces of legislation that affect all schools
Awarding bodies Academic	Numbers of students using a board	Number of boards used
Vocational	Number of awards gained	Numbers of vocational courses
Quality	Starting an award, e.g. IIP	Successfully gaining the award

Source: Adapted from Freeman, 1984.

Johnson and Scholes (1993) assert that a balance needs to be struck between committing inordinate efforts to the detailed evaluation of many different strategic options and simply following a 'hunch' that a particular strategy is best. Certainly in practice the judgement of managers is an important means whereby the field of search for strategic developments is narrowed.

EVALUATING IMPLEMENTATION

Once strategies have been selected and implemented, a key question is 'Did the existing strategies produce the desired results?' Schmidt (1988) gives a model for evaluating an implemented strategy which starts with this very question. The model is given in Figure 12.1.

This model provides strategic managers with a series of questions to use in the evaluation of strategies which have already been formulated and implemented. Such a strategy review is usually initiated when a 'planning gap' (Schmidt, 1988) appears between the organisation's objectives and the expected results of current activities and short-term measurements are beginning to suggest that performance is likely to be below expectations. Higgins (1983) introduces the concept of 'tolerances' that will be accepted or tolerated before the triggering of action. These tolerances could well be linked to the measures given in Table 12.1. The main advantage of this model is that, after answering the proposed set of questions, a manager should be able to assess the origin of the problem and what must be done to correct the situation.

Three types of evaluation, strategic, tactical, and operational, would seem to link with the three likely stages of planning or decision-making. These ideas, from Lorange *et al.* (1986), have been adapted to be more applicable to education in the UK.

Strategic evaluation deals with the basic strategic direction of the school or college in terms of its relationship with its environment. It focuses on the school or college as a whole and might emphasise long-term measures. A timescale of three to five years would seem to be appropriate.

Tactical evaluation deals primarily with the implementation of the school development plan or college operational plan and is mainly concerned with intermediate, medium-term measures of up to a year. This would include most of what might be done within an academic year. The focus may be on the faculty or departmental level.

Operational evaluation deals with immediate, short-term evaluation including today, this term and up to the academic year. It focuses on immediate, short-term activities. It may be more concerned with what is going on in the classroom.

A hierarchy of evaluation is given in Figure 12.2, which includes the relative significance of different categories of evaluation, timescale and hierarchy within the school or college. At the strategic level, evaluation focuses on maintaining a balance among the various activities of the school or college as a whole. Within the hierarchy of evaluation it may be thought that strategic and tactical controls are most important to the strategic or senior manager. At the faculty or departmental level, evaluation is primarily concerned with that department rather than the whole-school or college position. Tactical evaluation dominates. At the classroom level, the role of evaluation becomes one of developing and enhancing teaching and learning in a practical way, for example the implementation of the details of the

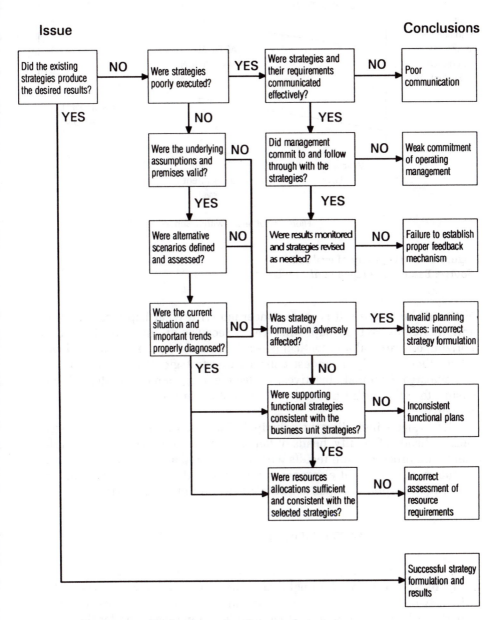

Figure 12.1 Evaluating an implemented strategy
Source: Schmidt, 1988

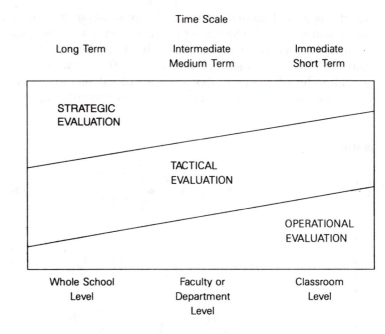

Figure 12.2   Hierarchy of evaluation
Source: Based on Lorange *et al.*, 1986

National Curriculum. It is more concerned with what happens this week and this term and perhaps this year. Because of the short-term time horizon, operational and tactical controls are most important at this level, where there is only a modest concern for strategic evaluation. To help achieve organisational objectives, strategic managers have an obligation to ensure that the entire hierarchy of evaluation is integrated and working properly.

All managers including the principal, SMT, as well as middle managers such as heads of faculty, heads of department need to decide what implementation processes and results will be monitored and evaluated, focusing on the most significant elements in a process – those that account for the highest proportion of expense or the greatest number of problems.

METHODS OF EVALUATION

In designing evaluation, Hunger and Wheelen (1993) advocate a focus on measurement of only meaningful activities and results, regardless of the difficulty of measurement. Key performance or key results areas are those aspects of the school or college that must function effectively for the entire organisation to succeed (Stoner and Freeman, 1992). These areas usually involve major organisational activities or groups of related activities that occur throughout the school or college. These, therefore, are areas which merit constant monitoring and evaluation for maximum effectiveness. For example, if co-operation between departments is important to school performance, some form of qualitative or quantitative measure should be established to monitor co-operation.

Within key performance areas, it is also important to determine the critical points in the system where monitoring or information collecting could occur, concentrating on the most significant elements in a given operation. If such strategic evaluation points can be located, then the amount of information that has to be gathered and evaluated can be reduced considerably, involving only the minimum amount of information needed to give a reliable picture of events (Stoner and Freeman, 1992). Too many evaluations can create confusion. The Pareto Principle has long directed attention to the 20 per cent of the factors that determine 80 per cent of the results. Another useful consideration is the location of operational areas in which change occurs. Since errors are more likely to be made when such changes occur, monitoring change points is usually a highly effective way to evaluate an operation.

The need for timing evaluation so that corrective action can be taken before it is too late is self-evident. Evaluations that monitor or measure the factors influencing performance are therefore particularly critical, so that advance notice of problems can be achieved. Although an evaluation may be seen as a priority, the timing of a priority can be problematic, as there are so many issues for consideration at any time that it is difficult, if not impossible, to have just one priority. Nevertheless, not everything can be top priority, and the responsibility of fitting priorities together in a planned order and the timing of different evaluations and initiatives lies with the principal and other senior staff.

The problems of time, and the attitudes to it may be strongly linked to whether the evaluation is voluntary or imposed. In general terms, too little time seems to be allowed not only for collection of data but also for reflection and thought about what to do with the information once it has been gathered. Caldwell and Spinks (1988) point out that the time involved in evaluation may be substantial. They suggest a cyclic approach is best, wherein only a few programmes are evaluated in depth each year. This limits the size of the task for any one year and a schedule can be drawn up to include all programmes over a number of years. In a cyclic approach to programme evaluation, all programmes are evaluated annually. In a large school, however, it is suggested that only one-fifth of the programmes be evaluated in depth each year in a major evaluation. In that year the other four-fifths of the programmes receive minor evaluations that are far less demanding in terms of time. In this way the evaluative process is a continuing one and all programmes are thoroughly reviewed on a five-year basis. In a small school with fewer programmes, a three-year cycle might be appropriate. Each organisation will decide an appropriate balance of short-term and long-term evaluation in relation to key performance areas.

An emphasis on reward for meeting or exceeding standards, rather than punishment for failing to meet standards, is likely to be more productive.

Heavy punishment of failure typically results in goal displacement. Managers may 'fudge' reports and lobby for lower standards. Clarity on the potential benefit for students may convince teachers and any others involved with the evaluation to regard it as worth while. Teachers are more likely to base their attitude on their assessment of the resulting benefit to the children in the classroom, if not immediately, then at some foreseeable time in the future. Viewed in this light, evaluation can revitalise the school and, it is hoped, release energy for its further development. Its aim is to improve understanding of what the school is trying to achieve and is achieving and to maintain morale. MacBeath *et al.* (1996, p. 70) in examining schools' self-evaluation, concluded:

> If the study of 23 Scottish schools demonstrated one thing, it was that the process of self-evaluation was in itself invigorating and generative for a school. Pupils, parents, and teachers were 'grateful' to be asked. As one teacher put it, 'This is the first time in thirty years of teaching I have been asked for my opinion.' This is both a sad and perhaps unlikely commentary on a school, but perhaps it contained an implied caveat 'with a complete honesty which was listened to and heard'.
>
> The Scottish Office Education Department was firstly relieved and secondly highly encouraged by the response of schools to the self-evaluation initiative. They were relieved because, from the outset, the sceptics waiting in the wings had foretold disaster if pupils were given the chance to comment on their schools and teachers. They were encouraged because of the positive response, not just from head teachers and School Boards, but from teachers and parents; in fact from everyone who had taken part in the exercise.

The final, and perhaps most important question to be asked is, so what? What is the application and use of the evaluation having completed it? What action has resulted? What changes have been made in the school? Has there been evidence of fresh or revitalised thinking? Are there procedures set up beforehand to ensure the evaluation will have some effect or will the evaluation merely gather dust on a shelf?

CONCLUSION

Hunger and Wheelen (1993) feel that it is surprising that the best managed companies often have only a few formal objective evaluations. They focus on measuring the critical success factors – those few things whose individual success ensures overall success. Other factors are controlled by the social system in the form of the corporate culture. To the extent that the culture complements and reinforces the strategic orientation of the firm, there is less need for an extensive formal control system. Peters and Waterman (1982, pp. 75–6) state that

> the stronger the culture and the more it was directed toward the

marketplace, the less need was there for policy manuals, organisation charts, or detailed procedures and rules. In these companies, people way down the line know what they are supposed to do in most situations because the handful of guiding values is crystal clear.

The purpose of evaluation is to inform practice. It is only by evaluating what is being done now and what has been done in the past that the future can be planned with confidence. This is true not only for individuals but also for groups and indeed the whole organisation. It allows for all the differing views and perceptions to come together to make a whole. It is by improving on what is being done well and also by putting right the things which are not going so well that a better provision is made for those who are at the heart of education, that is, the students.

If evaluation is to inform practice then it needs to be an integral part of what happens in the school or college, a positive, encouraging aspect of the work that is being done. Most of the time positive factors come out of evaluation, so it can be uplifting and encouraging to repeat the process, rather than threatening or negative.

It is important that *all* those teachers who are affected by any process are involved in *all* the steps of an evaluation. That is, in the planning, execution and review of the evaluation and not just the execution. Holly (1987) suggests that self-evaluation is more likely to be internalised and lead to action than is external evaluation. Self-evaluation is done

- *by* the members of staff – with appropriate support;
- *for* the members of staff; and
- *for* and *with* the participant practitioners.

In this way, ownership of the evaluation and its findings can be created and further encouraged if confidentiality is respected and if each stage is seen as being acceptable to all those concerned.

This chapter has placed monitoring and evaluation at the heart of responding to the ever-growing expectations of schools and colleges, and has emphasised that the processes can lead to a real energising of the school community. They also limit the waste of time caused by choosing an inappropriate direction, or by choosing the right direction but going off track. Monitoring and evaluation are far from a bureaucratic gathering of information, but a real focus on what it is critical to do and how far those critical aspects of performance have been achieved. In both the evaluation of strategic options, that is the choice of direction, and the evaluation of implementation, that is whether the goal is nearer, an intelligent and incisive use of evaluation techniques can build confidence, vigour and the real sense of purpose which comes from the ongoing commitment to be self-critical and to learn.

REFERENCES

Caldwell, B. and Spinks, J. (1988) *The Self-Managing School*, Lewes, Falmer.

Freeman, R.E. (1984) *Strategic Management: A Stakeholder Approach*, Boston, Mass., Pitman.

Gronlund, N.E. (1981) *Measurement in Evaluation and Teaching*, New York, Macmillan.

Hardie, B.L. (1995) *Evaluating the Primary School*, Plymouth, Northcote House.

Higgins, J.M. (1983) *Organisational Policy and Strategic Management*, (2nd edn), New York, Dryden.

HMI (1994) The Keynote speech to the BEMAS National Conference 16–18 September, UMIST, Manchester.

Holly, P. (1987) Making it count: evaluation for the developing primary school. In Southworth, G. (ed.) *Readings in Primary School Management*, Lewes, Falmer Press.

Hunger, J.D. and Wheelen, T.L. (1993) *Strategic Management* (4th edn), New York, Addison Wesley.

Johnson, G. and Scholes, K. (1993) *Exploring Corporate Strategy* (3rd edn), Hemel Hempstead, Prentice-Hall.

Lorange, P., Morton, M.F.S. and Ghoshal, S. (1986) *Strategic Control*, St Paul, Minn., West Publishing Company.

MacBeath, J., Boyd, B., Rand, J. and Bell, S. (1996) *Schools Speak for Themselves*, London, National Union of Teachers.

Peters, T.J. and Waterman, R.H. (1982) *In Search of Excellence*, New York, HarperCollins.

Ohmae, K. (1988) Getting back to strategy, *Harvard Business Review*, November–December, pp. 149–56.

Nixon, J. (1992) *Evaluating the Whole Curriculum*, Milton Keynes, Open University Press.

Schmidt, J.A. (1988) The strategic review, *Planning Review*, July/August, pp. 14–19.

Steingraber, F.G. (1990) Managing in the 1990s, *Business Horizons*, January–February, pp. 50–61.

Stoner, J.A.F. and Freeman, R.E. (1992) *Management* (5th edn), Englewood Cliffs, NJ, Prentice-Hall.

Tilles, S. (1963) How to evaluate strategy, *Harvard Review*, Vol. 41, no. 4, pp. 111–21.

West-Burnham, J. (1992) *Managing Quality in Schools*, Harlow, Longman.

13

THE PLACE OF EXTERNAL INSPECTION

Marianne Coleman

INTRODUCTION

The move towards school and college autonomy has been accompanied in England and Wales by a somewhat contradictory increase in central power and influence over educational institutions. The introduction of the National Curriculum for schools, the publication of league tables for schools and colleges and, since 1993, new arrangements for inspection of schools and colleges have all increased this influence.

Inspection of schools and colleges is of all aspects of provision, including the management and planning processes themselves. In England, typically, inspection is followed by the production of an action plan picking up on the major findings of the inspection. However, the extent of the impact of inspection on planning and strategic management is difficult to assess. Bailey and Johnson (1997, p. 185) refer to the relationship of strategy to incremental change, where developments are consistent with both: 'existing strategy and past experience', and also to situations where there may be more dramatic change of a discontinuous nature, when 'an organisation and its environment are increasingly mismatched' (*ibid.*).

For some schools and colleges, inspection may simply contribute to incremental change. For others, the inspection process may have a more dramatic effect and bring about discontinuous change. This possibility may be particularly relevant to schools and colleges that are seen to have 'failed', or to be in need of special measures. A further alternative is that inspection may usurp, or considerably modify, previous processes of internal evaluation in strategic and development planning in schools and colleges.

The first major section of this chapter briefly reviews the nature of inspection first in schools and colleges in England and Wales, and then within a wider international perspective. Consideration is then given to the importance of the concepts of strategy and planning in 'frameworks' and reports produced by Ofsted and the FEFC. A growing amount of research is being undertaken on the effects of inspection on education in England and Wales. The final major section of the chapter reviews some of the research that relates specifically to the relationship between inspection and management and planning processes.

INSPECTION

Ofsted inspection

Ofsted inspection is carried out according to a structured framework over which schools have no influence. The main issues on which inspectors of schools in England and Wales report are

the quality of the education provided by the school;
the educational standards achieved in the school;
whether the financial resources made available to the school are managed efficiently; and
the spiritual, moral, social and cultural development of pupils at the school.

(Ofsted, 1995a, p. 5)

In order to come to conclusions in these areas, the team of inspectors observe a range of lessons, inspect a sample of pupils' work, interview staff and pupils and collect extensive documentation relating to the school, including the school development plan. The details of the conduct of the inspection are clearly outlined in Ofsted publications (1995a; 1995b; 1995c; 1995d) and quality of provision is graded on a one to seven scale. Once the governing body receive the written report from the inspection team, governors are responsible for drawing up an action plan, within 40 days, showing what the school plans to do about the main issues raised in the report.

In the first round of Ofsted inspections, the aim was that schools should be inspected every four years; subsequent rounds of inspection will occur every six years.

FEFC inspection

In apparent contrast to the Ofsted framework, the framework devised for FEFC (1993, p. 7) inspection is 'sufficiently flexible to allow for the different experiences and traditions of the sector's colleges and that it must also be sensitive to each institution's own aims, objectives, targets and criteria for success'.

However, set criteria are outlined in the inspection documentation and clear guidance on inspection and planning is given (FEFC, 1993; FEFC, 1996a and b). The broad areas graded in FEFC inspections are: the curriculum areas of the college; governance and management; and quality assurance. In each case the quality of a college's provision is assessed on a five-point scale. Nevertheless, in contrast with the Ofsted framework, several features of the FEFC scheme involve the active participation of the college in the inspection. This can be seen clearly in some of the proposals for the revised inspection framework (FEFC, 1996b, p. 6), which maintains the main features of the first framework established in 1993:

a. regular visits to each college by the designated college's inspector;
b. continuation of the four-year college inspection cycle, leading to published reports;
c. the planning of inspection in conjunction with the college;
d. the inclusion of a college nominee in the inspection team;
e. the requirement for each college to produce a self-assessment report;
f. the involvement of both full-time and part-time registered inspectors on inspection teams;
g. the assignment of inspection grades.

However, the revised framework clearly states that 'The institution's self-assessment reports will be the starting point for inspection activity' (*ibid.*, p. 10). The self-assessment report should be 'integral to strategic and operational planning and other quality assurance arrangements' (FEFC, 1997a). Following inspection, colleges must develop an action plan dealing with any weaknesses in their provision. This must be produced within four months of the publication of the report.

The wider context of inspection

An increase in concern about the achievement of pupils and the improvement of schools is common to many countries:

> Many OECD countries, strongly influenced by economic doubts and difficulties, have been reassessing the quality of their school systems, looking at how far they succeed in educating the young to the maximum extent in the light of increased economic competition with other countries.
>
> (CERI, 1995, p. 13)

A concomitant of this reassessment has been a fresh emphasis on accountability, target-setting and the monitoring of targets. As a result, there has been an increase in inspection and other forms of external evaluation for schools throughout the OECD and elsewhere. In a comparative study of seven OECD countries, external evaluation in England is seen as being at the most extreme end of a spectrum of evaluation, where 'schools are not only evaluated through inspection, examination results and other indicators, but are publicly compared' (*ibid.*, p. 18).

This is in contrast to other systems where the onus of evaluation may fall more on the schools themselves rather than on external inspectors. A conclusion drawn from the OECD survey leads to support for the responsibility being taken by the schools rather than an external agency: 'not only is [this type] of self-review likely to be more cost-effective (i.e. both cheaper and more effective) than some of the more elaborate accountability mechanisms, but through it schools can truly become learning organisations' (*ibid.*, p. 47).

Work on internal evaluation has led to the conclusion that

> any effective evaluation of contemporary schooling must involve an element of self-evaluation, which in turn must involve the willing participation of the whole staff of a school. Without that active participation, the impact of any evaluation programme is likely to be severely limited.
>
> (Nixon, 1992, pp. 23–4)

The possible spectrum of approaches to evaluation is shown in Table 13.1. The left-hand side of the spectrum represents the aspects of evaluation which may be related to external inspection, whilst the right-hand side represents evaluation as part of a developmental process. It is difficult to place inspection systems accurately on this spectrum. However, whilst Ofsted inspection is probably situated to the left of the spectrum, the slightly more flexible approach of FEFC, the involvement of one member of college staff and the growing importance of self-assessment, places the FEFC inspection to the right of Ofsted on the spectrum. The evaluation and accreditation procedure for the European Council of International Schools (ECIS) is further still to the right, stressing self-study as the most important part of school evaluation. In the ECIS system, self-study is followed by a visit from a team which provides a professional assessment of the conclusions of the self-study and evaluates the school 'in terms of its own philosophy and objectives' (ECIS, 1987, p. 4). However, the report that follows the visit from external assessors does still provide an impetus for 'developing plans for improvement and initiating concrete steps towards their realization' (*ibid.*, p. 42). The stress on the involvement of the school is continued by ensuring that the process of working towards improvement as a result of the outcome of evaluation is through the activities of the committees that first identified the need for change.

A further example of the co-operation between schools and external evaluators can be found in South Australia where schools are required to provide three-year plans that include a shorter-term one-year action plan. It is the issues that are identified by the school within the plan that provide the focus for external inspection: 'The SDP is at the heart of the reviewing process' (Ofsted, 1993, p. 9) and in addition: 'Schools are required to use the SDP as a focus for internal review and development in the years when an external review is not taking place' (*ibid.*).

Having outlined different types of inspection, the next section gives specific consideration to the place of strategy and other management issues within two inspection frameworks, that of Ofsted and the FEFC.

Table 13.1 Dimensions of evaluation

Objectives approach	Process approach
Summative	Formative
External	Internal
Formal	Informal
Generalisation	Case particular
Product	Process
Judgmental	Descriptive
Preordinate	Responsive
Analytical	Holistic

←——————————————————→
Ofsted   FEFC   South Australia   ECIS
←——————————————————→

Source: After Clemett and Pearce, 1986, p. 36.

THE IMPORTANCE OF PLANNING AND STRATEGY IN INSPECTION 'FRAMEWORKS' AND REPORTS

Inspection frameworks

The references to management issues, including planning and strategy, in inspection frameworks are relatively limited. The first paragraph of the Ofsted framework (1995a, p. 5) states that 'The inspection process, feedback and reports give direction to the school's strategy for planning, review and improvement by providing rigorous external evaluation and identifying key issues for action'.

Specifically, *Guidance on the Inspection of Schools* (Ofsted, 1995b; 1995c; 1995d) states that 'School development planning is likely to be a useful process if it involves all staff productively in [these] elements of planning, implementation and review. Inspectors should decide whether, taken together, they form the basis of an effective strategy for improvement'.

When taken with the fact that the key issues for action specified in the report: 'should provide a clear and practicable basis on which the appropriate authority and school can act' (*ibid.*, p. 48), it seems likely that, at least short term, if not long term, planning must be heavily influenced by the findings of Ofsted inspection. Certainly, Ofsted (1994, p. 7) identify the planning process as being extremely important in terms of school improvement: 'even schools suffering from high levels of deprivation can achieve genuine improvements through careful, rational planning and the commitment of teachers, heads, pupils and governors.'

Glover *et al.* (1996a, p. 136) identify the Ofsted model of planning as being 'highly rational and technicist . . . Educational objectives need to be explicitly defined and selected and then implemented through action plans . . . The model can be seen as approaching the educational equivalent of formal strategic planning'.

Just as Ofsted inspectors wish to see the school development plan, FEFC inspectors expect to see the mission statement of the college and its strategic and operating plan. The requirement of the inspectors to comment and make judgements on cross-college aspects of provision including governance and management is part of the inspection process.

Inspection reports

There is a varied coverage of issues within the section of FEFC reports devoted to governance and management, and specific references to strategic management may be quite brief. For example in a report published in 1997, where governance and management is graded as 1 (provision which has many strengths and very few weaknesses) the comments specifically on strategic planning comprise one paragraph out of 94:

> The governors and a wide range of staff are involved in the college's strategic planning. The planning process is thorough; there is a management calendar and a schedule of meetings for staff and governors. The senior management team has a good understanding of strategic planning and works with the college's other teams to help them relate the college plan to their own areas of responsibility. There are development plans for each service and curriculum area down to section level, with appropriate operational objectives established and agreed.
>
> (FEFC, 1997b, p. 7)

Comments on mission statements may be limited to a description of the mission statement, or the fact that one exists, rather than a comment on its relevance or quality. For example: 'the college's mission statement commits the college to respond flexibly to the education and training needs of the community by maximising opportunities for achievement and success' (FEFC, 1997c, p. 3).

An initial search on the Internet of the summaries of 1995 FEFC reports numbers 60/95 to 128/95 (68 in all) published between June and October 1995, showed little stress on strategic management as a topic. In all, only 32 of the summaries contain the words 'strategy', or 'strategic' or 'planning'. In addition, this usage was not always in terms of strategic management of the college as a whole, but included references to specific strategic issues such as 'an accommodation strategy' or 'the information technology strategy'.

Strategic management and planning are also dealt with relatively briefly in Ofsted reports. Typically there may be four or five paragraphs on leadership and management and three or four on the efficiency of the school in an inspection report of 150–200 paragraphs.

An analysis of 66 Ofsted reports (Levacic and Glover, 1994, p. 19) identified the extent to which the reports commented on the 'attainment of rational planning', both in terms of where the school had achieved a level of planning and where it was recommended.

Of the 12 categories listed under rational planning only 'Financial control' was mentioned in all reports. Strategic planning was recognised as existing in only eight of the 66 schools and recommended in 18.

RESEARCH EVIDENCE RELATING INSPECTION TO STRATEGY AND PLANNING

The most obvious link between inspection and planning is likely to lie in the development of the action plan following the inspection report. An HMI survey of 85 schools inspected in 1993–94 found very positive responses to the need to produce a post-inspection action plan (Ofsted, 1996). The survey (*ibid.*, pp. 3–4) indicated that most of the schools

had addressed all of the key issues from the inspection (96%);

had made adequate preparations for their action plans (91%), which in a third of schools enabled work to begin on the plan before receipt of the published report;

had set out a clear timetable and identified the person responsible for each aspect (74%); and

had made discernible progress at an early stage in tackling some of the key issues in a way which was leading or likely to lead to improvement . . . (61%).

For schools under special measures, 'the action plan was likely to replace the school's development plan (where it existed)' (Earley *et al.*, 1996, p. 7). The relationship between the post-inspection action plan and longer-term development planning remains unclear. Some advice to primary schools on development planning states that

Schools need to be clear about the relationship between this kind of action plan [Ofsted] and action planning as part of the continuous development planning process. In practice the two should be combined and this will have considerable implications for the way the plan is led and managed.

(MacGilchrist *et al.*, 1997, p. 240)

Little research has been undertaken in respect of the impact of inspection on the action planning and longer-term planning of colleges. However, an evaluation of the work of the inspectorate (FEFC, 1997d) indicates that in the year 1995–96, the majority of action plans were received within the requested timescale and 'only two were considered inappropriate by college inspectors' (*ibid.*, p. 12). Certainly, the potential impact of the inspection process is considerable: 'Most colleges make extensive preparations for inspection, including staff development exercises, the analysis of students' achievements and the preparation of self-assessment reports' (*ibid.*, p. 10).

Advice to colleges is that their self-assessment report should include an action plan which shows, amongst other things, 'reference to strategic or operational objectives, as appropriate' (FEFC, 1997c, p. 8). The growing importance of self-assessment may lead to the production of action plans which are 'owned' by the college and therefore more likely to be integrated into a longer-term development planning process. Certainly the impact of an external inspection on the planning processes that take place in an inspected school or college appears to be dependent on several factors, including the degree to which the school or college does actually 'own' the recommendations, and the extent to which the institution correctly identify and carry out the intentions of the inspectors. Russell (1996a, p. 334) states that

> A clear report does not necessarily lead to an effective action plan. As one might expect, some other forces are at work, and these may be the culture of the school, the informal relationship with the inspection team, the staff and school attitude to external inspection or the perceived urgency of the recommended issue.

Russell (*ibid.*) reports that in 22 schools researched, issues identified in the Ofsted report were either avoided or only superficially addressed.

At the time of writing there is limited empirical research evidence relating to the actual or perceived impact of inspection on the development and strategic planning processes of schools and colleges. However, the research of Ouston *et al.* (1996) considered the relationship between the inspection and the school development plan, and analysed the responses of 170 of the first cohort of secondary schools to be inspected by Ofsted to research questions that included the following:

- Did the schools find the new pattern of Ofsted inspections helpful in their own development?
- What was the relationship between the Ofsted 'action planning process' and the school's development plan?

The majority of the headteachers of the responding schools considered that the inspection had been valuable to their school's development, with 74.1 per cent finding inspection moderately valuable, and 19.4 per cent very valuable. Of the heads, those in their first year and those who had been in post for more than ten years were the most positive. Those schools where there was moderate overlap between the school development plan and the governors' action plan following inspection rated inspection the most useful. Not surprisingly those where there was a large overlap felt that 'They had learned nothing new' (*ibid.*, p. 118), and those where there was no overlap felt that 'the inspectors failed to share their values and priorities' (*ibid.*).

A more recent survey on primary and secondary schools' post-inspection action planning (Maychell and Pathak, 1997) largely endorses the findings of Ouston *et al.* (1996). This survey indicates that 90 per cent of headteachers found both the oral and written feedback helpful for planning purposes. In addition, six out of ten schools had incorporated their action plan into their school development plan. Often this was where the key issues for action were similar to the priorities that had already been identified in the plan. Only one in ten secondary headteachers stated that the action plan and the school development plan remained quite separate. Between six months and one year after inspection, almost all schools 'had at least *begun* to implement *most* of their key issues' (*ibid.*, p. 13).

According to heads, the most important factors facilitating implementation were the commitment of the people involved and an understanding of the issues/process of action planning prior to the inspection. As with the research of Ouston *et al.* (1996), negative responses occurred where heads felt that the inspection and action planning process had made very little difference or had led to low morale and stress.

The research undertaken by Ouston *et al.* (1996) and Maychell and Pathak (1997) was conducted within a few months of the inspection taking place, and took the form of a survey of headteachers. Longer-term research, or research with respondents other than heads, may indicate findings that show a less positive relationship between the inspection and consequent planning decisions.

Follow-up research (Wilcox and Gray, 1996, p. 96) with 24 schools, undertaken a year after inspection and then after a further six to nine months, indicated that 'Only about a quarter or so of the recommendations could be said to be at least substantially implemented and nearly 40 per cent remained essentially unimplemented'. A reason suggested for this was that the head might block change because he or she was unconvinced of the importance or validity of the finding of the inspectors, but a further reason could be that recommendations might have involved a change in the practice of teachers. The difficulty of planning for any change involving teaching practice as a result of Ofsted findings has also been identified by Brimblecombe *et al.* (1996), where only 30 per cent of classroom teachers stated any intention to change following inspection findings, in contrast to 40 per cent of middle managers and nearly half of senior managers. Brimblecombe *et al.* (*ibid.*) hypothesise that the further from direct involvement in the inspection process, the less likely a teacher is to feel commitment and involvement in inspection findings. Elsewhere, Russell (1996b, p. 109) concludes from her research involving interviews with over 30 teachers and headteachers in six schools inspected in 1994 that

> there is evidence both in inspectors' recommendations and in school action plan responses that the external view is not enough to prompt change, and that the internalisation of findings as school priorities will not happen without school staff being more closely involved in the process of forming judgements.

Consideration has so far only been given to empirical findings that relate to the impact of inspection on development planning rather than strategic planning. The long-term dimension of strategic planning makes it difficult to evaluate the effects of inspection on the process in the short to medium term, but the original timescale of Ofsted inspections does correspond to that of traditional strategic planning. In one school:

A four-year cycle was chosen as a suitable time-scale, because it fitted with the Ofsted cycle of school inspections . . . Strategic planning was suggested as the best way forward. This led to a small working party putting together a draft format for creating a four-year strategic plan.

(Edwards, 1996, p. 136)

However, it may be that inspection will have less impact on the longer-term strategic planning of schools and colleges than it does on their shorter-term development planning via the action plan. Strategic planning is heavily dependent on external issues and the context of the institution (Caldwell and Spinks, 1992). The headteacher of one school, recalling inspection experience, stated:

I cannot remember a time when long-term policy-making in schools has been so difficult because of the uncertainties created by a rapid succession of government initiatives. The advocates of carefully-costed three- to five-year school development plans remind me of those retired colonels during World War I who in their London clubs with their maps and flags confidently explained how easily the stalemate on the Western Front could be broken.

(Roberts *et al.*, 1995, p. 87)

In research in four schools identified by Ofsted as highly effective, Glover *et al.* (1996a, p. 137) found that rather than being affected by issues raised in the inspection 'Strategic planning is dependent upon the way in which the leadership of the school interprets the needs of the school at the time of planning and also upon the relationship of the school to its community'.

The impact of their recent Ofsted inspection was not generally mentioned by the schools as determining their thinking; instead, planning was seen to be most strongly influenced by the external environment of the school, and the unique internal culture of each school: 'In discussion with the four heads it became apparent that they saw the long-term development of the schools as a most significant part of their work, but that this had to be seen against the local "market" situation' (*ibid.*, p. 140).

In only one of the four schools was development planning based in any way on the comments of the Ofsted report (*ibid.*, p. 251). In all four schools there were very different approaches to strategic and development planning. They covered a spectrum of management styles from the formal to the fluid, but in all of them there was evidence of 'a clear idea of their purpose and awareness of appropriate leadership style for the given situation' (*ibid.*, p. 261).

In the school with the most 'fluid' management style, the flexibility of strategic management meant that financial decisions were constantly being reviewed, but that decisions were strongly rooted in agreement on aims and objectives:

The processes by which the management team drives decision-making seem to ensure that shared educational values and aims are constantly acknowledged . . . The OFSTED inspectors' criticism of the poor link between development planning and the budget at

Uplands may reflect the lack of formal system, but not the reality of planning within the school where the aim is to meet changing demands to best effect.

(Ibid., p. 254)

The importance of strategy being based in the values of the institution is emphasised by West-Burnham (1994, p. 80), who claims that strategic planning 'moves management away from a response based on expediency into the value-driven approach which is founded on consent and consensus'.

CONCLUSION

Strategic planning and management are not always carried out in a linear and predictable fashion, and it is possible that the impact of an inspection is such that the planning process of a school or college may be significantly altered by an unexpected set of inspection findings. This may be particularly true of schools in England and Wales, where the inspection process is entirely external to the school. Alternatively, the findings may simply recommend strategies that have already been identified (Ouston *et al.*, 1996). Even in institutions where there are unexpected inspection findings, the underlying culture of the organisation may temper the long-term effect of the inspection process. Bailey and Johnson (1997) refer to the political and cultural perspective of the formulation of strategy. The role of interest groups in determining the choice and implementation of strategy, and the internal culture of the organisation may be much more influential than is allowed for in the 'technicist' model of strategic planning where there is a clearly identified logical flow from decision to action. Bailey and Johnson (*ibid.*, p. 189) draw attention to the cultural influence of 'deep rooted assumptions which are rarely talked about' and which 'can play an important part in strategy development'. It is possible that such deep-rooted assumptions such as professionally held beliefs about the nature and purpose of education, as well as the articulated values of the individual institution, are an important underlying influence on strategic thinking in schools and colleges.

Whilst the inspection findings must influence the immediate action plan of schools and colleges, the perceived impact of external inspection on strategic planning and management will only be tested by research that takes place at an appropriate interval or intervals after the inspection. The long-term nature of strategic management therefore makes it difficult to estimate the full impact of inspection. However, the research data relating to inspection and planning that are available appear to indicate the following:

1) In the short term, inspection findings are perceived as generally helpful, certainly by senior management (Ouston *et al.*, 1996; Maychell and Pathak, 1997).

2) In the longer term the effect of inspection on planning appears to lessen (Wilcox and Gray, 1996).

3) The ownership of inspection findings may be weak, particularly for those other than the senior management of the institution (Brimblecombe *et al.*, 1996; Wilcox and Gray, 1996).

4) The external factors pertaining to the school or college may have more influence on strategic thinking than the inspection findings (Glover *et al.*, 1996b).

5) The individual culture of the institution is an underlying and important influence on strategy (Glover *et al.*, 1996b; Russell, 1996b).

It does appear likely that the impact of the inspection findings on planning may be reduced over time by a range of factors, in particular, the values and culture of the institution and the impact of external factors specific to the school or college. In addition, research relating to evaluation indicates the importance of shared understanding and ownership if the evaluation is to be effective. This may cast some doubt on the long-term efficacy of an externally owned and motivated inspection.

Despite the apparently obvious relationship of inspection to the strategic planning process, it therefore appears unlikely that inspection has deep or continuing influence on long-term strategy. However, short-term action plans are dependent on inspection findings. At minimum, the impact of inspection has further augmented the requirement for schools and colleges to write their development plans, strategic plans and mission statements, and has encouraged a continuing focus on the concepts of planning and strategy.

REFERENCES

Bailey, A. and Johnson, G. (1997) How strategies develop in organisations. In Preedy, M., Glatter, R. and Levacic, R. (eds.) *Educational Management: Strategy, Quality and Resources,* Buckingham, Open University Press.

Brimblecombe, N., Ormston, M. and Shaw, M. (1996) Teachers' perceptions of inspections. In Ouston, J., Earley, P. and Fidler, B. (eds.) *Ofsted Inspections: The Early Experience,* London, David Fulton.

Caldwell, B. and Spinks, J. (1992) *Leading the Self-Managing School,* London, Falmer Press.

Centre for Educational Research and Innovation (CERI) (1995) *Schools under Scrutiny,* Paris, OECD.

Clemmett, A.J. and Pearce, J.S. (1987) *The Evaluation of Pastoral Care,* Oxford, Blackwell.

Earley, P., Fidler, B. and Ouston, J. (1996) Governing bodies, external inspections and 'failing schools', paper presented to the European Conference on Educational Research, University of Seville, September.

ECIS (1987) *Guide to School Evaluation and Accreditation*, Petersfield, European Council of International Schools.

Edwards, M. (1996) Primary school case study. 1. Client orientation in a first school. In Fidler, B. (ed.) *Strategic Planning for School Improvement*, London, Pitman.

FEFC (1993) *Circular: Assessing Achievement, 93/28*, Coventry, FEFC.

FEFC (1996a) *Circular: Strategic Plans 1996–97 and Beyond, 96/14*, Coventry, FEFC.

FEFC (1996b) *Circular: Review of the Further Education Funding Council's Inspection Framework, 96/12*, Coventry, FEFC.

FEFC (1997a) *Circular: Self-Assessment and Inspection, 97/13*, Coventry, FEFC.

FEFC (1997b) *FEFC Inspection Report 03/97*, Coventry, FEFC.

FEFC (1997c) *FEFC Inspection Report 13/97*, Coventry, FEFC.

FEFC (1997d) *An Evaluation of the Work of the Inspectorate 1996*, Coventry, FEFC.

Glover, D., Levacic, R., Bennett, N. and Earley, P. (1996a) Leadership, planning and resource management in four very effective schools. Part I. Setting the scene, *School Organisation*, Vol. 16, no. 2, pp. 135–48.

Glover, D., Levacic, R., Bennett, N. and Earley, P. (1996b) Leadership, planning and resource management in four very effective schools. Part II. Planning and performance, *School Organisation*, Vol. 16, no. 3, pp. 247–61.

Hargreaves, D.H. and Hopkins, D. (1991b) *The Empowered School: The Management and Practice of Development Planning*, Cassell, London.

Levacic, R. and Glover, D. (1994) *OFSTED Assessment of Schools' Efficiency: An Analysis of 66 Secondary School Inspection Reports*, Milton Keynes, Centre for Educational Policy and Management.

MacGilchrist, B., Mortimore, P., Savage, J. and Beresford, C. (1997) The impact of development planning in primary schools. In Preedy, M., Glatter, R. and Levacic, R. (eds.) *Educational Management: Strategy, Quality and Resources*, Buckingham, Open University Press.

Maychell, K. and Pathak, S. (1997) *Planning for Action. Part 1. A Survey of Schools' Post-Inspection Action Planning*, Slough, NFER.

Murgatroyd, S. and Morgan, C. (1993) *Total Quality Management and the School*, Milton Keynes, Open University Press.

Nixon, J. (1992) *Evaluating the Whole Curriculum*, Milton Keynes, Open University Press.

Ofsted (1993) *Aspects of School Review in South Australia*, London, HMSO.

Ofsted (1994) *Improving Schools*, London, HMSO.

Ofsted (1995a) *Framework for the Inspection of Schools*, London, HMSO.

Ofsted (1995b) *Guidance of the Inspection of Secondary Schools*, London, HMSO.

Ofsted (1995c) *Guidance of the Inspection of Nursery and Primary Schools*, London, HMSO.

Ofsted (1995d) *Guidance of the Inspection of Special Schools*, London, HMSO.

Ofsted (1996) *Planning Improvement: Schools' Post-Inspection Action Plans,* London, HMSO.

Ouston, J., Fidler, B. and Earley, P. (1996) Secondary schools' responses to Ofsted: improvement through inspection? In Ouston, J., Earley, P. and Fidler, B. (eds.) *Ofsted Inspections: The Early Experience,* London, David Fulton.

Roberts, M., Carpenter, B. and Stoneham, C. (1995) The first phase of Ofsted: two schools' experience. In Brighouse, T. and Moon, B. (eds.) *School Inspection,* London, Pitman.

Russell, S. (1996a) The role of school managers in monitoring and evaluating the work of a school: inspectors' judgements and schools' responses, *School Organisation,* Vol. 16, no. 3, pp. 325–40.

Russell, S. (1996b) Schools' experiences of inspection. In Ouston, J., Earley, P. and Fidler, B. (eds.) *Ofsted Inspections: The Early Experience,* London, David Fulton.

West-Burnham, J. (1994) Strategy, policy and planning. In Bush, T. and West-Burnham, J. (eds.) *Principles of Educational Management,* Harlow, Longman.

Wilcox, B. and Gray, J. (1996) *Inspecting Schools: Holding Schools to Account and Helping Schools to Improve,* Buckingham, Open University Press.

14

UNDERSTANDING STRATEGIC CHANGE

Jacky Lumby

THE EXPERIENCE OF STRATEGIC CHANGE

Change is an ever-present reality for all those working in education. The obligation to change originates from multiple sources, including new legislation, inspection, pressures from staff, parents and students, new technology developments, all in the context of the need to survive in an increasingly competitive environment. Despite the universal and ongoing opportunities to perfect the management of change, and frequent newspaper articles celebrating 'hero' leaders who have turned 'failing' schools or departments around, for many the experience of change has been often bleak: 'Reform is badly needed, yet people's experience with change is overwhelmingly negative – imposition is the norm, costs outweigh benefits, the few successes are short-lived' (Fullan, 1993, p. 353).

The experience of change has accrued negative connotations for many, who recognise that it is often played out symbolically, with micro-factors indicating macro-failure. O'Donoghue (1995) describes the efforts of a new headteacher, Sister Mary, to introduce a more collegial approach in a convent primary school in the west of Ireland. A previously rigid seating arrangement in the staffroom, which indicated a strict hierarchy, was rearranged to promote a more collegial and social environment: 'Unfortunately, despite her many attempts to retain this new seating style, Sr. Mary's efforts were soon thwarted by the invisible army of "fairies" who miraculously managed to have the chairs moved back to the aforementioned angle by break time each morning' (*ibid.*, p. 111).

Over a long period of struggle to change the attitudes and practice of the staff, the fact that 'teachers' rear ends invariably return to the security of their long-frequented haunts!' (*ibid.*, p. 90) came to be to all staff the visible symbol of failed strategic change.

Such seemingly petty trials are a common experience in education, and can lead to a realisation that the best intentions and clear logic are rarely enough. Theorists engage with this most complex of management processes, but the analysis of the challenges of the situation may reinforce a sense of inadequacy. Those leading strategic change in schools and colleges may be left with a conviction of the inevitable failure of managing such a delicate process.

DEFINING STRATEGIC CHANGE

Defining strategic change is problematic in itself. How is the change judged to be strategic or otherwise, and how is success recognised? Middlewood in Chapter 1 discusses strategic management, and suggests that planned strategy is concerned with changes which are long term and affect the whole organisation. Bush in Chapter 3 links strategy to the evolution of the culture of an organisation. In defining strategic change it might therefore be logical to conclude that effective strategic change can be identified by its large scale and its impact on culture. However, the cumulative effect of tiny changes could result in real strategic progress; thus seemingly small unimportant changes can be part of a strategic change process. Strategic change can therefore, at any point in time, be concerned with shifts in culture or whole organisation capability, but also may take the form of small, seemingly insignificant contributions to a longer process.

Perhaps strategic change could be recognised and success assessed when the results of all the small changes have accumulated sufficiently to achieve a major shift, but recognising that moment is also problematic. If the process were as simple as planning a change, setting a target and achieving it by an agreed date, then educational leaders might arrive at a point where they could each state with confidence, 'I have achieved my strategic objective'. Unfortunately, this neat, linear sequence seems increasingly remote from reality. Rather than a sequential or cyclical process of planning, implementation and evaluation, strategic change, as it is experienced by many, feels quite different. The targets may evolve or change over time. The planned point in time to judge success or otherwise may never arrive. Success criteria remain elusive. Strategic change is bounded by paradox, existing through both long-term, major change and small, often symbolic, contributions to the process and may never reach the moment of completion.

Recognising the anarchic flow of organisations does not negate the value or impact of development/business plans and their implementation, nor the necessity to attempt to assess milestones and progress. Rather it puts the visible process of planning and implementation as a tip of the change iceberg. A maelstrom of changing circumstance and apparently illogical political responses lurk beneath the public domain plans, sometimes buoying them up, and sometimes dragging them down until they become submerged and lost.

THE EDUCATION CONTEXT

Managing strategic change in education presents particular problems. The nature of teaching impacts on both the individual teachers and their engagement with change. Fullan (1993, p. 33) argues that 'classroom press' affects them in a number of ways: 'It draws *their focus to day-to-day effects* or a short term perspective; it *isolates them from other adults,* especially meaningful interaction with colleagues; it *exhausts their energy . . .* It *limits their opportunities for sustained reflection* about what they do.'

Teachers therefore face genuine difficulties in summoning the time and energy to think and plan long term. Simultaneously they have huge power to block and circumvent plans, because as Marris (1993, p. 220) claims, teachers may 'have little part in the decisions which determine the policy of the organisation; but collectively, they have great power to subvert, constrain or ignore changes they do not accept, because after all, they do the work'.

This chapter will argue that strategic change in education may be assessed using a variety of criteria. The achievement of quantitative measures is part of the picture. However, strategic change can also perhaps be recognised retrospectively, when an individual manager feels that there has been a movement in the values, attitudes and consequently practice of sufficient people in the organisation. It will rarely be universal movement, and will always be relative. One person's strategic progress may be viewed by another as a retrograde step. Rather than being vague and unsatisfactory, such recognition moves away from the normative, rational approach of clear plans and measurable evaluation to a recognition of success as it is experienced by many, as partial, judged rather than measured, and often, when it arrives, less relevant than was expected in the light of interim history.

THE PROCESS OF STRATEGIC PLANNING

The requirements of Ofsted and the FEFC demand detailed planning of the change process. Such scientific managerialism accords ill with modern writers on change in business, who stress the decentralisation of decision-making and the need to liberate and empower all to respond quickly to a fast-changing environment (Peters, 1988; Moss-Kanter, 1990). Wallace (1992) details the obstacles that impede planning in education:

- The multiplicity of goals, some of which came and went, that competed for attention at any time.
- Unpredictable crises and issues affecting innovations and other work.
- The inability to predict some shifts in central government and LEA policies.
- The combination of uncertainty about some external innovations or the arrangements for their introduction and clarity about others.

- The inconsistency between academic and financial year planning cycles.
- The moderately high degree of control retained by headteachers over internal workings of the school coupled with a lack of control over the flow of external innovations.
- The number and scope of the externally imposed innovations.
- Routine planning for maintenance of the yearly round of existing practice being strongly influenced by the external innovations.
- Difficulty in securing certain resources.
- The time-consuming effort required to co-ordinate action to achieve goals.
- Limited evaluation of progress (adapted from Wallace *ibid.*, pp. 155–6).

When plans are achieved, their value can be perceived as limited. Morgan (1993, p. 55) argues that plans

> quickly become straitjackets because of the political and other alignments that are created. They are often inflexible, and their implementation often mobilizes cynicism and resistance from many quarters. All too often, they become an end in themselves, saluted in annual reports, and launched with great fanfare, but fizzling in implementation because all the real energy has been put into the creation of the plan itself.

In contrast, the chapters from Jayne and Lumby in this volume (Chapters 6 and 7, respectively) offer examples of the process of planning proving of value to schools and colleges.

STRATEGIC CHANGE TIMESCALE

Plans often relate to short timespans. Although strategic plans may cover a three-year period, the plan to which staff are more likely to refer is the one-year operational plan, and this does not begin to address the timescale needed to achieve pedagogic change: 'A school has many choices as it starts on the road towards improvement of pedagogical practices. It is a complex and long journey; often it takes 4–6 years before a new classroom practice is implemented and benefits all students in a school . . . There is no quick fix' (Dalin *et al.*, 1993, p. 119).

However, others believe that such absolute statements are untenable, in that the ability to achieve speed of change and to implement plans is contingent on a number of factors, including the power base of those leading the process. Eccles (1993) believes there is a need to retain the more orthodox view of planning, arguing that planned sequential change is more common than believed, and can happen quickly when those steering it have significant power.

The literature abounds with examples of how plans went astray. There are far fewer documented instances of where senior management made a plan and implemented it quickly and apparently successfully, but they do exist. Plymouth Polytechnic faced a number of problems following incorporation:

> In a very limited time-scale, we unashamedly adopted a very top-down process, in which I (then deputy director) wrote a series of papers, consulted with senior colleagues, obtained advice and approval of the then 'shadow' board of governors, making only minor amendments before implementation . . . I believe there are times when what has been called 'transformational leadership' simply will not work – and this was one such!
>
> (Bull, 1994, pp. 87–8)

A top-down, speedy process of planning and implementation appears to have brought the required changes, though no evidence is presented as to their long-term stability.

Gee (1994, p. 134) also describes major changes introduced as a clap of thunder:

> I offered no choice to staff about the establishment of a discrete personnel office, the effective functioning of a finance office nor the establishing of a marketing and communications office. I introduced a college newspaper and formed an access and equal opportunities unit. The opponents of change were worried. Those first actions had been neither consultative nor slow to implement. I acted decisively and introduced the new.

How far the changes introduced by Bull and Gee were strategic is a moot point. They were structural in both cases, and in the initial months of a new order (in one case, the polytechnic becoming incorporated, in the second following the appointment of a new principal). Price (1994) points out that structural reorganization is the classic top-down favourite for inducing change. The mere creation of a number of different organisational units and processes, with the concomitant cohort of staff whose vested interest lies in their jobs in the new structure, can result in strategic change achieved very quickly. However, the tactic, even if repeated frequently, as has been the case in many colleges particularly, has limitations. It is remote from pedagogic practice, and the new processes can be resisted by many.

RESISTANCE TO CHANGE

Ansoff and McDonnell (1990, p. 416) argue that if senior management apply strong pressure, then temporary coercion may be effective, but that resistance is natural and will resurface. They further posit the equation that 'Resistance to change is proportional to the size of the discontinuities introduced into culture and power, and inversely proportional to the speed of introduction'.

Internal resistance

Ansoff and McDonnell's (1990) exploration of the phenomenon of resistance is detailed and provocative. They conclude that 'reasonable people *do not* do reasonable things, if by reasonable we mean analytically logical things' (*ibid.*, p. 416). This statement is well illustrated by reference to the Irish convent primary case study. The new headteacher attempted to modernise the school and improve the schooling received by pupils, and was surprised by the illogic of responses. The suggestion that the school acquire a telephone, which one would assume would be of benefit to all, was opposed by all staff on the grounds of cost and inconvenience. The apparently unimpeachable improvement of a healthy eating policy for children, banning sweets at break 'infuriated Mrs Flood'. The factor the head had omitted to consider was that the local sweet shop was run by Mrs Flood's father (O'Donoghue, 1995).

A similar hostility to attempts to achieve a more collegial approach are outlined by the head of a secondary school, and involve animosity between groups of staff, as well as between the head and staff:

> A minority of staff have attempted to sabotage the system by outright antagonism to certain newly appointed staff and by becoming thoroughly unreasonable towards the pupils, both *en masse* and individually. Stress comes from trying to maintain happy working relationships, not so much between the staff and me, but between warring factions of staff.
>
> (Dunham, 1995, p. 118)

In the examples above, the best interests of the children are not the deciding factor in staff attitudes. In both cases, the headteacher expects a logical response and receives a political one. As Newton and Tarrant (1992, p. 105) assert, the actual merits or otherwise of any proposed change may be quite irrelevant:

> People will resist positive innovation if to do so is their only or main influence over the system. If the manager says A, then the powerless will say Z, whatever the merits of A and Z and all the schemes in between. If the manager is very authoritarian, the workforce will say A but do Z, a wrecking or sabotage response.

Ansoff and McDonnell (1990) list the circumstances in which individuals will resist change, including the following:

• Any threat to their power over decisions or resources.
• Any perceived potential reduction in rewards, reputation or prestige.
• Any feeling of incompetence to carry out the proposed changes.
• Uncertainty as to how the proposed changes might affect them (adapted from Ansoff and McDonnell, *ibid.*, p. 408).

As most changes are likely to involve one or more of these factors, resistance is endemic. Leaders of change are sometimes confounded by the apparently illogical reaction of others who are hostile to changes which appear patently in the best interests of students or of staff. In fact, antagonism to change may be entirely logical and reasonable on the part of staff. If only logical analysis of the change itself is taken into account, then a hostile reaction may appear irrational. If the total experience of staff is considered, then a reluctance to take on additional work, which is nearly always the result of proposed change, is entirely logical. In this sense, resistance to change is always understandable. Attwell (1994, p. 34) describes the experience of introducing strategic curriculum change into a consortium of further education colleges in Wales, and recounts the difficulties of resistance with some sympathy for the position of staff:

> The biggest barrier to change is the conservatism of staff within the college itself. Many have invested time and effort in developing the existing curriculum and in accumulating teaching and learning materials to deliver their courses. Any change to the status quo offers only more work for them. More radical programmes of change have implicit threats for their professional and personal life and practice.

If the resistance of staff sometimes comes as something of a suprise to headteachers and principals, that of students is likely to be even more unanticipated. Rudduck (1991) recounts the attempt to move a primary school from a Victorian use of desks to a more open-plan system. The feelings and problems of staff had been thought through and incorporated. Those of the children had not. The staff were suprised to find the children stealing pencils and hiding them in little caches in an attempt to recreate a sense of personal area or ownership, rather than community space. As she asserts (*ibid.*, p. 57):

> Where innovations fail to take root in schools and classrooms, it may be because pupils are guardians of the existing culture, and as such represent a powerful conservative force, and that unless we give attention to the problem that pupils face, we may be overlooking a significant feature of the innovation process.

External resistance

Resistance can also come from external coalitions. The attempt to establish a nursery was resisted in one primary school by the local playgroup, residents, some parents and some governors resulting in 'a formidable coalition of interest sets' (Meadows, 1992, p. 273). The power struggle may also relate to underlying inequalities such as gender. A woman principal may face particular difficulties in addressing external resistance. Gee (1994, p. 135) admits her miscalculation:

> No educational manager should underestimate the personal and political networks that operate in all communities. I recognised their existence, but I assumed that because it was in the best interests of the college to move quickly, they could be overcome. Little did I reckon with the power of the sports club, the party political group-

ings, the church and the pub – networks that for a woman in the north west were hard to penetrate.

Drawing together the threads of the examples of resisted change, leaders attempting strategic change may consider the likelihood of the following:

- Logic and rationality are unlikely to prevail.
- Staff may work against the best interests of the pupils/students and even their own best interests if the desire to thwart change is provoked sufficiently.
- Speedy change can happen, but only when the power base and circumstances are right.
- Strategic change is a chimera, which, when it arrives, may look and feel different from what was anticipated.

APPROACHES TO ACHIEVING CHANGE

Drucker (1992, in Wilkinson and Pedler, 1994, p. 91, emphasis added) asserts that 'In knowledge and service work, partnership with the responsible worker is the *only way*; nothing else will work at all'.

This absolute position, that a collegial approach is the only way to achieve strategic change, is supported by other eminent authorities. Fullan (1992) refers to the 'over-riding problem of ownership'. The concept of collegiality is attractive:

Collegiality has become a very popular notion . . . There is an obvious logic to the idea of greater involvement leading to greater ownership and commitment to decision making, policy development and other change processes. Advocates from different backgrounds have encouraged collegiality for at least three reasons:

- Increased professional accountability (Campbell, 1985)
- increased participation in organisational development (Herzberg, 1966)
- as an alternative to the headteacher's power (Hargreaves, 1992).

(adapted from Newton and Tarrant, 1992, p. 92)

The professional culture of teachers strengthens the normal human hostility to being told what to do. Consideration of the failure of change often leads to a belief that insufficient involvement of teachers was at the root of the failure. Analysing the series of disasters at the convent primary, O'Donoghue (1995) concludes that the underlying cause of failure was the principal's inability to build staff support.

Wideen (1994, p. 97) documents the process of change in one London school from the perspective of teachers:

At Lakeview the innovation became less of a threat because the teachers were in control; they owned the innovation. With the ownership of the process a reality, the innovation itself began to generate information which acted in turn to alter their prior values about teaching.

The idea of ownership is seductive and, as in the Lakeview school, can no doubt be a powerful force to drive strategic change. However, as Rudduck (1991) points out, the term has become key partly because it remains undefined. If ownership, defined as all staff agreeing on the direction and objectives of change and on the specific means to achieve it, is the prerequisite of successful change, then it would seem to preclude the majority of institutions ever achieving it. Holder (1996, p. 9) argues against the practicality of such a view:

Anyone sitting through a few staff meetings would observe the difficulty of getting people to change their views towards those of the group, or even to acknowledge the views they already share. It is very hard work. This is not to question the value of sharing views, but to question the necessity of coming to a shared view before anything more can be done.

There may be difficulties in shifting the values and beliefs of staff. Even more problematic, there may be a refusal to become involved in a collegial process at all. Even where collegiality appears to be achieved, there are doubts as to the nature of the process in action:

In the more dominant cultural perspective, collaborative cultures express and emerge from a process of consensus building that is facilitated by a largely benevolent and skilled educational management. In the micropolitical perspective, collegiality results from the exercise of organisational power by control-conscious administrators.

(Hargreaves,1992, p. 83)

The very difficulty of achieving any universal 'ownership' may mean that a manipulative process is substituted, whereby an appearance of consensus can be maintained while accommodating enforced change or irreconcilable differences of view. Collegiality may be the orthodoxy of the professional in education, but it is often impossible to achieve. It may also be impractical because of the need to introduce change quickly in response to external mandate or the need to survive. If collegiality and ownership were indeed Drucker's (1992) 'only way', it would condemn many educational organisations to paralysis.

The other end of the spectrum from collegiality is to adopt a coercive approach, where staff and structures are changed through a top-down decision. The examples from Bull (1994) and Gee (1994) earlier in this chapter demonstrate this approach in action. Ansoff and McDonnell (1990) argue that coercive change is expensive and disruptive. The process may be expensive in two senses. First, the amount of ongoing managerial energy and time which must be devoted to enforcing the change would be great. The minute the focus slips to other activities, the change may revert to the previous stasis. Secondly, there may be a need for a large amount of resource to implement the plans laid out by the leader. However, such a high-risk and resource-greedy process may be justified or unavoidable at times when the incrementalist, slow-but-steady approach cannot maintain or increase the quality of learning experience, or threatens the survival of the organisation. In just such circumstances, Gee acted alone, but eventually, a proportion of staff became involved in planning and implementing change.

The term 'proportion of the staff' is perhaps key to understanding a third approach, which is based on a recognition of the impossibility of achieving total consensus, but the need to minimise resistance and to create the degree of support which will mean change is not totally blocked. The adaptive approach aims for coalition, not consensus, and moves by incremental steps in the general direction required. Detailed plans may be available for external scrutiny but are not the controlling framework for the real process of strategic change. Morgan (1993) argues for a style of leadership which avoids planning and plans as they attract opposition, and moves forward towards a final vision, but without a clear picture of the stages to get there. Such managers know where they are going, but don't have a step-by-step route. They have plans, but are not constrained by them. Morgan (*ibid.*, p. 47) quotes a manager who finds an appropriate simile for this approach: 'The process can be like pushing a piece of rope across the top of a table; it's slow and difficult and you need patience. You'd love to run to the other side and pull it, but you can't do that'.

The determination to avoid or deflect resistance can be further developed. Ansoff and McDonnell (1990), Meadows (1992) and Bull (1994), from business and from different phases of education, all argue for the need to build political support and to move by addressing fundamental alignments. This view is not cynical manipulation, but a recognition of, in their view, the lack of realism in targeting consensus and universal ownership. Pfeffer (1993, pp. 203–4) suggests a process to identify action:

- Decide what your goals are, what you are trying to accomplish.
- Diagnose patterns of dependence and interdependence; what individuals are influential and important in your achieving your goal?
- What are their points of view likely to be? How will they feel about what you are trying to do?
- What are their power bases? Which of them is more influential in the decision?
- What are your bases of power and influence? What bases of influence can you develop, to gain more control over the situation?
- Which of the various strategies and tactics for exercising power seem most appropriate and are likely to be effective, given the situation you confront?
- Based on the above, choose a course of action to get something done.

Building a power base in this way, eschewing plans which are too detailed and approaching change as a series of small adjustments, may result in incremental change over time which amounts to a transformation of culture and organisational capability (Ansoff and McDonnell, 1990). The adaptive approach to strategic change achieves the major by minor adjustments, indirect approaches and political intelligence. It rests on the twin beliefs of the possibility of substantial progress and the necessity to settle for the achievable.

LEADING STRATEGIC CHANGE

Whichever approach to achieving strategic change is chosen, it is clear that there is a role for leadership. Research in four London schools found that the majority of innovations had been introduced by heads (Wallace, 1992). Weil (1994), as editor of *Introducing Change from the Top in Universities and Colleges,* acknowledges in her introduction that 'the title of this book will raise eyebrows'. However, the volume brings together a series of personal accounts which demonstrate the critical role of the head of each organisation in achieving strategic change. Their methods vary, emphasising that, in contradiction to Drucker's (1992) view, there is no one best way. The accounts illustrate a pluralism of both conceptual understanding and consequent practical approach. Change is in evidence as both imposed and agreed by consensus, as both slow and speedy, as successful and as failure. In any one organisation it would appear that there are a number of possible ways to achieve strategic change.

Personal accounts of change leaders are reassuring to those struggling with seemingly insuperable difficulties in achieving change (Meadows, 1992; Webb, 1994). They offer testimony to the real difficulties faced, and the limited success often achieved: 'It is important to have ambition, but it is also important to settle for what one can achieve. One lives to fight again' (Meadows, 1992, p. 273).

Fullan (1994, p. 19) asserts that 'productive educational change roams somewhere between overcontrol and chaos'. Certainly those locked into a change process recognise the bounded nature of what they can hope to achieve: 'You can't "manage change"; you can only go along with it and do your creative best to exploit it' (FEU, 1993, p. 85).

Meadows (1992) describes his change process as no more than 'high-class fumbling'. The complexity of the task is conceded, but not allowed to daunt. Rather, partial success is a matter for pride. Strategic change must be attempted, and those engaged with the attempt must be supported by both reflection and conceptual understanding, but also by acknowledgement of what it is realistic to expect them to achieve. All are engaged in a learning process, where even failure has positive value in offering lessons:

> But most of all we have learned that change is not an option. So we are still trying to learn not to be afraid of it. We want to be like the good surfer; we want to ride the waves of change and enjoy them, not fight them and go under . . . That means we have made mistakes and we will continue to make them but we think we've learned, a century and more after Mark Twain learned it, that 'he who grabs the cat by the tail knows 80% more about the cat than anybody else'.
>
> (FEU, 1993, p. 90)

'Success' and 'failure' of strategic change can be redefined to encompass the reality of the experience of those in schools and colleges, taking the educational process as a paradigm, where any experience can be converted to positive learning and an increased capacity to manage change.

REFERENCES

Ansoff, H.I. and McDonnell, E.J. (1990) *Implanting Strategic Management* (2nd edn), Hemel Hempstead, Prentice-Hall.

Attwell, G. (1994) Curriculum development: the case of Gwent Tertiary College. In Crawford, M., Kydd, L. and Parker, S. (eds.) *Educational Management in Action*, London, Paul Chapman.

Bull, J. (1994) Managing change or changing managers? In Weil, S. (ed.) *Introducing Change from the Top in Universities and Colleges*, London, Kogan Page.

Campbell, R.J. (1985) *Developing the Primary School Curriculum*, London, Holt, Rinehart & Winston.

Dalin, P. with Rolff, H. in co-operation with Kleekamp, B. (1993) *Changing the School Culture*, London, Cassell.

Drucker, P. (1992) *Managing the Non-Profit Organization*, Oxford, Butterworth-Heinemann.

Dunham, J. (1995) *Developing Effective School Management*, London, Routledge.

Eccles, T. (1993) Implementing strategy: two revisionist perspectives. In Hendry, J., Johnson, G. and Newton, J. (eds.) *Strategic Thinking: Leadership and the Management of Change*, Chichester, Wiley.

FEU (1993) *Challenges for Colleges: Developing a Corporate Approach to Curriculum and Strategic Planning*, London, FEU.

Fullan, M. (1992) Causes/processes of implementation and continuation. In Bennett, N., Crawford, M. and Riches, C. (eds.) *Managing Change in Education*, London, Paul Chapman.

Fullan, M. (1993) *The New Meaning of Educational Change* (2nd edn), London, Cassell.

Fullan, M. (1994) *Change Forces*, London, Falmer Press.

Gee, R. (1994) Survival is not compulsory. In Weil, S. (ed.) *Introducing Change from the Top in Universities and Colleges*, London, Kogan Page.

Hargreaves, A. (1992) Contrived collegiality: the micropolitics of teacher collaboration. In Bennett, N., Crawford, M. and Riches, C. (eds.) *Managing Change in Education*, London, Paul Chapman.

Herzberg, F. (1966) *Motivation to Work*, New York, Wiley.

Holder, B. (1996) Is blurred vision healthier? *Management in Education*, Vol. 10, no. 3, pp. 8–9.

Marris, P. (1993) The management of change. In Mabey, C. and Mayon-White, B. (eds.), *Managing Change*, Milton Keynes, Open University Press.

Meadows, E. (1992) One school's response to parental choice. In Bennet, N., Crawford, M. and Riches, C. (eds.) *Managing Change in Education*, London, Paul Chapman.

Morgan, G. (1993) *Imaginisation: The Art of Creative Management*, London, Sage.

Moss-Kanter, R. (1990) *When Giants Learn to Dance*, London, Unwin Hyman.

Newton, C. and Tarrant, T. (1992) *Managing Change in Schools,* London, Routledge.

O'Donoghue, D. (1995) The implementation of change: a case study of a convent primary in the west of Ireland, *Compare,* Vol. 25, no. 1, pp. 85–95.

Peters, T. (1988) *Thriving on Chaos,* London, Macmillan.

Pfeffer, J. (1993) Understanding power in organisations. In Mabey, C. and Mayon-White, B. (eds.) *Managing Change,* London, Paul Chapman.

Price, C. (1994) Piloting higher education change: a view from the helm. In Weil, S. (ed.) *Introducing Change from the Top in Universities and Colleges,* London, Kogan Page.

Rudduck, J. (1991) *Innovation and Change,* Buckingham, Open University Press.

Wallace, M. (1992) Flexible planning: a key to the management of multiple innovations. In Bennett, N., Crawford, M. and Riches, C. (eds.) *Managing Change in Education,* London, Paul Chapman.

Webb, R. (1994) Two tales from a reluctant manager. In Weil, S. (ed.) *Introducing Change from the Top in Universities and Colleges,* London, Kogan Page.

Weil, S. (ed.) (1994) *Introducing Change from the Top in Universities and Colleges,* London, Kogan Page.

Wideen, M.F. (1994) *The Struggle for Change: The Story of one School,* London, Falmer Press.

Wilkinson, D. and Pedler, M. (1994) Strategic thinking in public service. In Garratt, B. (ed.) *Developing Strategic Thought,* Maidenhead, McGraw-Hill.

GLOSSARY OF TERMS

CEF	College Employers Forum.
CERI	Centre for Educational Research and Innovation.
DES	Department of Education and Science.
DFEE	Department for Education and Employment.
ECIS	European Council of International Schools.
ERA	Education Reform Act 1988.
FEDA	Further Education Development Agency.
FEFC	Further Education Funding Council.
FEU	Further Education Unit.
GM	grant maintained.
GNVQ	General National Vocational Qualification.
HEADLAMP	Headteacher Leadership and Management Programme.
HEI	higher education institution.
HMCI	Her Majesty's Chief Inspector of Schools.
HMI	Her Majesty's Inspector.
HRM	human resource management.
INSET	in-service education and training (of teachers).
ITE	initial teacher education.
LEA	local education authority.
LMI	labour market information.
LMS	local management of schools.
MCI	Management Charter Initiative.
NAO	National Audit Office.
NC	National Curriculum.
NCE	National Commission for Education.
NFER	National Foundation for Educational Research.
NPQH	National Professional Qualification for Headship.
NQT	newly qualified teacher.
NVQ	National Vocational Qualification.
OECD	Organisation for Economic Co-operation and Development.
Ofsted	Office for Standards in Education.
PI	performance indicator.
PIT	Pool of Inactive Teachers.
PRP	performance related pay.
SDP	school development plan.
SMT	senior management team.
SMTF	school management taskforce.
SWOT	strengths, weaknesses, opportunities and threats.
TEC	Training and Enterprise Council.
TES	*The Times Educational Supplement.*
TTA	Teacher Training Agency.
TQM	total quality management.

AUTHOR INDEX

SUBJECT INDEX